SILENT
GESTURE

SILENT
GESTURE

The Autobiography of
Tommie Smith

Tommie Smith
with David Steele

Temple University Press
PHILADELPHIA

Temple University Press
1601 North Broad Street
Philadelphia, PA 19122
www.temple.edu/tempress

In the series, *Sporting,* edited by Amy Bass

Text design by P. M. Gordon Associates, Inc.

♾ The paper used in this publication meets the requirements of the American
National Standard for Information Sciences—Permanence of Paper for Printed
Library Materials, ANSI Z39.48-1992

Library of Congress Cataloging-in-Publication Data
Smith, Tommie, 1944–
    Silent Gesture : the autobiography of Tommie Smith / Tommie Smith with
David Steele.
        p.   cm.
    ISBN-13: 978-1-59213-639-1 (alk. paper)
    ISBN-10: 1-59213-639-7 (alk. paper)
    1. Smith, Tommie, 1944– 2. Track and field athletes—United States—Biography.
3. African American athletes—Biography. 4. Olympic Games (19th : 1968 : Mexico
City, Mexico) 5. Olympics—Participation, African American. 6. Sports—Social
aspects. I. Steele, David. II. Title.
    GV697.S65A3 2007
    796.42092—dc22
    [B]

                                                                    2006051455

Frontispiece: Silhouette of Tommie Smith, adapted from a photograph
of Rigo23's sculpture at San Jose State University.

2 4 6 8 9 7 5 3 1

Contents

SILENT
GESTURE

Welcome Home

I HAD TRULY BELIEVED that I would be six feet under before something like this took place. But I had lived long enough to see it, and to be part of it. My alma mater was welcoming me back. It was embracing me as one of its own, as a part of its history and of its legacy and of its contribution to American society. And it was going to immortalize me with a statue right on the campus grounds I once walked.

Thirty-five years earlier, I had thought I would never see the city of San Jose, the campus of San Jose State College, my home on the west edge of campus, or my wife and son ever again. On the night of October 16, 1968, I had stood on a platform on the infield of the Olympic Stadium in Mexico City, with a gold medal around my neck, black socks on my feet, and a glove on the right fist I had thrust in the air. My head was bowed, and inside that bowed head, I prayed—prayed that the next sound I would hear, in the middle of the Star-Spangled Banner, would not be a gunshot, and prayed that the next thing I felt would not be the darkness of sudden death. I knew there were people, a lot of people, who wanted to kill me for what I was doing. It would take only one of them to put a bullet through me, from somewhere in the crowd of some 100,000, to end my life because I had dared to make my presence—as a black man, as a representative of oppressed people all over America, as a spokesman for the ambitious goals of the Olympic Project for Human Rights—known to the world.

That was my victory stand. Not only because I had won the gold medal in the 200-meter final a half hour earlier, in world-record time. This was my platform, the one I had earned by years of training my body and my mind for the ultimate achievement. The athletic achievement paved a road toward my quest for a social victory, where everyone would be listening to and watching my statement about the conditions in which my people and I were living in the greatest country in the world. I never said a word as the national anthem was playing. My silent gesture was designed to speak volumes. As hard as I had worked to climb the victory stand, I had worked just as hard to earn the platform that the stand provided. For me, and for all of those who had participated in the struggle to bring me there and to put that platform to its best use, this victory stand represented more than just a place to accept a medal.

And because of what it meant to all those who opposed me, who hated me for what I had done before and was doing now, it very well might have been my last stand. Live another 35 years? I felt blessed that I lived another 35 seconds, after raising my fist, after descending the platform, after waving my fist again, after walking out of the stadium and into the uncertainty of the rest of my life—the uncertainty being how much longer I might even survive. But I lived on, and I lived long enough to step onto campus again, 35 years later to the day, and to see and hear San Jose State University honor what we had done—myself and John Carlos, who had stood with me with a fist raised on that stand, who had also attended San Jose State, who had felt the same weight of what we did and wondered how much longer he would live after it. The school was acknowledging our sacrifice, telling us that the act and the sacrifice had not been in vain.

I had received threats in my own little home that I shared with my first wife and my eldest child, then less than a year old. I had been forced to scrape by for a living to support my family, and eventually I lost that marriage from the strain. I had been denied an opportunity to take my track career to its fullest potential. I had been left no choice but to leave California, my home, to start over, and then to leave my adopted home of Ohio, where I had moved away from the mainstream, away from the turmoil brought on by my name—moved underground, I thought. Ultimately I had come back to my home state, restarted my career, and started a new family, but stayed at a distance from San Jose, teaching and coaching in southern California and coming to terms with the life path I had chosen. I saw that second marriage disintegrate but found a third, and fought both to educate my students and athletes and to have the opportunity to educate them better. I also searched for a peaceful location in which to live, where for at least a little while the hate mail, condemnations, and death threats might not find me.

Maybe none of this would have happened had I done nothing on the victory stand. It doesn't matter, though. I have never regretted it and never will. If the city and school at which the first planks of my stand were built were content with leaving me on the outside, then I would have to live on the outside.

Yet now, 35 years later, they were again opening the door for me.

So, on the morning of October 16, 2003, I stood in the quad near the entrance to San Jose State, with the traffic on San Fernando Street rushing by, and looked around at the place where so much had begun, and where I had thought so much could have ended. I can't say I was filled with joy, or relief, or pride, or even redemption. I stood with my wife of the past three years, Delois, and one of the men responsible for that day's commemoration, Alfonso de Alba, executive director of the campus's Associated Students, the independent student body organization. Delois and Alfonso were full of happiness and antici-pation. But my mind wandered to other anticipations, not that far removed from the one I felt on the victory stand in Mexico City. The sight of the city and the campus brought those feelings out.

In the years since 1968, whenever I was invited to a function in San Jose, I was nervous. I always thought, "I don't want to end where I started." How many minds do you think are still out there saying, "Oh, that nigger Tommie Smith, I'm gonna take him down where he got started"? I've been around too many people who think like that, have heard too many things in San Jose—when I was going to school —to feel welcome there. It's because of thoughts like these that I have not gone back often. Oh, I was invited back a handful of times after Mexico City to be honored by the city or by the school. In 1994 the Bruce Jenner Classic, a prominent international track meet in San Jose, held a special ceremony in tribute to me, and I attended. That was the first time I had been back in the city in several years. In 1997 I was inducted into the San Jose Sports Hall of Fame. A year later, on the 30-year anniversary of the victory stand, San Jose State gave me its annual award as Outstanding African American Alumnus. At that point I had been an alumnus for nearly three decades, but then, as now, I remembered to be gracious. I could have gone unrecognized forever, or at least while I was still on this earth.

It was not that I felt totally uncomfortable with, or even hostile to, San Jose State. I never could feel that way, really. My five years on the campus had shaped my life more than anything else. Those years pointed my life in the direction of social integrity. My first year in college, the 1963–64 academic year, was a shock in every way, athletically, academically, and socially. It took no time at all for me to realize how much I had not learned in my life before that—not as a little boy, one of 12 children, picking and chopping cotton in east Texas in the late 1940s, and not during my years in Lemoore, in central California farm country, going from the fields to the classroom to the practice field and back to the fields, through grammar school and high school. Until the day I got on a plane to San Jose in the summer of 1963, I had no knowledge of social integrity. I discovered it in abundance at San Jose State, for better and for worse.

Much of what I am today—and no doubt who I was on the victory stand—developed at this school. Part of me was formed here. Now the school was saying I was, and am, part of it.

More specifically, the students were saying I was part of it. This commemoration was their welcome back. The administration had signed off on it and was giving its blessing to it. That was as close as the faculty, officials, and administrators of San Jose State had ever come to expressing any sentiment more positive than indifference toward Tommie Smith or John Carlos. In some ways, they had not even waited until we returned from Mexico City to begin ostracizing us. Long before the Olympics, we had been made to feel like less than true members of the college. In the days following Mexico City, I would have welcomed mere benign acknowledgment in place of what we did get from the leaders of that branch of the state college system. Now, 35 years later, having them stand in support was appreciated, even if it was belated.

But this was not their show. The students had put this together, and it was they who opened the door and opened their arms. They were where I was four decades earlier, and they made me feel truly welcome. They were one-third of my age. They were doing something great, much as we had tried to do when we were there—not exactly the same, but they were doing something, and in doing it they were acknowledging what we had done.

The signs of their appreciation were all over campus this morning, and I mean that literally. Along the same pathways on which I used to draw stares—because I was a black man and an athlete in the 1960s with the nerve to show off an armload of books—banners snapped in the autumn breeze. On one side was the photo that's instantly recognizable the world over, of Carlos and me with gloved fists raised. On the other side of half of these banners was a reproduction of me in action that seemed damn near lifelike. The young man on those banners had no facial hair, a short Afro, unshaded eyes (which indicated how early in my college years this was, because the sunglasses I wore during my later races became a trademark), and the letters "SJS" running diagonally across his chest. That man was the athlete at his peak, not yet the activist depicted on the other side.

He did have beautiful form, though. That kid on the banner was going through the turn—I didn't know if the photo of me was from the 200 meters, 220 yards, 400 meters, or 440 yards—but I was coming around the curve. Over the years, my technique, for the turn and every other segment of a race, was honed to perfection, with every movement in place for maximum effectiveness. My expression on the banner . . . well, I had none. I didn't look tired; I didn't even look like I was exerting myself. Every description of my running style referred to how easy I made it look, how smooth, how fluid, how effortless. But it wasn't ever easy or natural to run as fast as I did. The results were worth every extra ounce of effort I put into the science and physiology of running fast, as taught me by the greatest coach who has ever lived, Lloyd C. "Bud" Winter.

Coach Winter had built the San Jose State track program into the unit known worldwide as Speed City. Four of us, as well as Coach Winter, made it to Mexico City. All of us won medals. Two of us went a step further, using what made us well known to make our message heard. Coach Winter has been gone a long time now, since 1985. The track program he built has been gone almost as long, brutally chopped away in 1988 for lack of money, our once state-of-the-art track surface now used as a parking lot for football games.

Across the pathway from my banners flapped the banners for John Carlos, his image frozen in full, explosive, scowling charge. The differences between us were obvious from the way we ran. Of course, when we opened our mouths later in the day, we reminded everyone and each other of those differences.

Together on this morning, the two of us loomed over campus—in my mind, for the first time since our return from Mexico City. It would have taken a mighty effort for a student to ignore us, to turn away this time, as so many had 35 years earlier. This morning few of them did. The point of the entire day was to not ignore or turn away.

As nervous as I was being there, I was not nearly as nervous as I had been in the days leading up to this event. On the previous Saturday I had attended the annual health walk sponsored by the 100 Black Men at Lake Merritt in Oakland, another of my old stomping grounds, up the highway from San Jose. I knew my day at San Jose was drawing near, and I knew the attention it had attracted would only grow. All I could think of was that I had never believed I'd see it happen.

But here we were, and I felt overwhelmed. A lot would happen that day, and keeping up with it mentally as well as physically would be a challenge. So before the official events began I decided to focus on the students themselves, the ones who were walking the paths I had walked. I cleared my mind, providing space to store information from what I was observing. How much had the campus changed, and how much had the students changed?

A lot of them looked at us that day and figured we were just a couple of old black folks, no one special, could be anybody—and only later matched the aging faces with the fresh young ones on the banners, posters, T-shirts, programs, and fliers all over campus. And even then they might not have understood why these men, whose action was captured for the ages in that photo, did what they did—or even understood what they did besides raise their fists on the victory stand.

I thought back to what I must have been thinking when I walked these same grounds in 1968. I realized that today's students and I probably had similar thoughts—about society and change and what America really represents and what it ought to represent—but these students likely were thinking of these things because of Carlos and me, because this day was dedicated to us, because we had done what these students ought to be doing today, nearly four decades after we opened the door for them and showed them the way. On any other day, they might not have been having these thoughts.

The students responsible for this event surely were thinking something close to what we once had thought. My mind turned to Erik Grotz, the young white Associated Students board member who had taken the first steps toward this event the previous spring. That a 23-year-old white male was the originator and the catalyst for this event might have been the most interesting thing to me. It all started with his curiosity about us. Then in December he introduced a resolution in an Associated Students board of directors meeting to honor us with this entire project—campus visit, ceremonies, salutes, banquets, and the statue. He pushed for us to receive the school's annual Unsung Heroes award in recognition of our special place in the history of the college. Much of the ceremony surrounding the first football game of the season in August, against Grambling, centered on Carlos and me. We participated in panel discussions, were praised in speeches by the likes of Cornel West, and were introduced at the game to the first sellout crowd at Spartan Stadium in more than a decade.

Erik Grotz had set in motion everything that was to happen on this day, getting people to support him in something that not long before he had little knowledge and less understanding of. By pursuing this, he grew to recognize the Mexico City victory stand for what it truly was: not an athletic thing, even though it was done at an athletic event, but a socially generated act that happened to culminate on the world's biggest athletic stage. One of the people he enlisted for his cause was walking with my wife and me: Alfonso de Alba, who himself had grown up in southern California, as a Mexican-born immigrant, understanding the global impact of what Carlos and I had done.

In fact, it was his destiny to take the baton on this project: Alfonso de Alba was born in Mexico City on October 16, 1968. That fact gets a laugh from many, including me, but that element of fate is hard to ignore, and Alfonso decided not to. Once he learned of his prophetic entry into the world, he realized he could not honor it any better than to clear a path of his own toward social justice, on the very campus where I had, and to lift this project as much as he could. He found his platform as a student leader at San Jose State.

Similarly, Erik Grotz's platform is not athletics. He used his platform as a recognized student leader to perpetuate the legacy of Tommie Smith and John Carlos. He used it to send the true message of this day and of this project: this is what educated and aware young people can do, and must do. "See these men?" he was saying. "They are your proof."

I can only hope the students today get his point better than so many people in the world got ours. Our point is missed even now: it wasn't a black athlete on the victory stand giving accolades to his triumph in athletics, but to his triumph socially. If there ever was a time to understand that point, it's today, with so many of the same problems back with us again. The present government is at war for an unclear reason, taking and losing lives to force its version of democracy on other people. It is undermining the Constitution here and abroad and denying the rights guaranteed in the Constitution to its own citizens in the same way as in the '60s. The groundswell of activism will grow from the students, as it must.

But it's going to have to happen in a different way, and the students will have to awaken themselves to do it. The mindset has changed. The students, and society as a whole, have allowed their concerns to shift from society to technology, which has its place and its positives, but which shrinks human interaction, thought, feeling, and concern. When someone is satisfied with pushing a button to accomplish something, or with communicating through computers rather than in person, the prospects for awareness and change through political and social means are diminished.

As I prepared for the ceremony, I realized that this event would be a test of how much today's students are willing, prepared, and able to think. And in my mind, I tested them. I kept an open mind, but I watched and listened and looked into their faces for signs of recognition and understanding. I am an educator, and have been for years, and wanted to be one for many years before that. If the students of San Jose State were not more educated by the end of this day, the day would be a disappointment.

There were plenty of opportunities for them, and for me, to learn —almost too many. I decided to deal with each as it came along and leave it up to the organizers and to my wife Delois to steer me to the right place for the moment. The day began in the student union at about 10 in the morning, with John and me participating in a panel discussion on activism, in our day and today, along with three San Jose State students, campus communications professor Dr. Marquita Byrd, and the moderator, campus sociology professor Scott Myers-Lipton. An hour later, the discussion moved into the atrium of the student union, with John and me talking informally to the students for another hour, answering all sorts of questions about ourselves, the Olympic protest, and the role of athletes as role models for the campus and greater society. That was a lot of talking with which to start the day.

A barbecue on the Seventh Street Plaza, pretty much directly in the middle of campus, lasted from about noon until our next speaking engagement. The barbecue included entertainment from a live band playing music from our day—they billed it as "the protest era." Several student groups performed for us in their own cultural ways. A Mexican American dance troupe performed. A Vietnamese group did a stage show that alluded to our protest and tied it to the struggle of their people at the same period in history. A group of Pacific Islanders performed a dance in our honor.

The black fraternities and sororities did a step show that recognized our contributions. I enjoyed this immensely, partly because the members all came by afterward to pose for pictures with us, and partly because under other circumstances, I would have been a fraternity member back in the day. I had other priorities back then, mainly academics and athletics. They had their platform; I had mine. It was encouraging to see them using theirs in this way.

It was far more encouraging to see that it was not only the black students, or the students of color, gathered on the plaza under the sunny sky during that barbecue. The blend of colors among the students, from all nationalities, was breathtaking. They all lined up to pose with us, speak to us, shake our hands, and ask for autographs on posters, fliers, and shirts being sold to commemorate the day and to raise funds. Carlos and I signed and signed until we were dragged away from the table to speak before the crowd; then we went back and signed some more until we were dragged away again for our next appearance.

When we did speak to the gathering at the barbecue, we each expressed our awe at being here. I said what I believed this day to be: a momentous time in history, the two of us together on stage on the campus we had walked decades ago. Carlos praised the former school president, Dr. Robert Clark, who had supported us by speaking out against the outpouring of condemnation. That tribute was fitting, too: one of the buildings bordering Seventh Street Plaza, visible from where we stood, was named for Dr. Clark.

Dr. Clark deserved that honor for a number of accomplishments as president, including what he had done in our defense. When the pressure was on to officially denounce these two unpatriotic radical Communist race agitators who dared disrespect that flag, anthem, and country, he made his feelings clear about our reasons for doing what we did and our right to do it. Dr. Clark issued an official statement that concluded, "They do not return home in disgrace, but as the honorable young men they are, dedicated to the cause of justice for the Black people in our society." He immediately got a taste of what we had gotten in the months leading up to the Olympics and ever since the victory stand. You can go to the Martin Luther King Library on campus today and look at the inch-thick stack of hate mail he received.

I saw a lot of old friends at the barbecue that day. My old roommate was kicking off his final year as a campus administrator before retiring—St. Saffold, the football and basketball player from Stockton, not far from where I grew up in farm country, who later played pro football and then came back to San Jose State to mentor the next several generations of students of all colors. Old track teammates were there, such as Jerry Williams, who once managed to beat John and me in a race and never let me forget it, and who later sued to become one of the first black firefighters in the city of San Jose; and George Carty, who came to San Jose State after I had finished running and stayed in the area to become a track coach and high school teacher.

A few old heads from the struggle on campus made the trip unannounced, like Loye Cherry, who was a few years ahead of me and was one of the activists back when being an activist was even more new and dangerous. Loye came in from Oakland, where he is now the minister of a large Baptist congregation, and he caught me by surprise, telling me he just wanted to take advantage of the day set aside to honor us.

Our wives were there, of course. Delois and John's wife, Charlene, and all of the old crowd sat together at the picnic table, ate ribs and chicken and baked beans and salad and rolls and hoo-rahed around like in the old days. Not me as much as the rest, although I enjoyed being with everyone, but John definitely raised a ruckus, as he can do. That's what I call all the noisemaking and attention-getting people can do, hoo-rahing, and John has a gold medal in hoo-rah. He showed off his skills when the local TV reporter, a man named Lloyd LaCuesta— who was one of the first journalists to speak to us when we returned to San Jose State, as he was a fellow student at the time—sat down to interview John and me together at the picnic, there in the plaza. 'Los was 'Los, in every way. For that time, while the spotlight was on the two of us, he pretty much took it for himself and shared it with people of his choosing, whether they wanted to or not. At that point, he wanted Erik Grotz, the young white cat who conceived the whole plan for honoring us, to join in. He got the young man in there, even though it was pretty clear that Erik wanted to be there a lot less than John wanted him there.

There was one absence from the day's events, someone both notable and noticeable by his absence. Everyone asked about him. Those of us who knew him, especially Carlos and me, were not surprised that we didn't see him there. I finally made a point to mention him late in the day at the final panel discussion. A very critical figure in this entire project is not here, I said—Dr. Harry Edwards. Harry Edwards was there at the beginning of the project and throughout the struggle, but not in Mexico City, where our lives were on the line. I guess I shouldn't have been surprised, then, that he would not be here, I added. It got a little chuckle. It was the truth, though. It was Harry Edwards himself who had said to both of us, we ought to be the captains of our own ships. Harry is his own captain. John is his own, and I am my own. Two of the ships were docked in San Jose that day, and in reality there wasn't much reason for that third ship to be there.

The rest of the day, we talked. Oh, did we talk, talked in the morning and talked in the afternoon until we were all talked out. The two morning discussions, before the barbecue, were pretty much a direct dialogue with the students, although the first panel session was moderated and included the two faculty members. It was the three students on the panel, though, that livened things up for me. I was glad to see the room so full, some 300 spectators, most of them current students, including a good segment of athletes. I knew nobody had ordered them to attend, just as I could tell no one had to twist the arms of the students on the panel with us. They were very engaged in what we had done and what needed to be done now.

One young man in particular—a Vietnamese American junior named Justin Nguyen—was so eloquent and dedicated that I had to acknowledge him during the discussion and speak to him afterward. All three students—the others were a young white woman, Mary Moran, and a young black woman, Ambra Kelly—spoke their pieces well, but Justin was very self-assured and seemed to have a real grasp of the connection between my time and his, as well as a view of the world similar to ours at the time. For one thing, he thanked Carlos and me for what we had done and compared us to, of all people, Galileo, who was excommunicated from the church for advancing a dangerous and unpopular idea: that the earth revolved around the sun rather than vice versa. Justin knew about Speed City, which is only a rumor to most people his age. He said he hoped his children would one day attend this school because he would be proud of the legacy we left.

Justin, Mary, and Ambra reflected the passion and commitment that John Carlos, our Speed City teammates, and I brought to the struggle 35 years earlier. They stood out that day, even as the crowds gravitated toward us throughout the afternoon. The other students were curious about us and the world in which we had lived, and about how similar it might be to their own today. The rap session in the student union atrium after the panel discussion was very informative to us as well as to them. The crowd—again well populated by athletes—threw question after question at us about our responsibilities, and theirs, in being role models and leaders on campus and in society. Many of them had no prior knowledge of our history on this campus. Some said that now that they knew, they would take a more active role in the issues that affected them as athletes and as members of the community—even to lead. Some said they began to study up on us more when they heard about the commemoration, or promised themselves they would do so now that they had seen and heard us. And I hope they do.

The final panel discussion was coordinated by the campus Africana Center and the Black Student Union—the descendents of the Black Student Union in which we were involved, which was one of the first ever started on a college campus. This event was less of an interaction with the audience; the two of us were alone at the table answering questions from the audience read by the moderator. The venue was spectacular: the brand-new campus library, doubling as the main branch of the city library system, named for Dr. Martin Luther King. The atrium where we spoke was packed, and under other circumstances we could have spoken for hours. The students and everyone else who wanted a glimpse of us and an earful of our recollections about 1968 didn't mind standing behind the full seats, in the hallway, the doorway, and along the wall.

John and I answered the questions, even the difficult ones. The entire experience hit home the hardest when we were asked what we felt and thought as we stood on the victory stand with fists raised. I admitted, as I always do, that I was scared, that it was something I felt I had no choice in doing. And, I said, I had thought about death threats, and not just the ones that might be carried out in the stadium. I had been harassed at home, right there in San Jose. I'd gotten letters, of course, and phone calls, and people driving by the house and yelling, or throwing things, or just stopping and sitting and waiting for a reaction before pulling away. They would do this when I was home, and they'd do it when my wife and infant son were there by themselves—and when my wife went shopping to buy Similac for little Kevin, spending the precious few dollars I had to feed our child, money I barely scraped up because I had lost jobs because of my beliefs . . .

And I couldn't go on. I didn't want to go on. I normally am not a big talker anyway. This time, though, the memories of what my wife and son endured because I chose to take a stand overwhelmed me.

Thankfully, my partner had no reservations about talking. He never has. He didn't in 1968, after the victory stand, and he doesn't now. At every session, John Carlos talked himself almost completely out. He started the day worn out; he did not get to campus as early as I did because he had an attack of kidney stones the night before. But that didn't slow him down, or even slow the pace of his talking. At the first panel discussion, we both said we might occasionally need reminding of what the question was, in case we got off track on something else. John just went completely off track on every question.

He was asked, for example, how he and I spread the word of a possible protest for human rights at the Olympics, and by the time he finished answering, he had veered into making sure schoolchildren in San Jose had crossing guards, how he and others had helped get them to take the proper math courses, the reasons drugs and crime afflict the black neighborhoods, how steroids are ruining young athletes, and how the CIA had infiltrated the movement on campus. And on and on and on. All valid topics, of course, and all related to the issues at hand and, in fact, the question asked. But it takes a John Carlos to articulate it that way.

He approached the rap session in the atrium the same way, and he repeated the process at the dialogue in the library. In fact, the library session ended up being cut short after we had taken only three questions. In truth, we were both exhausted, and John was clearly fighting those kidney stones. But the reason we took so few questions was that John spent about 20 minutes answering one of them. He had the audience riveted the whole time. Don't ever think John Carlos doesn't know what to do when he has a stage.

That wasn't the first time one of our speaking engagements together had been cut short when John got hold of a microphone. Sometimes he doesn't even need the microphone, as long as he has an audience. That's the way the cat does it. That's the way he did it 35 years earlier. Think of the comment that has stayed in so many minds from those days surrounding the victory stand. It's when Carlos says to the reporters fighting to get to him that nobody had better come at him, because the next person that comes at him, he's going to kick his ass. That's what people remember, even though I spoke at length to Howard Cosell the day after the victory stand.

Lee Evans—who played a large role in the project even though he never had his opportunity to do what we did—has pointed out frequently that somehow, after Lee and I and Harry Edwards laid the foundation for months before the Games, John became the spokesman when it was over. He was the spokesman in Mexico City, the spokesman at the airport when we left, and the spokesman when we arrived back in the United States. When we were invited to places on campus afterward, he did most of the talking.

News wants excitement, and he can excite you. But that's another difference between us: to me, being excited isn't all that's necessary to get a point across. If you have a listening audience, I'm good for that. If you have an audience that likes movement and likes to be aroused, then Carlos is your man.

Carlos did say something earlier in the day that illuminated our relationship perfectly: that he was more in the mindset of Malcolm X, while I was more aligned with the philosophy of Martin Luther King, but rather than letting this keep us apart, we brought our approaches together, and when they intersected, those who opposed us had to take notice, to the extreme. I had voiced that thought about Dr. King and Malcolm myself, but he was the one who put us in those roles. He was right on with that. Our differences are very distinct, and for that reason we conduct our own lives and are far from the permanently linked pair so many like to portray us as being. But we are not rivals, either. I'm my own man, and so is Carlos. Anyone who watched and listened to us that day understood our link and our separateness.

We surely were linked on that day, and more proof came in the final event of the day, a black-tie banquet in our honor at the Fairmont Hotel in downtown San Jose. The dinner, at up to $150 a head, was also designed to kick off the fundraising for the statue. Again, so many of the people I grew to know and appreciate before, during, and after my time at San Jose State were there. St. Saffold and Jerry Williams were there. Dr. Robert Fuller, who as president of Oberlin College in Ohio hired me as a coach, administrator, and instructor in the 1970s, when no one else would give me a job. My fellow coach at Oberlin, one of the three black men hired there when hiring black coaches in college was unheard of: Cass Jackson, who coached football after being a player and assistant at San Jose State. Bob Poynter, who coached at San Jose City College and who has been a towering figure in track and field in the area for decades. Frank Slaton, who played football and sprinted at San Jose State when I was there, who took a stand of his own in the aftermath of Mexico City and who still coaches high school track in the area. A whole bunch of my old teammates and my rivals at other schools, whom I'd met at meets then and have seen at meets around the state at all levels since.

The students had planned this event as well. The model of the proposed statue was on display, and the artist whose design was chosen in the competition was there. We were saluted by a photo film essay, a jazz trumpet solo, and more live music from the band that had played earlier in the day. The keynote speech was given by Dr. David Horne, a black educator who at the time was an associate professor at California State University at Northridge and whose other positions included executive director of the California African American Political Institute in southern California. I can't lie, I had never heard of him before he stepped up to the podium. I can't say, however, that I'll forget his speech either: he talked about how as a teenager growing up in Florida, he was inspired by the sight of Carlos and me with fists thrust in the air before the world. It made him proud, he said, to be a black man at a time that it wasn't fashionable, or safe, to be a proud black man. Now, he said, the sight of us reminded him of all the beautiful things about the 1960s when he was growing up: the music, the spirit of revolution, the awakening of his soul and the souls of so many others. Apparently he came up with all this off the cuff—he had only a couple of notes with him at the podium, he said, because he didn't know what kind of a function it was going to be.

But his memory of the victory stand must have been very strong. Dr. Horne ended his speech by pumping his own fist in the air several times, saying it was a salute to all of us who sacrificed ourselves for our people's benefit. "Huhn! Huhn! Huhn!" he shouted. It came off like something the old Black Panthers would have done—which was funny to me, because, of all the misconceptions that have spread about the victory stand for the past 35 years, the one about us being Panthers and giving what they called a "Black Power" salute has gone the furthest. That is, if it's not the one about the Olympic officials taking John's and my medals away in Mexico City. John and I made it clear that day, once again, that our medals were safe and sound at our respective homes. Anyway, at our table at the dinner that night, John was loving it; he was saluting and shouting back at Dr. Horne. When Dr. Horne came back to the table, both John and I gave him big hugs of appreciation.

Even that, however, was not what stood out most to me about the evening. Throughout the banquet there was a steady stream of proclamations and salutations and commendations from the administration of San Jose State University, the city of San Jose, and the county of Santa Clara, California. The first commendation we received, in fact, came from the newly appointed president of the university, Dr. Joseph Crowley. He brought us onto the stage at the front of the ballroom. He read the proclamations on the awards plaque to us, commemorating this as Tommie Smith and John Carlos Day. And when Dr. Crowley finished reading the plaques, he told us, "Welcome home," shook our hands, and then embraced us.

Yes. The president of San Jose State University hugged Tommie Smith and John Carlos. No, I would never have imagined living long enough to experience that. Nor could I have imagined hearing those words from anyone within the San Jose city limits or the borders of this campus: welcome home.

Now, it was not as if no one with a title or prefix on his name at San Jose State stood with us in 1968. Dr. Clark, for one, spoke up for us after Mexico City at great cost to his standing on campus and with his peers in other parts of the country. Also, at least two professors at San Jose State will always stand out in my mind as men who helped shape me when I needed shaping most: Dr. Bruce Oglivie and Dr. Thomas Tutko. Their names ought to be recognizable as, respectively, the foremost sports psychologist and sociologist of all time, men who pioneered in their fields. When either of them spoke in the years after I graduated, I made a point to go see them if I could, no matter how long the drive was. Dr. Oglivie in particular was special. I took his class as a junior, and in that class and in personal conversations with me, he truly made me understand that I was not dumb. At that time, convincing me of this took some doing, because of my own background and the campus culture. He was amazing.

But besides those exceptions, I cannot honestly tell anyone that the administration has ever made me feel welcome—back, home, or any other way. Not until right around the time the movement to commemorate us began, with the students. And realistically, it's still the students. The administration hasn't done anything more than what it did that night. What has it done? It has given a couple of kudos to us to keep itself alive in this awareness project. For 35 years it was up to the faculty and administration to make us a part of this campus's history, to impart our impact to generations of students, and to create an awareness of us among them. The awareness project in motion now is all coming from the students. How, then, can I feel welcome from anyone but the students? Besides the select handful I mentioned, I didn't feel anything from the faculty and administration when I was a student, I didn't feel anything after I graduated, and I didn't feel anything that night or since then.

For the official segments of the campus, city, and county, the time to acknowledge and embrace and recognize us was that third week of October 1968, when we were sent home from Mexico City. What were we sent home to? When we got onto the campus, it was just the status quo. Nothing. No celebration. At best, we were considered outside the mainstream, even more than we had been during our college years, and that period was no time for those outside the mainstream to wait for recognition. At worst, we were simply infamous. Those who didn't believe what we did was necessary, who thought there was no reason for it, or who knew the reason but didn't want us getting any accolades for it—they were not going to give us any notice for being back. Not even to congratulate us for winning a gold and a bronze medal for the country they believed we disgraced. We received positive reactions from some, but the negative far outweighed the positive, and many made it clear how negative they planned to be.

I'm gonna take him down where he got started. If I had found a reason not to feel dread on a day like this, I would have embraced it like no one had ever embraced anyone or anything before. But after all I have seen, known, and heard, how could I just dismiss that kind of threat? Again, grateful for it all, but wary. And observant, with eyes and ears wide open.

Those eyes and ears saw and heard, at the end of the night, waves of people, family, friends, admirers, students, and officials eagerly waving me over to a little table off to the right of the stage in the ballroom. On it stood a model of the statue that would, God willing, be erected in honor of John and me. There I stood looking at myself in miniature, on a victory stand, head lowered and fist thrust high. What do you think? I was asked, over and over again.

What did I think? What could I think?

2

October 16, 1968

I CANNOT SAY what I remember most about that night in Mexico City because I remember everything. How could I possibly forget anything about it? Every detail, from the position of the starting blocks to the feeling of crossing the finish line—and after I crossed the finish line. What happened that night, October 16, 1968, was history, and you'd better believe I was aware of what was going on every second.

It began long before the starting blocks on the Olympic Stadium track for the men's 200-meter final. But the starting blocks are, yes, a good place to start. As I stood behind the blocks, my whole life went through my head, as a child in Texas and in California, as a student in grammar school and high school, and all my experiences in college, especially the political times, and now, 24 years old and the fastest man in the world, standing at the starting line at the XIXth Olympiad ready to prove it. You'd be surprised when you are to call upon everything, how quickly you can remember nothing. But I had no choice; I had to remember this. It would be devastating for me to forget any of it; I could not forget, because to forget was to lose sight of what I was there for. Of course, I was there to win the race, but winning the race meant much more than picking up the gold medal. It meant the sacrifices that Tommie Smith had gone through the previous year and a half—the catcalls, the threats on my life, the letters in the mail, the mock tickets back to Africa, all the different names they were calling us. I was afraid for my wife Denise and my son Kevin, who was just a baby then; I was afraid for their lives because everyone knew where we lived.

Usually a runner just before a race will stretch, shake, jiggle, somehow exercise the legs, arms, muscles, ligaments, tendons—keep the body loose and warmed up. But I was exercising my thought processes, seeing how many Thank-you-Gods I could send up, because whoa, did I need some help. I thought every gun in the world was pointed at me. I knew politically I was a negative because I didn't have an education, or I didn't have the education I wanted; in fact, I had not yet graduated from college. I had been fired from all the little $2.50-an-hour jobs I'd had, and that was usually washing cars at San Jose State as an athlete to make money besides your scholarship, which was $85 a month and $25 a semester on books. That was my full scholarship. Heavy duty, huh? Holding 11 world records. Thinking back on it all these years later, I'm about to start crying all over again. And even with all that, I knew it might not matter much at all, because I also was thinking, My goodness, when I win this race, I won't live to see my gold medal.

Now, even with all that going through my head, I still normally would have been warming up my legs at the starting line. But I was afraid to do anything because of my injured leg. In the semifinal heat less than an hour earlier, I had strained my left adductor muscle, high up on my thigh near the groin. That's the muscle that keeps the legs straight in line. Oh, I knew all my muscles, all the physiology of running, the science of sprinting; I had learned it for four years, and I knew what that muscle was, what it meant, and how much I needed it. By that time, I had also figured out how I could get through the race and win it with that muscle injured. I had put on a couple of sprints on the practice field before I got there, and walking across the field I had hoped the excursion would have been a little faster, but no one had a pulled muscle but me, so no one had that worry but me. I was shaking the arms a little bit and the muscles within my butt trying to keep the deep muscle warm. My legs, no; I was afraid that if I shook one leg the other one wouldn't shake, and I didn't want to do any damage to the adductor muscle.

So I had all these things going through my mind—and I had to worry about John Carlos in the next lane. Anybody who knew anything about the sport of track and field at that time knew that John Carlos was plenty to worry about. I knew better than anyone; we ran together at San Jose State College. We were not teammates, at least outside of the United States Olympic team; he had arrived at San Jose State as a transfer from East Texas State College when he was a junior and I was a senior, and he sat out that year because transfer students are ineligible to participate in athletics for their first year. When he became eligible, my eligibility had ended. Regardless, we were the two best in the world in this event. On the day we both made the Olympic team, I ran the 200 meters in 19.9 seconds, the fastest I had ever run. Carlos ran a 19.7, which would have been a world record, except that his record was disqualified because the spikes he used were not approved. But it still gives you an idea of what kind of an athlete he was, one of the best that ever lived. That's who I was trying to beat to win a gold medal.

So as I stood behind those blocks, I prayed a little bit, and I cried a little bit. With all these things in my mind, I knew I couldn't fail—not that I must not, but I could not, with a capital C. Had I failed to win, everything would have been in vain, it would have been a waste.

By everything, of course, I include the reason for the death threats, the feeling that I would not live to enjoy my gold medal, the reason both John Carlos and I were even on the track in Mexico City: the Olympic Project for Human Rights. Read that name again, very closely, and put aside what you thought you knew about what happened on the victory stand in Mexico City that night. This was not the Black Power movement. To this very day, the gesture made on the victory stand is described as a Black Power salute; it was not. Nor was it only about black athletes talking about boycotting because they don't like what's going on. It was the Olympic Project for *Human Rights.* It was more than civil rights; that's why it was called human rights. It's just that pressure was taken by the black athletes; we stepped out and did what should have been done by young groups much earlier. It wasn't dope-smoking, arm-pumping punks, as the other protesters of all types from that era are portrayed. We were students, and we were very dedicated to the Olympic Project for Human Rights. What we as black athletes took on for the whole world was a very basic platform that should have drawn support from everybody everywhere. But one no one else wanted to join us. For example, white women faced the same things we did, and years later, in the 1970s, when they realized that the power structure was in the hands of the white man and that what we were fighting for is what they also should have been fighting for, they took up the fight for themselves.

These women then said, "We would have helped you, because we understand what you're going through." At the time, though, they looked at us black athletes like racist dogs who didn't know what we were talking about. So all alone in the fight, we took the bull by the horns, and we did the best we possibly could.

Of course, the very fact that we were lined up to compete in this race meant that we did not choose to boycott. But just as clearly, something was to be done on this stage; something had to be done. As difficult as my situation was, that fact made it even more imperative that I succeed in this race. Look at it this way: Your kid is hungry and thirsty, he's yelling in your face, you know you have to feed him, but you can't even go to the store, and your wife is looking at you and saying, maybe you should go out and make some more money. And you know both of them have a point, but you can't do anything, because something is stopping you, and you have to overcome that before you can satisfy them. Well, my race was no different, except I had no time to get out of it or to do it another way.

The only way was to win this race. You win, you get a gold medal; second, you get silver, third you get bronze, fourth you get forgotten. That's it. And this wasn't a dual meet at San Jose State, this wasn't a conference meet, this wasn't a state meet, this wasn't a national competition. This was the world; the only place you can go from here is down. There was no other place like this. There was no other place where we could present our platform. And to do that, there was no other place to finish but first.

That thought brought me back to how I would finish first. As I have said, sprinting is a science. A lot of people can run fast. If someone scares you, you probably can run fast, but it wouldn't be sprinting. Your poor body would be going in five different directions, because sprinting is not your forte. My coach at San Jose State helped teach me the science of sprinting: Lloyd C. "Bud" Winter, in my mind the greatest track and field coach who ever lived. I absorbed his lessons and studied how to make the body go where the mind tells it to go. My degree is in sociology, and the mind and body play into the study of sociology, and that plays into the pursuit of sprinting excellence. So I had honed my technique, my positioning, the use of my muscles, and my ability to call on all of it in an instant, almost without thinking of it at that moment. So nothing I did on the track before and during a race lacked precision and design and meaning.

For instance, the type of start we learned let the legs relax during the "get set" position, so when you call upon them to react, they have the freedom to react. My buttocks were about 4½ inches above my head in the "get set" position, my head was directly on my shoulder, I wasn't looking up or down, so when I came up in a running position, the head came up with the shoulder, instead of the head coming up and then the shoulder, or the shoulder and then the head. They were very well coordinated, so I didn't have to worry about the degree of head or degree of shoulder coming up. My front leg was at about a 45-degree angle. As the starter said, "Come to your mark," I rocked back in the blocks; at "Get set," I rolled forward, then I rolled up. I leaned on my hands, not the fingertip but the first joints near the nail, at a pressure of about 85 or 90 percent, a lot of pressure, so when the gun sounded the explosion was from the rear and the hands didn't come up first. When I did come out, my right hand came up as I pushed from my back leg, the right, and the left leg, in front, came out. The coordination of the feet and hands had to be perfect. The goal is to be relaxed but in a ready position so when the gun sounds, the only thing you want to think about is forward momentum. You couldn't buy forward momentum. If you thought, "I gotta get out, I gotta get out," then the gun sounds, and out of the corner of your eye you see the other guy leaving you and you're wondering why you're not going—it's because you didn't call on your muscles to react.

And that's just to start the race the right way. Now, starting a race was critical for me because of my size. At 6 foot 4 and about 180 pounds, I was much bigger that just about everyone else I ran against at that time. Being as tall as I was and weighing what I did, it was like a big truck with big tires. Once you get rolling you're moving, but in the first few feet, even a Volkswagen can beat you. So I had spent a lot of time working on my starts on the San Jose State track, on the south end of campus on 11th Street. I had my technique down pretty sharp. I had also made sure everything about the positioning of the starting block was perfect as well, to accommodate my frame and my leg span. All things considered, particularly my size, on a scale of 1 to 10, I would say my start was an 8½ or 9. When I set the world record for the 200 meters and 220 yards on a straightaway, in my junior year, I was the first person out of the blocks; I had a good meter and a half on everyone for the first 10 meters, and that's exceptional for me. But everything clicked perfectly for me that day. Besides, I always knew that I could compete at 100 meters, where the start is even more critical to success. I had run a 100 in 10.1 seconds when the world record was 10 flat. At the time I already held the world records at 200 and 400 meters, so I was a tenth of a second away from holding all three sprint world records. That achievement tells you how good my start generally was.

My start this time would determine a lot more; the first three steps would determine how well I would run the turn, and because of that pulled adductor muscle I was very afraid that I might be too far behind the leaders. I already knew that one of the leaders was going to be John Carlos. I knew he'd be coming out of that turn at about 21 miles an hour, and he would be impossible to catch. So in those few seconds before the race that encapsulated three years, with all the other things going through my head as we stood behind the blocks, I also went over my race plan. My plan was to come out easy because of the adductor pull; to put too much pressure on it would throw me out of the race early, and putting too little pressure on it would throw me too far behind to come back on people like John Carlos and Peter Norman of Australia. Norman and I had passed the Olympic record back and forth between us during the heats; I tied it, then later he broke it, then I broke his record. If I do either too much or too little in this race, I might as well not run. I had to redline it all the way—keep it on the redline, just as in a car. You go any faster, your engine's going to blow up, and you go any slower, you get beat. So you have to keep it redlined, right in between, and hope you come out on top. I promised myself, if I could do 15 really strong strides, I'd shut it down afterward. I was looking at going 80 percent out of the blocks, 85 percent on the turn, 90 percent three strides out of the turn, 100 percent for those 15 strides, then shut it down to low power about eight meters before I hit the tape. I figured those 15 strides at full power would be all that adductor muscle could take.

I couldn't hide that injured muscle; everyone knew about it. In fact, as we lined up, I heard the announcer say, "And Tommie Smith has a pulled muscle; he's getting in his blocks now; we'll see how this race goes; I'm not sure if he'll be able to run." I heard him, and I wanted to say, "Man, why don't you just shut up and let me run my race?"

The injury had happened in front of everybody, at the end of the semifinal heat earlier in the day. I know why it happened. As I came to the finish line, I slowed down out of control; when you're running almost 30 miles an hour and you don't think about slowing down or gearing down as you do in a car, you're going to strip your gears, you're going to mess your transmission up, and that's exactly what I did to the body. My leg kind of strayed as I slowed because I wasn't completely concentrating, because of the pressures of that race—not only running fast and keeping muscles coordinated but also the proposed boycott and the approaching moment where I would run the race of my life, and for so many other lives. If the mind is not totally straight, it cannot communicate to the body precisely what it has to. Otherwise, I would not have lost the coordination I had always trained myself to have. In fact, I had never had a serious injury such as this before. The injury was as much sociological as it was physical.

It was a very sharp pain, and I hit the ground because I didn't know what happened. They took me off in a prone position and when I looked up, you know who I saw? My coach, Bud Winter. And I said, well, everything is okay, Bud is here. What made Bud a great coach is that he made the most difficult things seem easy by the way he explained them. The techniques he taught were different from every other coach's, and he explained them with a humanistic feel, not with a scientific approach: if you do this or that, this or that will happen. He just talked to you about what would work, and you try it and get a feel for it, and you realize, wow, this isn't very hard. When you did it, he'd give you a little cheer—"Way to go, Tom-Tom." He made it easy for a tall, gangly athlete to get it all together. Bud was a very, very attentive coach; he recognized talent and he worked with it.

Bud had more great athletes than any other coach that ever lived. I remember the day before the race, he came to the Olympic Village, and he took me and John and Lee Evans, all his San Jose State athletes, out to train. There was a track near the Olympic Village, right outside the dormitories, that athletes trained on instead of going all the way over to the stadium or the practice track. I wish someone had taken movies of the scene, because it felt like one of the most incredible moments ever in track and field. There was me, specifically tuned to win the 200; Lee, specifically tuned to win the 400; John, who could win the 200 or the 400; and also Ronnie Ray Smith, another athlete from San Jose State running a leg of the 4-by-100 relay. One coach, from one college, had four athletes at the Olympic Games, all attending at the same time. In fact, seven of us had a chance to qualify for the Games, four of us did, and each of us medaled. We had a camaraderie at that college that very few colleges across the nation had, and we had that because we had a coach like few others.

That is why I felt relieved to see Bud Winter as I was carried off the track. My eyes were closed and I was in pain, but I was aware of the reaction around me; I think Carlos and Lee were both there. Bud and two or three others escorted me into the training room, which was adjacent to the track, maybe 75 meters from the finish line. It was a big, spacious room with a nice, clean table, and I got up on one of the tables, and I said, "I'm gonna be here for a while, maybe forever." They iced the injury—and remember where the injury was. You put ice cubes in your groin area and your head starts hurting; you don't mess with the groin area unless you mean business, and I suppose they meant business because they crammed that ice on there. I thought, "Oh no, why me?" But they isolated it, they cooled it down, they stopped the swelling, they stopped the bleeding if there was any, and left me in there, ice on and ice off, for about 45 minutes, until about 40 minutes before the final—that's how little time there was between the semifinal and final, how little time I had to heal. Bud stayed with me the whole time. Then they got me up and walked me out to the practice field, which was only 2½ minutes away walking. It had gotten dark by then. We walked up the stairs very carefully, maybe a flight of 45 or 50 steps up to the practice field. This was the test.

I started jogging, and the whole track stopped; I could tell it stopped because I couldn't see anybody moving. I said, "Oh God, help me, help me." I started picking up speed a little bit, raising my knees, bringing my arm out, going at about 60 percent. Nobody spoke to me; they had been surprised to see me come out of the training room. They wanted to see if the leg was going to work, just like I did; they wanted to see if it was going to blow up in my face, or if I would even be able to start the race or finish the race. I kept jogging, and I thought, this feels pretty good. So I backed off until about 25 minutes before the race. The injury was still fresh, so nothing had atrophied yet and nothing had stopped working completely. The ice had worked. I walked and jogged a little. I thought I'd better save everything I had for the starting block. Then came time to go to the track, and the organizers, wearing their little white hats and blue coats, keeping everything moving efficiently in the biggest track meet in the world, said, "All the 200-meter athletes please line up." They said it in broken English, but I knew what they meant: Hey man, time for you to run, the time for truth is now.

I remember what I wore: the uniform was comfortable, and I wore it with pride of the country it represented, that I represented. I was wearing black socks, which of course came into play later that evening. There was no such thing as black sports socks back then. They were dress socks, which usually are not what you wear for athletic competition. A pair of good dress socks at that time cost about $1.50; I bought that pair for 89 cents. They're now in the USA Track and Field Hall of Fame in Indianapolis. I have the rest of my uniform. I also kept the outfit we wore in the opening ceremonies, the hat and slacks and coat. I don't have the Hush Puppies; I remember I kept them after I returned to San Jose and wore them until they wore out, then I threw them away. I didn't have the funds to buy shoes, so I wore those out.

I was in lane 3; Carlos was in lane 4. At a lot of meets the better lane assignments go to the guys with the best times in the preliminaries, and 3, 4, and 5 are the best lanes. In Mexico City, though, the lanes were drawn by lot, a blind draw. Larry Questad, a young runner from Stanford University, was in 5, and I believe Peter Norman had 6. The lineup did please me. For the races on a turn—which today means anything above 110 meters—the starting blocks are staggered as the lanes go further out. So Carlos was ahead of me, and I like to see people ahead of me. I don't want to use the word "chasing," but I like it better to see a person out in front if me. And I knew that Carlos was the runner I had to beat. I ran against people on my United

States team—even people on my own San Jose State team—that were faster than the best guy from another country in that final in Mexico City. Still, at the start I couldn't look at Carlos's butt. That would have caused the control of my body, my technique, my balance, to backfire. Your mind is not controlling his muscles, but when you look at him, your mind ends up running to his beat, his form, his rhythm, and you begin to run Carlos's race. You never look at any other racers; if you do, you might as well go help them run. You tell them, "Here, you take my energy of 14 years and run with it because I won't need it, I want to watch you." Nor do you look at the finish line; you learn that early. It's on the other side of the track, around the curve. I remember a grammar school meet where a kid got caught up looking at the finish line on the other side of the track. The gun went off, he went, and when he came to the turn, he ran across the field to the finish line. He ran to where he was looking. You can't look at the crowd, either. Definitely don't look at the starter. That's why he has a gun, to make noise, so you have no need to look at him. When you're in your starting blocks, you hear your heart beat, everything is turned into yourself, and the only other sound you hear is the starter saying, "On your mark, get set," and the gun. After "get set" there was usually a pause of two: one-one-thousand, two-one-thousand, then the gun. There was one difference in Mexico City, though: it was all done by whistles. One whistle meant "come to your marks," two whistles meant "get set," then the gun. It was done so there would be no language miscommunication, runners trying to understand Spanish, having to know the words for "on your mark" and "get set."

Have you ever been stopped by a policeman? The first thing in your mind when you see the red light and hear the siren isn't even a thought, it's a panic; your adrenaline gets pumped up, then the thinking process kicks in. That's about the way you feel in the get-set position. You think about that, that moment, anticipating a sound, and once you hear that sound, you hear nothing but patters of feet, trying to get to that finish line to pick up a gold medal or silver medal or bronze medal. That's it. There was no payment, just gold, silver, or bronze. Although I had held 11 world records at one time, more than any man in track and field history, there was no way to make a living in track and field then; if you did get a few pennies here and there, it was not in the same amount as the athletes are getting today. Especially in my case, there certainly would have been no financial reward because the political push we had for the Olympic Project for Human Rights would certainly have killed any chance to profit from winning a gold medal. But I was there to prove a point, not to make a buck.

As the on-your-mark signal came and I backed into the blocks, I quickly scanned the people in front of me. Not that this is what I normally do, but I knew this would probably be the last time I'd compete against these people, especially in the Olympic Games. I wanted to get as much out of it as I possibly could, so reflection would give me as much of a feeling of accomplishment as possible, knowing that this was it, and it would be finished in less than 20 seconds. But I couldn't think too much about that. At this moment, everything you've learned about running was all on the head of a pin. Everything had to come to a point right then. The race yesterday was no good today, the race for the world record three years ago was no good today. Everything that was good today would only be good for today. All your thoughts had to be concentrated on what was happening right now. What your body had to do, you've trained to do, so you could do it without thinking about it—but you had to be prepared, in the blocks, to call on it in an instant. The psychological encompasses the physical and mental; if the physical wasn't right and the mental wasn't right, nothing would go right. So that big old P-S-Y-C-H aspect was just sitting there waiting to gobble everything up so that later on down the line, when you take dead last at the worst time in your life, you ask yourself why, and then you become suicidal. The feeling of being on that starting line is like having diarrhea—you can't think of anything else except getting relief from what ails you, and the quicker you get there, the sooner you'll feel that relief and the greater that relief will be. So what do you do? You get there as fast as you possibly can. But there in Mexico City, getting there would be a problem.

I felt the tape on my adductor muscle. I knew that I could run in less than full health. I had done it at the Olympic training camp in South Lake Tahoe, in what was the real Olympic trials—the ones that replaced the trials in Los Angeles that were diluted by the United

States Olympic Committee out of fear that the athletes would either follow through on their proposal to boycott or make a gesture of protest of some kind. I had toured in Germany about two months before Lake Tahoe, and I had to rush back to join my teammates. I was eating in another country, rushing to catch a plane, worrying about getting back in time, and it all put pressure on me and affected my insides. Not to make a pun, but I had to run in Lake Tahoe with the runs, and when you do, all your strength exits you before you can use what you put in your body. I was truly in no condition to race, not against the likes of John Carlos and the rest. And that internal physical pressure was not the only pressure; the athletes had received a letter from the USOC saying that if we were contemplating an "embarrassment" to the United States at the trials or at the Games, we would be ordered to leave the team. But I think God Almighty protected me because he knew there was a message that was needed; he kind of picked me up, patted me on the back, and said, "You worked this hard, you have so much to say, I'd better put you in there so you can help yourself and somebody else in the process." So with all of that, I ran a 19.9.

They gave the get-set signal, and I thought, "The time is nigh." Everything was culminating in this moment: all the things that had happened because of the proposed boycott, and the years that I trained, not only in school training with a coach, but also in the summer when I worked in the fields with my father, in what we'd call the Bottom, that wide area in the central California Valley where my family and I had moved from Texas when I was little. It was the West-lake area, a great big farm area that extended from down near Stratford all the way up to Avenel. If you drive down there, to Stratford, and look at all that land, you'll be looking for a long time. The farmland goes on as far as the eye can see. That is Westlake; that's where we had to work at night, and it would be quite a night. When I was at Lemoore High School, a typical 24 hours would go like this:

I would go to my first class at around 8 in the morning, and after school I went to football practice from 3 to 4:45. I'd rush to shower, if I had time, then rush to catch the late school bus by 5, and hope the bus driver wouldn't be late. I'd get home at 5:30, and my father would be waiting for me on the front porch. We'd jump in the old pickup and go to the field, about eight miles away, to start work by 6, because that's the time the hands change on the 12-hour shifts. And I'd work in those fields all night, 12 hours, and get home and have to be ready to be back in class at 8 in the morning, which meant I might get some sleep and I might not.

That's what I had gone through to get out of Lemoore, to San Jose State, to the Olympic Games, to arrive there as part of the Olympic Project for Human Rights, and to reach this starting line, in the starting blocks. All of this came to mind as I waited and listened . . . On your marks . . . get set . . . one-one-thousand, two-one-thousand—gun. And off to the races we went.

I guess prayer does things, because when we came out of the turn I was within striking distance. The adductor muscle did hold up on the straightaway, doing exactly what it had done in all the races in which my whole body was healthy. It felt extraordinarily good when I came out of the turn and I realized there was a body and a half in front of me. I do think there was somebody else half the length of my body in front of me it; it could have been Peter Norman or someone else from another country—but I also knew I was in an attack position. I had not lost contact with the rest of the field. After 14 years of hard work, 14 years of dedication to the sport, putting all this together in one last attempt to make my body function to its optimum, it did happen. And I'm very thankful that it did happen, because if it hadn't happened, I wouldn't be doing this book.

Carlos was about three meters ahead of me at that point. That's when I suddenly opened up at full throttle, for those 15 strides that I felt my body could handle. I was conscious that I was gaining on people because their bodies got bigger; which means either they're coming back to you or you're going toward them. In some cases it's both, but in this case I know Carlos wasn't coming back toward me. I was coming toward him at such a rapid pace that the attack, I think, was a surprise to him, and I don't think he could recover from the initial blow of someone going by him that fast. Even though everything you hear while you're running is a blur because you're concentrating on your form and not the crowd, I heard the crowd, a big loud cheer, when I went by Carlos. I don't believe they were cheering for me. I think they were cheering the way I went by him and the form I used to go by him, rather than Tommie Smith beating John Carlos. Who in the hell cared whether Tommie Smith beat John Carlos, with all the political business that had gone on before? Besides, we were on the same team, the same country.

Now, of course Carlos's story is a little different; his story is "I let Tommie Smith win." It's very embarrassing to say you went to an event such as an Olympic Games and let somebody beat you. Number one, not only is it embarrassing, but it's also quite stupid. I know Carlos is a buddy of mine, but the truth is the light. Number two, when you're in a race like that and you don't put up your 100 percent best and you get beat, you can be disqualified. So there are a lot of ramifications to Carlos saying that. He should keep quiet because it's not very smart to say you let somebody beat you, in any race.

Besides, there is this you have to consider: the 80 meters I ran full-throttle is probably faster than any man or woman had run before. It was such a burst of energy, such a burst of speed. Some people have a burst of energy, but their ability cannot equal their burst of energy, and they don't get the result to match the energy expended. In this particular instance, I got that burst of energy and I had the speed to match the energy. That was one of the biggest bursts of energy I'd ever had in track and field, because it was the highlight of my track and field life. It was the finale of my career, and it was in the Olympic Games. I opened up at 100 percent, and it came out at 115 percent of the normal me. Of course, in the last 10 meters my hands went up; I lost more than a couple of strides, two and a half or three good strides, and I still came in at 19.83 seconds, a world record. I do believe that if I had not thrown my hands up, 19.5 would not have been too much to imagine. But at that particular time it didn't matter. I don't want to get caught up with what I could have done; I want people to know that the 19.83 meant as much to me as a 19.5 would have, because of the win and because of the platform. I had to put the last nail in the platform for the Olympic Project for Human Rights. That gold medal had to be won by someone who really believed in the Olympic Project for Human Rights and the contention that it helped everybody, not just the black athletes.

The hands didn't go up because I was trying to look cool, to be Mr. Big, or to try to become famous. I already held 11 world records, so I didn't need to be famous. People all over the world already knew what I represented in terms of human rights, so I didn't need to say, "Look at me, I'm great, my hands are up." It was a moment of elation, a moment of accomplished ecstasy in which I had no choice. In fact, my hands went up before I realized they were up. For all the athletes who are reading this, it's not a good idea to throw your hands up 10 meters before the tape. It's dangerous—number one, because you throw out of line the coordination of the muscles, the legs and the arms, and number two, you could be beaten, because you cut about 50 percent of your power and momentum forward. That didn't happen to me, because I was going fast enough to hold it—my strides were nine, nine and a half feet, and neither Peter Norman nor John Carlos could have closed the distance between me and them fast enough. But, my goodness no, it wasn't a smart move. As it turned out, both of them crossed the finish line in 20 seconds flat, and Norman edged Carlos at the tape. It was the fastest 200-meter race up to that time.

For me, it was a happy ending; it was a happy culmination of all the races I'd ever run, and all the practices, as well as all I had endured with the pulled muscle, the political scene, with me not having finished school yet and my having to go back and face all the racist attitudes at the time, the ones that had generated the idea of the Olympic Project for Human Rights in the first place. It all came together then, and I was very glad it was over. It seemed like 200 years had come to an end, because I had worked so hard to get to the finish line first and achieved one of the highest accolades for any athlete in any sport.

I didn't know I was smiling when I crossed the finish line, either. Again, that's not the thing to do, because it gives the appearance of being very cocky, very unsportsmanlike. You want to cross the finish line with the idea of sportsmanship, not with an attitude of "I am the best, I knew it before I started out, here I am, so give me my medal." But I knew I had a distant look in my eyes. That was a look of tiredness, of fright because there were threats on our lives, and exhaustion from having just finished a 200-meter race with all the odds against me.

When I hit the tape, I felt I was looking at nothing in particular, but I guess at everything. Nothing really mattered at that time: recuperate and get out of there, and I mean *get out of there.* You win a gold medal, you strive all these months and all these years to win it, but at that moment I was more concerned that I would not make it out of Mexico City alive. We had received death threats all along, all of us in the Olympic Project for Human Rights, but mostly myself and Dr. Harry Edwards, more than the others combined, because of our activism and the proposed boycott. We continued to get death threats in Mexico City, and yeah, that scared us. I got notes saying, "You won't run in Mexico City." Yes I would, I thought, what would keep me from running? But when you get this, you think either the guy is crazy, or he's going to physically harm you. When I approached the blocks, yes, the death threats were on my mind, deep on my mind. But I was going to run the race unless somebody took the race away from me, because I had come too far to stop. I tried to give it as little thought as I could, but when somebody threatens you, you don't just flick it off the cuff of your sleeve and say, "Ah, the guy is crazy." To give you an idea of what was on my mind during the heats, when I pulled the adductor muscle in the semis, it was a very sharp pain unlike any other pain I had felt before, and I had pulled a few muscles before. I honestly thought that I had been shot. I looked down and there was no blood, so I was happy that I had pulled a muscle, that I had pulled something on the inside rather than having had something pierce me from the outside.

I knew that even though I had achieved the ultimate in my sport, because I worked on an Olympic Project for Human Rights platform, there were people out there who looked at me and the others as dumb jocks who didn't know what we were talking about anyway and therefore had very little to say, and to use the Olympic Games as a platform for political protest was a no-no. What I believed, instead, is that you take what you do best, which for me was running in track and field, and use it as a platform for something good, to get something done. The Olympic Games was a part of a platform that I was able to use because of what I had accomplished, to make people realize what's going on in this country. You can't not use it. What we did was aimed at no individual but at society in general, so if people take it personally, they should look within themselves; they might find that their beliefs are as racist as society's.

But in order to use that platform, I had to win the race. There was no way I could lose; if I had lost, I would have lost everything. The whole year and a half that we had talked would have been in vain because I wouldn't have been able to do what I did by winning the race. I didn't have the weight of history on my shoulders, because I didn't know what kind of historical perspective this particular stand was going to take. I knew what it meant to me, but I didn't know what kind of effect it was going to have on history. I knew it was something that was needed; I knew it was something that had been too long dismissed because there was really no help for athletes who wanted to speak, or couldn't speak, or did speak without its being reported, and this certainly was a time for something to happen in the world of athletics. So there was a lot on my shoulders, and on the shoulders of whoever would be in that position, whoever had been involved at different times with the Olympic Project for Human Rights. There was a lot that went on long before we went to Mexico City, a lot going on in the minds of others involved, a lot that I wasn't even aware of. I do know that I was walking around there more afraid than in my right senses. I carried a lot of weight, particularly a need to win this race, to facilitate this need I have, not just for myself, but for people I thought deserved it, the people who worked the fields in Texas and saw certain things that they knew weren't equal, seeing even things in grammar school that I knew weren't equal. I needed be in a position to do it, which meant the victory stand. Now, I didn't know at that time what we were going to do; it only came to me later on. I thought about what I might do, but it wasn't solidified in my mind until suddenly, like a snap, I realized, "This is it, this is what I want to do, it's strong enough to hold the attention of myself, and, therefore, it must be strong enough to hold the attention of others."

Now I had to be very smart or very careful in how I was going to approach the situation. The American public was against it, not so much what was done, I believe, but how and where it was done. If this had taken place in Los Angeles, they could have cut to a commercial; anyplace in this country, they could have rationalized cutting to a commercial and cutting off the ceremony by saying, "The USOC warned that this might happen." So we would have been stone caricatures of dummies to let someone tell us how bad we were and how wrong we were and then leave ourselves no recourse, knowing we would not have the audience. What we did was a smart move, a very smart move, and it was so strong that people could not believe we had the audacity to speak out in the eyes of the world about something that was wrong in our country.

Now I know I'm not popular because I did it. There are a lot of people who aren't popular and are now dead. I just thank God that I'm not popular and I'm alive, so I can continue to at least listen and learn and help out wherever I can. I've been a track and field coach for some 30 years, and I know I've helped athletes out by not telling them, "The white man is bad, he should be shot, throw a rock at his head." What I tell them is that people are people, give them a chance to prove themselves wrong, regardless of color. Shake that white man's hand and go on down the line, because he's human also. Look at him in the face, talk to him like he is a human being because he is. Let him show his racist tendencies; see if he believes some of the things that are racist. If he believes such things, then you talk to him about why he's saying them. We all need education. The tendencies of racism come from the systems long before us, and we don't know where they all came from or how long they have been developing and taking root.

That is what this book is about, not about how Tommie Smith raised his fist in the air on the victory stand. So much led up to it, and so much has gone on since then, in his life and in this world. I don't want this to be the Jesse Owens story—Jesse was great, he ran a race, his mouth was so dry it was like cotton, he ran a race against Germany and he beat Nazism and Hitler. I don't want to hear that bullcrap. I want to hear a humanistic point of view; I want to get Jesse to that race, because that's just as important as Jesse running that race. How did I get to that race, and where did I go when it was over?

A S FAR BACK as I can remember, my father would tell me, "When you could, you wouldn't, and now you want to but you can't." That stayed with me the rest of my life, and I've taken that message, dissected it, and gotten as much out of it as I could. What I see in what he said is, "Don't wait for tomorrow to do what you could do today, because tomorrow is not promised." I didn't totally understand it in high school, but it evolved for me a little more in college, and I can see now and I understand why I felt the way I did at certain times at San Jose State. I know I won't be around forever, and I tend to think that whatever I do today will have an effect on what will happen tomorrow, but if I don't do it today, what will happen tomorrow— I'll have nothing to say about it?

But what I say now is what I have always said. Tommie Smith to most people was a radical and a militant, and that has very little to do with what's happening today. Everywhere I go, people recognize who I am, and they know what I did in Mexico City. I do resent that in these conversations all they remember is Mexico City. But, again, the impact of Mexico City is greater than the impact in my sociology classes at Santa Monica College, where I taught for 27 years. I want my students to realize that Mexico City is not the only way to bring about change. It can be brought about in the classroom and in the understanding of the books and of that particular instructor—not just the passage in the book but how the instructor brings that passage to life, what the instructor has to say about the passage, and, in the students' own terminology, what they believe in that passage. Sociology teaches us that difference of opinion is the glue of society, that freedom of speech is critical, that the thought process is free. Many times in your thought processes you can't, or don't, say how you really feel. That's the worst misuse of education.

In my case, most people don't agree with how I did what I did. They think that it was needed but that the Olympics was not the place to do it. I disagree; if you are one of the world's greatest in a particular field, as I was in athletics, you have an avenue, and you have a responsibility to use it, especially if you have something to say about society and how people are treated, people who are not in the position to say it themselves or who don't have the ability to say it. I know there are those who believe only in the goodness of America, not the negative part of America, but America has its negative issues, just as everything has its negative issues. I pinpointed that particular negative issue in Mexico City: simply that the ideals of this country are not applied to everyone. There are those who know and believe and live those truths about America but don't say anything—but that doesn't mean they are socially asleep. As Malcolm X said, "Every shut eye ain't asleep." My father sometimes would sit in a chair in the living room with his eyes closed; we thought he was asleep, but he was not; he was aware of everything but was too tired to keep his eyes open, or he was thinking. Other times, people cannot speak about the system because it might cost them their job or their social standing or the almighty dollar. I believe the almighty dollar doesn't represent the person; the person represents the almighty dollar. What Tommie Smith did is he represented a lot of people who didn't have the freedom or the platform—at least the worldwide platform—or the avenue to speak. Other people don't have to agree with your message, but it can still be said and needs to be said. I didn't look to educate all people, only those people who had the cranial capacity to use what we did to do good for someone else. The victory stand was a human rights stand, and even if what happened on the victory stand was not fully understood, if it was confused as a civil rights stand or a black athletes' stand, at least it opened up the thought process, and it affected how people think about these issues to this day.

I've been told by people in the system, people who hold high stakes in the system, that it would have been better for me not to do what I did because I could have gotten a better job and therefore more money. That was not the issue with Tommie Smith; Tommie Smith's issue was human rights, being a black person, a black athlete in particular. Some people would sum that up in one sentence: I don't like America, I don't like my surroundings, so I'm being a militant in letting people know that some things needed changing. The latter part of that is true: some things did need changing, among them the constitutional rights of black people and stomping out the race issue as much as possible. It wasn't just me as a black athlete unhappy about how I was treated; it was a systematic battle over more than one issue. I was willing to fight and sacrifice for what I believed in, and stay within the guidelines of the law of the land. I don't think the victory stand was outside the law of the land. It only took what I had to say to the rest of the world, and according to white folks, that was the insult of what Tommie Smith and John Carlos did: they took it to the rest of the world. They told me numerous times that I was an athlete and I should have remained an athlete and not gone outside the athletic realm to bring up a social issue. Well, my goodness, athletics in this country produces more revenue than any other single profession in the world. And what black people put into the system in this country, including the industry of athletics, was not equal to what we were provided in terms of our constitutional rights and the rewards of the system. My eyes were not shut and I was not asleep, and athletics was one of the ways I had then to voice an opinion that was part of my personality, but which I'd held inside, ever since the cotton fields of Texas in the early 1950s and in California in the 1960s.

Today very few people know that Tommie Smith did go to graduate school, that Tommie Smith did not major in physical education, that Tommie Smith holds a master's degree, that Tommie Smith is a college instructor, even that Tommie Smith held more world track and field records than any other man or woman in the history of the world. They see me as the person who stuck a fist up on the victory stand in Mexico City. I can't get out from under that; it was in the eyes of the world. Many years ago, I was invited to a track meet at Hawthorne High School, which has a great track and field tradition in southern California. Hawthorne was competing against Inglewood High School, and there were very few people in the stands because even with their success, Hawthorne's meets do not draw very well. I was sitting in the stands when the Hawthorne coach came up to me and introduced me to his wife, and she said, "Oh, Tommie Smith, I've wanted to meet you for a long time." That got the attention, the eyes and ears, of the people around me; people knew the name Tommie Smith because of the Olympic Games, the victory stand. I take insult from that sometimes, but I know at least that's a thought process; it gets out in the system, either for good or bad, and someone gets something out of it.

People around me now know that I am not afraid to involve myself in conversations or conferences that start to go in one direction, and that I am not afraid to change that direction just by a look, by a smile, or by opening my mouth and saying, "I don't necessarily see it that way." I've done this many times at Santa Monica College, and of course I'm not popular. But I'm respected, and that's more important to me than being liked. It's been a long time coming just to reach that level, and I'm not through moving yet. My degrees are in sociology, but I am in the department of physical education, as an instructor and track and field coach, and people have asked me why I don't go to the sociology department, or why I don't go on to a four-year college and coach, and so on. My answer is that I am doing what I like; in fact, I'm in contact with more students now than I would be in the sociology department. I also do ad hoc counseling, I set up programs for students to study, and in my track and field program I have a tendency to talk to my students from a humanistic point of view and not just an athletic point of view. I cannot totally separate the mind from the body; you cannot just talk about the body and not talk about how the body functions and why it functions. A human being is a very intricate organism that was created by a nonhuman, and man has tried many times to change the thought processes by some type of control process, to program a human and make it do what he wants it to do. What's more likely to happen is that by introducing that human to certain parts and aspects of the system, that human realizes that there are other things in the world to be concerned with. The thought processes get stimulated, the mind grows, and he finds that there is more to society than a straight path—and he decides based on what he has experienced whether to explore those other paths.

Thus, you can take the victory stand in Mexico City in a number of ways besides the one way it usually is portrayed. You can do the same in how you take Tommie Smith. But just as there is more to the gold-medal race in the 200 meters in the 1968 Olympic Games than what you thought you knew, and there is more to the victory stand in Mexico City that night, there is more to the man that climbed atop that stand, and more to the man that stepped down from it and into the rest of his life.

Out of the Fields

'M A COUNTRY BOY. I grew up in the country, and even though I have lived in big cities and have traveled all over the world, I don't think the country ever left me. Most of my memories growing up were of the outdoors, not inside—not watching television, not cleaning the carpet, not listening to my CDs or anything like that. None of that was even a possibility then, not TVs or CDs or carpets—well, carpet was, but not for us.

I was born on D-Day—June 6, 1944, in Clarksville, Texas, 35 miles west of the Arkansas border, on the Red River. Clarksville has about 3,000 people living in it, and it's the county seat of Red River County. Compared to Acworth, where I actually grew up, though, Clarksville might as well have been New York City. Acworth was 13 miles northeast of Clarksville, and while the U.S. Census claimed a population of 20, I don't know how accurate that was. I don't know if I knew of 20 people in that area, outside of my family. Acworth wasn't even big enough to be called a town, and if there hadn't been a post office there, no one might have had reason to know it was there. From our house, we could see another house only far off in the distance. This wasn't a town; this wasn't even on the outskirts of a town. We didn't live on the outskirts of a town until we moved to California. Until I went to college in San Jose, when I was 19 years old, I had never lived anyplace where a building was close enough to throw a rock at it. For a long time, living right next to other people gave me the creeps.

We were a big family, and we were poor. That should be no surprise: if you were black in the 1940s and living in Acworth in northeast Texas, you were poor. My father, James Richard, and my mother, Dora, had 12 kids in all—Willie Jewel, James Richard Jr., George, Lucille, Sally and Hattie (they were twins), Tommie, Ernie, Mary,

Gladys, Eugene (whom we called "Nudy"), and Elizabeth. Two other children died in infancy; one, a boy, would have been the oldest, and the other, another boy, was right before me. I never knew their names. So in all my mother actually gave birth to 14 children.

My earliest memory is of my dad leading a group of us, me and a couple of my older brothers and sisters, into the backwoods to go fishing. To get there we had to go through a marsh, and we saw little fish, only three or four inches long, swimming across the grass, so fast you couldn't catch them. I wondered why my father and brothers were walking past these little fish, since they wanted to fish—they wouldn't have to throw their hooks into them, I thought, all they had to do was bend over and pick them up. Then I bent over to try to pick them up, and realized why you couldn't fish that way; they were too little and too fast. But I thought that was the coolest thing in the world, to see those fish swimming across the grass.

We also used to go catch crayfish after the rain, in the ditches next to the road outside our house. It was a dirt road that ran between ditches that were three or four feet deep and 20 feet wide. I didn't see pavement for the first time until I was four or five years old, and I thought it was the coolest thing to see road that was hard and smooth and didn't move or make you dirty. But back then there was plenty of dirt; you couldn't avoid it. After we went crayfish hunting, we would cut off their tails and cook them. They tasted like lobster, or what I learned much later was what lobster tastes like.

That was the fun part. The rest of the time was work, in the fields. We were a sharecropping family; we worked on land owned by white people, lived on their property, and paid our way through the toil we put into their crops. Our lives and our livelihood were dictated by the crops and the seasons. It was mainly cotton fields, some corn and sugarcane as well, but mostly cotton, which meant we could be working any time of day or night. If you were picking cotton, all that mattered was what you picked, and you didn't stop until your bag was full of cotton. There was no quitting time in picking cotton. Chopping cotton, though, was done by the hour, so time to quit was when the straw boss said it was 4 o'clock. They were using automatic cotton planters by then, and they overplanted the fields. Chopping cotton meant taking a hoe and blocking it so the rows were three or four inches apart and taking the cotton away so the rest of it would grow strong. So when quitting time came, you'd better have your rows chopped because you weren't going to stay out there until midnight the way you would if you were picking. Once you got old enough, you were doing some kind of work in those fields, chopping or picking cotton, picking corn, even picking walnuts, whatever you could do to help out.

When I was too little to go into the fields, I used to go with my mother as she took lunch to my father and older brothers and sisters; usually it was a pail with biscuits on top and syrup in the bottom, and every once in a while some potatoes or beans. I used to see my family in the distance. They looked like they were bending with the atmosphere, shimmery and watery because of the heat rising. I didn't know the word "mirage" back then, and I wondered why it always looked like it was wet where it was most dry. Later, when I started working in those fields myself, I saw those mirages plenty more times in that hot Texas sun. Bringing them lunch, that was my first work in the fields.

And I remember feeding the hogs. We had to have our own meat, after all. I used to see my dad feed the hogs, saw him take the slop out. I got older and I joined everyone else feeding the hogs, raising the hogs, digging holes for the water so the little hogs wouldn't get heat stroke in the summer.

So those were all big parts of my life my first two or three years on this earth: the little fish in the marsh, catching crayfish after the rain, working in the fields, walking to school, going to church, riding in the wagon, feeding the hogs. You might look back at that now and say, *How nostalgic, I'd sure love to go back and relive those days.* Forget it. I don't think I want to relive any of those days. It sounds good now, but back then it was pretty rough.

We lived as comfortably as we could, considering where we were. Our home was not insulated, I can tell you that; we had a roof over our heads, even if it was a leaky one. The house was wood, or anything else we could find to build it, but mostly wood. We didn't have cement or stucco or anything like that, but it was good enough to keep us out of the weather.

While we did work a lot, we kids played a lot too, especially in the summer when school was out. There were no Boy Scouts or Little

League or organized basketball leagues. We played any games we possibly could think of, as many as we could make up. Our playmates were our brothers and sisters, since there were no other kids nearby. We didn't get into too many fights because a fight meant a belt, and a belt meant pain.

I can vividly recall two characteristics of mine from those days: I was a momma's boy, following her around everywhere, keeping an eye on her to make sure nothing happened to her, and I was very quiet. I would watch a lot. I watched so much I could imitate everybody physically or verbally—not openly, just to myself. Everything I saw in the family I thought was good. I would stick it in my mental compartment until I could use it later: how my mother ironed and cooked and cleaned, how my father hunted and fished, the routine my brother James went through when he came home from work.

I didn't associate much with grandparents, and I don't remember a lot of aunts or uncles or cousins. There were so many of us in our own family that we never had a shortage of people around. My mother—we called her Mulla—was at the center, the strength of the family, as it is in most families.

Mulla was a tall, strong, light-skinned woman. She was kind of a catchall for everything. She played multiple roles all the time, being a mother to all those kids and a wife to her husband, cooking, then working in the fields, then hearing the problems from the kids and problems from the dad. She didn't let on about her aches and her pains and her thoughts, although we knew what problems she had and where they came from. It was hard to get her to talk about what was bothering her; we'd ask if she was all right, and she'd always say, "Yeah, boy, I'm fine, I'm okay," and she'd keep rocking in her chair or cooking with a hand on her hip. When I became an adult and had children of my own, I began to understand what was going through her mind when the kids were asking these questions. I know what she was worrying about: where's the food coming from next, how am I going to get all this work done, what am I going to do if one of my children gets sick. She took it all on and held it in very deep, and I understand now that because there were so many of us, it was hard for her not to show it on her face and in her actions. That's why it always made me feel good to hear her laugh. She had a good laugh, and I never heard her laugh enough back then.

From following her around all the time, I learned from her. I absorbed her qualities; I was quiet because she was quiet, watching you closely rather than talking. She was also strict about being neat and clean. She sewed a lot of our clothes; she had to because it was much cheaper to do that than to buy ready-made clothes. We wore a lot of hand-me-downs, from our family and from other people. Rarely did I have something new to wear—at the beginning of school sometimes, and maybe Christmas. Later on I did become one of the better ironers around; in fifth and sixth grades I prided myself in how my Levi's looked. I hated to bend my knees because I might break the crease in the pants. If I had to wash my pants the night before, I would pull out the old washtub—no, we didn't have a washing machine—scrub those Levi's, hang them out on the line to dry overnight, press them in the morning, and wear them to school.

Mulla imposed order in the household. If we were not in the fields, there were things that needed doing around the house. We all learned all the necessary skills to survive; there was no dividing things up by who was a boy or a girl. If you were told to put on some water or some beans or get something out of the icebox, you were not going to say, "I'm not going to do that, I'm a boy." Mulla did what she had to do, including work in the fields, and Daddy taught us to do whatever was necessary to survive, whether it was hunting or fishing or chores around the house. Mulla was in charge of the domestic finances, and she made sure our basic needs were met, because we could afford nothing more. We grew a lot of our own food in our garden—green beans and cabbage and all sorts of vegetables.

We were not a touchy, huggy family; you wouldn't hear a lot of "I love you, dear" or "Come give Mulla a kiss." We saw how hard Mulla worked, we knew the sacrifices she made—she would give her last bite of food to us even if she was hungry—and we followed in her footsteps and worked hard and sacrificed for each other and tried to make things easier for her. And we stayed close, because she kept us close. We even looked at working in the fields, all hours through all kinds of heat or cold, as a family activity.

Of course, we had to live physically close too: we slept two or three to a bed sometimes, the boys with the boys and the girls with the girls. I usually shared a bed with Ernie, my younger brother, or we shared a corner of a room, or whatever we had to do.

And we had to work close in those fields, all of us, when we got old enough. During the hottest part of the hottest days of the summer in Texas, Daddy would work straight through. He would have us come out early in the morning when it was coolest and rest for a little while when it was hottest or have us sit under a shade tree or put our cotton sacks down and sit on them a bit—but he would continue to work. That's what stuck in my mind. His endurance was so amazing that later in life, when I was working as a janitor during the summer in high school and when I was training to run track in the hottest weather, thinking of what he did gave me the strength to continue.

The winter was no better. Just as we didn't have central air, we didn't have central heating, unless you count the warmest room in the house, where the one heater was. On the cold nights, we huddled in that one room before we went to bed. That was our entertainment, before television, huddling in front of that heater. Of course, getting wood for the heater was a chore too, and Daddy wasn't always the one to get it. You had to get that wood and light that fire before we went to bed so we would have it the next morning; if not, we had to get out from under the quilts early in the morning when it was freezing outside to get the wood and light the fire. Daddy wouldn't send me out if it were raining, though; he got it himself then. Then again if it was raining, that meant we had to get buckets and set them up around the floor. The roof leaked.

Daddy was the caretaker of the family. Whatever that family needed, he would provide the best he knew how. That's something else I understood better once I had my own family. But it's a heckuva lot different now—the jobs are better, the pay is better, you have central air and central heat, carpet on the floor, drapes on the windows. Yet in a way, it's harder now; we don't have to go through as much as we did then to survive, but we don't do it as well.

I didn't see Daddy as often as I saw Mulla, because he was always out in the fields, yet his strength stands out in my mind more. He was a physically strong man, from all the physical labor. The man plowed fields without a tractor, with just a plow and our horses, Tom and Button. He would hook them up to a single-side plow and turn the topsoil, and you would hear the grass roots pop with such force, you knew only a strong man and strong horses could do it. Anything around the house that required strength, like moving a log or a wagon, he did. In his late 70s he was still a strong man; on his birthday he'd stand on his head, and all his sons had to do the same. It was something to see.

Daddy was a staunch man with a deliberate gaze and deliberate speech. He didn't use big words, but you knew what he meant. When he looked at you sometimes with his red eyes, you knew that in a millisecond you had to go back and figure out what you did; in a matter of seconds you'd research the previous three days and hope you remembered what you did so you could straighten it out, or hope he didn't remember it so you wouldn't get a whupping. Mulla usually only had to say, "I'll tell your daddy when he comes home," and that usually was all the discipline she needed to apply. She did a little of the whupping herself, but Daddy did most of it. It wasn't considered "child abuse" then. We came up very straight, very strong and deliberate, and I can give thanks to my mother and father for that.

To me the coolest member of my family was my older sister Sally, Hattie's twin. She and I became close, I think, because she saw something in me that she appreciated: being clean, trying to look nice going to school, getting my studies done. She was very academically inclined as well. I just hit it off with her: I could talk to her, or feel comfortable about not talking since I was so quiet. Later in life she became the one who helped me start, and then continue, my athletic exploits, largely because she was such a fast runner herself. When I started to run track, she was the one who would say, "If you're good in this race, I'll give you a quarter," or, "Tommie, I didn't see your trophy." Sally was the one in the family who was interested in my meets, when my mother and father were too busy in the fields to attend. Sally was a very smart conversationalist, the kind who could take what you said, analyze it, and feed it back to you. And she was trustworthy; I could trust her and she could trust me. That camaraderie lasted our entire lives. It still hurts me that Sally was the first of my brothers and sisters to go; she died young, at just 47 years old, from diabetes.

I wish I could say that school was a pleasant memory, but it was not. For one thing, it was the first time I became aware—even though I did not know the word for it or understand the meaning behind it—of segregation. I think back now that I don't have to read or hear about it, because I lived it, and it continues to make me sad that human beings felt they had to be separate just to pretend that one group of a particular color was better than the other. I learned this in Texas, where I began school, in kindergarten.

We walked to school, a good two or three miles each way. Sally and Hattie and I would walk through the woods, we'd come out in a meadow, we'd walk through the meadow to a big old sandy spot, we'd go across it and go down another hill, go up the next hill, and the school was on top of the hill, next to the church and the cemetery. The school, the church, and the cemetery were all called Mount Olive. It sounds very romantic, but it wasn't.

The school had one big classroom with a big heater in the front in the middle, and we sat near the heater when we could. I remember some kids were reading different books; my sisters were reading *Br'er Rabbit*. The teacher—Ms. Carey, I remember—would go from one group to another, from group to group, and I wondered, why is she doing that? Then I realized that all the classes were in one room. Ms. Carey would teach one class, then move three or four seats over and teach the next class a different subject, then move three or four seats over and teach the next class. She taught all those different kids and kept track of them all, and if you didn't have your lesson or acted up, she would take you in the back room and spank you. There was nothing you could do about it even if you wanted to; there was no principal around, and the teacher was in total command.

After a while I realized that there were only black kids in that school. They were the children of our neighbors, if you could call them that considering how spread out our homes were. Their families lived like ours, on the land near the fields where they worked with us. Even the older people, who had lived on the land for years and could not work in the fields anymore, did little jobs in the fields or on the land or property. I can't say I knew them personally; I really only knew a few of them—the ones who were at our school or went to our church. They all had to travel a long way to get there just as we did.

I never did know where the school that white kids went to was located. I just knew they went to a separate school closer to town. I also knew they were riding to school in a wagon and we were walking; the only time we rode anywhere was to church, which was right next door to the school. The church also had nothing but black people in it. I later came to find that only black people were buried in the cemetery. That's how complete the segregation was. It fascinated me then, and I'd think about it later in life: Man, my education started in a segregated school in Texas, in one big room next to a church that I had to walk to every day.

Back then I almost never saw white people. The only time I did was when they came by to tell my father something or to have him do something, or we'd see them across the counter when we went to the store. We never lived around them, never really talked to them. I never had friends who were white; I remember how hard it was for me to get used to being around white people in school once we moved from Texas to California. My father worked for white people, in their fields. They owned the place he worked and the place we lived, and they owned what was grown in those fields and the produce of those fields. I saw him work in the rain while they sat in their cars or the covered wagons staying dry. I saw him working and doing things for them late in the night while they did not have to work. I saw him walk that horse in circle after circle, round and round, grinding the sugarcane we had cut all season, then go home with two cases of sorghum while the white man drove off with nine —off to a big house where he only had one son to feed and a wife who never had to wear an apron like my mother did.

We didn't go over to white homes to play, we didn't have dinner there, we didn't spend the night. To us, they were saying, "You do that and we do this, and since you work for me, you do as I say and don't try to come up to my level."

I was quite young and I didn't know exactly what I was seeing, but I knew somehow that what I saw wasn't the way it was supposed to be, and no one told me that what I saw was wrong. What I did see several times was my father pulling our wagon, with all of us in it, to the side of the dirt road so that a wagon with a single white man in it could pass. I saw the farm owners coming to our house and calling my dad outside, and my dad always saying "Yes, sir" and "No, sir" to them. I wondered why he had to say that. I thought that was just the way my father spoke to people. I didn't realize then that that was the way it had to be done, that he had a family to raise and protect. He also had to let those white men play around with him and tell dumb jokes around him when he came to pick up his share from them, and he had to chuckle and guffaw along with them. He did that the entire time we were growing up. I remember going with him one time after we had been in California for a long time, because we missed part of the Floyd Patterson–Ingemar Johansson fight to go get that check. So this was when I was in high school, or about to go into high school.

James Richard was from the old school, and he had to make his money the best he could. It didn't seem to bother him as much then as it bothers me now. But it meant that while he was addressing his straw boss in the field as "Sir" or "Mister," that straw boss would call him "boy." And the straw boss's 10-year-old son would call my daddy by his first name. I had to call the straw boss "Mister" like Daddy did. When Daddy came home, he couldn't let that frustration show through, but you could see the look of worry on his face, the deep scowl, the tiredness in his voice, the way he'd walk. Sometimes when he was at the table eating, he'd take a bite of food and lean back in the chair and just close his eyes and chew.

So the man and woman that provided the strength in our family needed strength themselves. Religion and the church provided that strength. My parents believed that going to church and serving God were better than sitting home and knowing nothing and doing nothing, and that believing in someone that was bigger than you are would make you much stronger. The orientation of going to church has helped me become a better person because I strive to become better at everything I do. Even in college I continued to go to church every Sunday, with my roommate, St. Saffold. We were the only two athletes getting up early going across campus to church every week.

On Sunday, my daddy's two workhorses, Tom and Button, became church horses. We'd hook them up to the wagon, jump in the back, and off to church we'd go. Everything in the church was wooden, including the floors, which would give you splinters if you dragged your bare feet across them. My father would put us in the front row with him, on the moaning bench. I first thought it was the "morning" bench, because we usually went in the morning, but it was where you helped the minister out by getting people into the spirit. We'd spend a good hour and a half to two hours in church, from 10:30 or 11 in the morning until about 1 in the afternoon. We were a very musical family—we had a piano in our house, and there were times we even sang while working in the fields—and we put our musical talents to use in church. My sisters sang together for years, and were known all over the Central Valley in California just as widely as was another group of sisters from the area, the daughters of a pastor —the Pointers. The Pointers moved into secular music and became best-selling recording artists in the 1970s. The Smiths were right up there with them in those days.

As I got older, of course, I began to get curious about what I had been told over and over again by the grownups about God and the Bible. I started reading the Bible, which can be difficult to interpret. As much religious faith as I had, and as much faith as I had in the way my parents raised me, I saw things in the Bible that prompted questions. I read that everyone is equal in God's eyes, that we are all children of God, that we serve him as one, thus no one is better than another. I believed in that, yet we went to a black church and whites went to a white church, and we went to one school and they went to another, and we walked to school and they rode to theirs, and we lived in a shack and worked in their fields and they lived in nice houses near town. I asked myself why this was. It was a long time before I got any answers I could comprehend.

I didn't dare ask my daddy, though. Rights and wrongs and laws and the Constitution were not topics that were discussed in our house. There was work to be done and hogs to feed and church to attend. We were very devout, raised to do the right thing regardless of whether the right thing was done to us or not. If we did right, we were told, God would provide and give us what we were due. Ask of him and it shall be given, we were taught. As I got older, I was asking on a daily basis.

As you might be able to tell, I was becoming an eager little person, still quiet but not one to sit still or to let something go by without my notice. I did as I was told and respected my parents and wanted to please them, but I felt antsy, even while sitting on the moaning bench in church. I also knew I already was showing myself to be a good athlete, the best in my class. I was a kid who wanted to get somewhere, anywhere. It wasn't long before I was going someplace, and, again, I was aware of it even if I couldn't be clear on exactly what was happening.

What I realized, when I was five years old going on six, was that over a span of several weeks, Daddy had gotten rid of a hog here, a couple of cows there, another hog here, a horse there—not Tom and Button, but the other animals we had were disappearing. I wondered, "How are we going to plow, what are we going to eat next year?" Then one day a big school bus pulled up, and we start loading things on this big bus, and we got on it, and we started driving. I could tell it was different from other trips I had taken; a few times, we had gone on a big truck to Commerce, also in East Texas, a couple of hours away, and we'd move into a little shack and put a couple of animals in the yard. I noticed right away that the shack was sitting next to the biggest cotton field I'd ever seen. Then the truck would disappear, and we'd go into that field and pick cotton until cotton season was over, through the rain and all. When it was all picked, the truck came back and took us back to where we had lived before. That's how we'd had to live.

This trip was totally different. We were on the bus for a couple of days. There were 40 or 45 people on this bus, filling just about every seat, with several families with a bunch of little kids like me. The white driver didn't want to stop the bus every time someone wanted to go to the bathroom, so when I had to go, or any of those kids had to go, he'd pull out a little jar, a pee jar, and we went in that jar. I think part of it was racist, and part of it was that he just didn't want to stop the bus for some bratty kids. To me the whole doggone trip was demoralizing; it was tiring, it was long, there was no chance for any fresh air with all those people crammed on that bus for two days. But that's how the Smith family moved from Texas to California, to the lush farm country of the Central Valley, in 1950. It wasn't even the whole Smith family, because I learned later that Daddy, even though he got rid of all those hogs and horses, didn't have enough money for all of us to come to California on that bus.

As soon as we got to California, we were put in a labor camp in Stratford, in the heart of the valley south of Fresno and northwest of Bakersfield. The camp was a couple of shacks in the middle of a field with grass six feet high. It was cold and foggy the morning we got off, and it was colder inside those shacks than it was outside. We stayed in those shacks for the next two and a half years—both shacks, because our family could not fit into one; we used one for the kitchen and the other for bedrooms. Working in the labor camp, I later learned, was how we paid for our bus trip from Texas. In exchange for leaving that life behind and taking root in beautiful, bountiful California, we worked the farms for the landowners, doing even more of the same tasks we did in Texas and doing them until we paid off the cost of getting us there. It was like that for everybody on that bus; they all had to live in shacks like that too, off the main road, with a common area and a communal shower and toilet facilities.

So we were back in the fields, cotton and corn and sugar again, with grapes and lettuce added now, chopping and picking and irrigating. My father drove a tractor—a step up from plowing with Tom and Button—and worked in one field or another every chance he got to support us and pay what we owed. The pay scale, if you could call it that, was four dollars a day, based on the ability to pick 100 pounds at between 1.75 and two dollars per 100 pounds. In today's dollars that would be about 35 dollars a day, and you were not working eight-hour shifts with a half hour for lunch. You worked until you were done.

As a result, school had to take a back seat temporarily. Education was important to my mother and father, of course, and it was going to be emphasized for all of their kids, but at that time, work came first. But none of us knew at that time that California, unlike Texas, was a lot stricter about school-age children being enrolled. This state did not allow exceptions for children to miss school because of work; there had to be a very good reason, and it had to be approved by the school district superintendent. We found out how the law worked about two weeks after we'd arrived in California, as we were on the bus that would take us from the camp to the fields, a big, typically raggedy bus full of raggedy workers—that is, we were dressed raggedy, because of the work we had ahead of us. A man named Smith, the principal of Stratford Elementary School, two miles up the road, got on the bus before it had a chance to pull away from the camp and asked if there were any children on the bus that were of a certain age. Principal Smith had gotten word, I don't know from where, that there were a bunch of children freshly arrived in town who were not attending school. Not knowing what it meant to be that certain age, a bunch of us raised our hands. Principal Smith said he was sorry, but all these kids had to get off the bus and go to school. My father didn't appreciate that and told him, in his very firm way, that nobody tells his kids what to do except him. Principal Smith said he understood; he knew the kids were needed in the fields, but they were of legal school age. "The law is the law," he said. That got my father's attention and calmed him down, because he prided himself on being a law-abiding citizen. Still, there was a standoff for about five minutes between him and Principal Smith. The principal won: we kids got off the bus and somehow—I don't remember how, whether there was another bus waiting for us, or whether we walked like we had back in Texas—we got to school and started going there regularly.

My parents really had to be pushed into letting us go to school there. However, we started listening to radio and television more and my father started talking to white folks in California more, and he started to see the world in a different way than he had in Texas. My parents came to realize that education was the only way out of the cotton fields. I figured that out soon as well. My father started reminding me of it all the time; when I was older, he would say to me, "If I'd had the chance you have, I wouldn't be doing what I'm doing, I'd be doing a lot better." That motivated me.

Still, it wasn't as if there was a lot of heavy discussion of the issues of the day going on in our house. My family did not get engaged in politics; we were more concerned with plain survival, and we took our guidance from the Bible rather than from man, left things up to God rather than to people. We knew some things that were going on and we knew enough to sense whether something was right or wrong, but we didn't get active about it, and no one really yearned to learn the history or background of some event or topic. My family were never active voters; back then it was difficult to vote, especially where we lived, in Texas and in California. It was a long trip to the polling place, and it demanded more education and information on the issues and candidates than we had access to. I really don't remember a lot of open talk about race; I grew up hearing about lynchings, but only once do I remember much discussion about one, once hearing the adults talking about it on the porch. I do remember when the *Brown v. Board of Education* decision came down; I was about 10.

Going to school in Stratford taught me a little more about how blacks and whites were treated. It was obvious, even at the very beginning in second grade, that there was a difference in the way the teachers treated me and talked to me and the way they treated and talked to the little blond-haired girl or blue-eyed boy next to me. When these kids raised their hands they were immediately called on. They could go to the bathroom any time they wanted. They got to go to the bin first and get the balls out to play, got to leave to go to recess first.

My first field test on segregation in California came in my first year in school there. One day my mother gave me a nickel to buy ice cream. With all I went through to get into school, being pulled off a labor bus and thrown into a classroom with maybe one other black in the class and trying to learn what these people wanted, which wasn't what I had learned from my background, it didn't take much to make me happy. I was real happy to get that nickel, and I was going to be happy to get that ice cream. I wiggled and turned in my seat all morning waiting for 12 o'clock to come. It came, I got the ice cream cone, leaned up against the building to eat it, and a little red-headed boy named Wesley Adams, I'll never forget him, came up and knocked the ice cream out of my hand and said, "Niggers don't eat ice cream." I looked at him in surprise and shock and didn't know what to do. Six-year-old kid with a nickel to buy an ice cream, goes to eat it in solitude, and some white kid knocks it to the ground and gives you a smirk. I just walked off. That's all I could think of to do. I thought of something better to do a few years later when Wesley Adams ended up in a class with me; I gave him a natural ass whupping, and then I made him fetch our cows from the field for a week. It was all payback for that ice cream cone.

Eventually, about two years after we had arrived in Stratford, we paid our debt and we moved from the labor camp to another labor camp very briefly, then into an actual house, outside of Stratford. I remember this move a lot more clearly than the move from Texas. The house was on Kansas Street, and it was big, bigger than what we had known. It wasn't anything fancy; it was still wood, and you got a foot full of splinters if you dragged your feet in it. It also didn't have windows, or it had windows but no glass to fill them, which meant that the house was very drafty. But it had three or four bedrooms, and we didn't have to go to a communal shower or bathroom (an outhouse was necessary, but we didn't have to share it with another family). And it was high, up on stilts, a good foot and a half up off the ground, so that you could look clear through from one side to the other, and enough room that once or twice a month you had to clean out the junk that collected under there. We could go under there relatively clean, and when we came out the other side you couldn't tell which kid it was.

We stayed on Kansas maybe three years, then moved to a nicer house on Jersey, about a mile further north, closer to Lemoore. This house was even nicer than the last one; I saw it as a home, finally. We even had a little lawn—more like a pasture, except there was no cow, but there was enough room for my mother to have a garden. It also had indoor plumbing, another first for us: faucets, a toilet we could flush, the whole deal. We were even able to get a television of our own; we watched I Love Lucy, and Daddy stayed up late watching westerns—I stayed up late with him for a while, until it was obvious that I wasn't getting up early the next morning, which meant the end of my staying up late.

It wasn't actually our house, of course. We were paying about $40 a month for it, maybe a little more, maybe a little less. But all in all, the Smith family was moving up; we were seeing the reward of hard work, and we had done plenty of hard work.

A little later we moved up even further, to another house on the same street, where we stayed for years and where my father stayed long after all of us kids left. He actually bought that particular house later and moved it, the whole structure, to a different location on the street, about 600 yards from the spot of the first house on Jersey, which had burned down after we moved out. He moved the house, added some rooms, and settled in.

The original move out of the labor camps, meanwhile, meant we were going to a new school, one that was only a mile or so away from our new house, Central Union Elementary, on 18th Street. Before long I began to show off my athletic prowess, and at Central

Union, it impacted the life of my family and me for the first time. We ended up moving from Kansas to the better house on Jersey in part, a big part, because one of the teachers wanted us to stay at the school. Daddy had planned for us to move completely out of the area, up north past Fresno to Madera. But one teacher, Mr. Focht, recognized that we were good athletes and good students from a good, stable, hardworking family, and told my father that if he kept us at Central Union, he would help find us a better place to live and a better job for my father.

Jim Focht would influence my life in many more ways before I finished at Central Union. I'm sure he did the same for countless other students in the area; he eventually became a school superintendent on the county board of education and served until just before he passed in the spring of 2003. That's more than 50 years, dating back just to when I was at his school. Back then, he simply improved my life and that of my family through his thoughtful action. Because we got a better place to live, we did not have to change schools; we could stay in one place, with school just a 15-minute walk away, where it was so safe that we could leave our doors unlocked at night.

Mr. Focht's influence also gave my father the steady income he had always yearned for. He got him a job as janitor and bus driver at Central Union, which got him further away from the life of the fields. It was very hard work, cutting grass and mopping floors, but he always was a hard worker, and he still did work in the fields and had us out there at times as well. But the steady money meant we didn't have to depend on crops and the effects of the seasons and the weather. Plus he was never far from home, and we always knew where he was. Things were not perfect; there were still times we were hungry, we still made do with hand-me-down clothes, and it was still a matter of surviving rather than living in luxury. But staying at Central Union and Daddy becoming the janitor was a big turning point for our family.

Mr. Focht was important in my life as well because, although he was white, unlike many of the white teachers, he always made you feel like you were sky-high. He'd always give you the benefit of the doubt; he wouldn't let you get away with doing wrong, but if you did something wrong, he'd let you know you were above doing this, that you were a better person than this thing you did. He'd make you feel that it was just a mistake that you knew you'd never do again—and you'd say, "Yeah, it was a mistake," and more often than not, you really wouldn't do it again. He'd pit your better judgment against your negative behavior; his goal was to make you think about what you did and why.

That approach made a difference in my life, largely because it went against everything the teachers and the system were doing to the nonwhite kids in that school. I started off wrong in Central Union anyway, because I ended up repeating a grade for no reason, other than walking into the wrong classroom. I left Stratford Elementary after the second grade, where my classroom had a "2" over it. With my background and limited knowledge—remember, in Texas everybody went to school in one big room with one teacher—I didn't think you changed anything just because a summer went by. So on my first day at Central Union, I went to the room with a "2" over it. That's how I ended up in second grade two years in a row. But I had it straight every year after that.

The kids in that school were a lot like me—the poor children of field workers. Stratford was a town, and people owned things there; those were the children of the farm owners or business owners or employees of those businesses, like banks and gas stations. At Central Union, further away from the town and in the boonies, the parents worked in the fields and didn't own anything. The workers in the fields were ethnically diverse, and so were the children in the school; it had Indians, it had blacks, it had Mexicans and other Hispanics. I had friends of all colors and shades. One was an Indian, Elmer Thomas; two of them were white, a redheaded kid named Danny and a kid named Ernest Drewrey. David, a tall kid like me, was black. We kind of hung out together; we had some things in common, like being among the better athletes. We were the ones everyone wanted on their team when they played kickball, and we usually got split up when we played football because you couldn't let all the best players be on one team.

I still stood out, on the playground and in class, because I was taller than most of the kids. I already was bashful and quiet, and being so big didn't make it better because I couldn't hide. I felt I had to study hard so that if a question were asked of me, I wouldn't get it wrong and stand out even more. I was far from a total introvert, but it was becoming a natural state for me to feel uncomfortable in school.

I was not a poor student at all; I could read and spell and do math, and I liked and appreciated those subjects. But communicating in class became a problem right away because I realized that we talked a little different than white folks did. We both spoke English, but it wasn't the same English; the southern black English I spoke and the black kids and some of the other kids spoke wasn't the English white folks wanted to hear, especially teachers. This problem started in Stratford and continued at Central Union. We didn't pronounce words the way they did; Texans and Californians don't speak the same anyway, and it was really exaggerated with us black Texans pronouncing words our way and hearing white Californians pronounce them totally different—like the word *road*, which when they spoke sounded to me like *roar-ahd*. We said *y'all, ain't, gonna, gotta,* all words that most of society, especially teachers, didn't appreciate. They made sure that you knew they preferred to see and hear from the little girl in the front row, the very prissy one, the one who had the right answer all the time because she had the opportunity to get it long before you ever did, because her family was oriented academically long before she was even born, while yours was oriented in the fields working for her family and usually didn't have the time or capability to educate you right or instill education as a value.

So the teachers made you feel inferior and substandard from the beginning, in the class in which they were supposed to be teaching you and preparing you. My fourth grade teacher, Mrs. Yenger, was the perfect example. To me, she was a very tedious so-and-so, one of those teachers who wouldn't give you a break. I never said much in her class because she was the type to make you feel bad if you were wrong, and I thought that was very detrimental to a youngster who had a hard enough time in life without getting a negative reaction to what you're doing compared to the blond-haired kid in front of you. The white people's way of looking at life, expressing it, and dealing with it were totally different from mine, and they were not doing anything to accommodate mine. It took me a while to understand why it was so difficult for me to communicate, but the effect stayed with me for an even longer time.

Mr. Focht was different. As a teacher he brought out the academic belief in myself, and as coach of the track team he showed me what can be accomplished through athletics. I was one of the best athletes in my grade then, but I would only show it off in the schoolyard, or around my family. My big sister Sally was also very athletic, and I had been racing against her for years, in the cotton fields and near the swimming hole. I'd also gotten fast running away from her, because by then she liked to do things like call me over, and when I got there and asked what she wanted, *bam bam bam,* she'd start hitting me, and I'd run away.

But I had never beaten Sally in a race, ever. One afternoon, when I was in fourth grade, Sally, who was in seventh grade, was in PE class outside while I was inside in Mrs. Yenger's class, and Mr. Focht was watching Sally beat everybody in races. He asked her, "Don't you have a brother that can run?" She said, "Yes, that's Tommie." He asked her to go and get me out of class, and of course I was as glad to get away from Mrs. Yenger as I was to see Sally. When I got out there I knew Mr. Focht had something in mind, because he had that little look in his eye, the one he got when he thought he saw something I was capable of doing. I was right: he wanted me to race, against Sally and a white kid, Coy Cross, who was also very fast, someone who got out of the blocks quick and was up to full speed in three steps. With my long legs even then, getting out fast was not my thing.

"Let me see what you can do," Mr. Focht said. I knew, and he had figured out, that as soon as anyone asks me what I can do or gives me a chance to prove myself, I can go far beyond their expectations. I felt it then, too: my first real big chance to do something, even though I wasn't sure what. So he put us on a starting line and said, "On your mark, get set, go"—and man, we took off, a 50-yard dash across the little lawn we called a playground. Coy Cross had no chance after the first five yards. And I destroyed Sally.

I was so happy, but I didn't really jump up and down and go, "Way to go, way to go." I looked at Sally and looked at Mr. Focht and kind of smiled. That was the first time I had fresh wind hitting my face, because there was no one else to pollute it in front of me, as Sally usually had done. It was the kind of sensation I learned to enjoy, like feeling the burn across my chest from hitting the tape hard, fast, and first. I went back to class feeling elated and surprised. I didn't win anything, I didn't get any money, but I recognized all that can be gained from sports anyway: hearing clapping and ovations, being appreciated. Mr. Focht had seen it and made me realize it. Best of all, I didn't get beat up. That was the first big race in my life, and even today, it's bigger than Mexico City.

Still, it wasn't something my parents cared about that much. They thought it was nice that I could run so fast and beat Sally, and that Mr. Focht thought so highly of me. At the same time, they didn't see how that fit into the world they saw for me, which was defined by work, school, and God. I was still going into the fields before and after school, picking and chopping and irrigating cotton. So when I went and told Daddy that Mr. Focht wanted me to run, he told me: "Mr. Focht is a good man; he helped the family out, found a house for us and a job for me, so you can go on and run." He turned away, then turned back again and said, "If you run and you get second place, you'll have to be back in the field with the rest of us next Saturday." And he would have found out somehow if I had gotten second place, even if he hadn't been there. From then on, every time I got on the starting line, even when I was in college, I thought I'd be in the cotton fields if I got second place. That's where I got the impetus to beat folks—and not just beat them, to positively destroy them.

I understand why Daddy looked at athletics that way. He was an athlete in his day, back before he had all us kids; he had nine brothers, and they formed a baseball team in Texas that would travel around the area and play other organized black teams. I have vague memories of seeing him play when I was very little; what I remember most was how hard they hit the ball, and how they had to scoot so fast to get to it, and how it hopped up one time and hit Daddy in the head and raised a big knot. But there was no future in a black man playing baseball back then, not when you had a family to take care of.

That was a big reason why, from the beginning, Mulla and Daddy did not come to see me run. Sally supported me and kept up with how I was winning. But to be honest, I don't remember even one time that my parents saw me run. It just did not interest them, and they certainly were not going to travel a distance to an unfamiliar place to see me. Not to see someone just playing. That's all it was to them, just play. So they did not see me win my first trophy, for a race in the fourth grade at a meet in Bakersfield. It's a little wooden trophy, four or five inches high, with "AAU" on it. I still have it. I can't remember what race I won to get it, but that's the one I'm most proud of, because it's the first. I cherished that thing; I set it on the mantle and kept dusting it off, so that everything else on that mantle was dusty except that trophy. I've kept everything I could hang on to over the years, all the medals from international meets in faraway nations, from every state in the union, and from Mexico City, of course—but that little four-inch-high trophy from a race in fourth grade stands out among the rest.

Eventually, I played all the sports, especially basketball, which I took a liking to because of my size, speed, and agility. Somehow I was far more coordinated in basketball than I was running, until I learned the science and technique of how to run much later on. I played Little League baseball, pitching and playing centerfield. The coaches lied about my age one year so I would be eligible to play, telling me to remember that my birthday was June 12, not June 6. I kept thinking that was my real birthday until 16 or 17 years after I got out of college. My second wife, Denise, found my birth certificate and asked why it said the 6th instead of the 12th. You can still find some old biographies of me that say my birthday is June 12, because that's what I'd thought for so long. There also was flag football, where I was able to get through holes and run before anyone pulled my flag.

Eventually, I was able to do things most grammar school kids couldn't do. As I entered eighth grade, I was long-jumping 17 or 18 feet, and I could come close to dunking a basketball. In fact, one time in a tournament at Stratford, my old school, we were losing by one point with one second left, and Mr. Focht called a play where they would throw an inbound to me, and I would jump from under the basket and catch it and dunk it as soon as I touched it, before I landed back on the ground. This was in eighth grade. If Michael Jordan did that today, he would get a standing ovation. It didn't work, but it amazes me to this day that anyone even thought we could try, or that I could do that at that age.

Mr. Focht took us everywhere he could within a 25-mile radius of Central Union. He took us to meets held at Lemoore High School, which was big for me because I knew that eventually I was going to go to that school, and even Bakersfield Junior College, which was a very big deal. My runners at Santa Monica compete at meets at that school, and I was running there in elementary school. I didn't have track shoes; I'd run in black high-top tennis shoes that Mr. Focht was able to get for me somehow. I put taps on my shoes, because that was the thing to do then; I liked the noise they made. Or I ran in my bare feet around that dirt track at Lemoore High, before all-weather surfaces were even thought of. The first time I ever wore track shoes was at a meet at Lemoore High, when I was in eighth grade; I borrowed a pair from one of the Lemoore High runners, a size 12, when my feet were more like a 9½ or 10. They looked like clown shoes on me. The photographers from the newspaper were there; about three hours before the meet, a bunch of them were standing around taking pictures, and I happened to be standing at the top of the long-jump runway. They wanted to take a picture of me leaping. Mr. Focht gave me a look, and I nodded and took off down the runway—clop, clop, clop in those huge shoes. I jumped 23 feet, walked back, took off the shoes, sat down and waited for the meet to begin. I guess I gave the photographers what they wanted. They pretty much used me, because they got a big kick out of those big shoes, but I didn't mind. I really did just want to please everybody more than anything else.

My mind, though, was very competitive even then. It wasn't that I wanted to go out and destroy somebody in order to hurt them—they were out there for the same reason I was—but to go out and get more points than they did. I never thought that my competitiveness could take me a long, long way. I never thought then about going to the Olympics, because I didn't even know what the Olympics were. I wasn't trying to imitate or emulate anybody; I didn't look up to anyone in sports back then, because I didn't really know about anybody. Besides, we were raised not to look up to athletes, or any other men, as idols; we learned in church and from Daddy that God is everything. Even when I was in college, I didn't have any athletic idols, even though I knew all the big athletes then on the national scene in football, basketball, baseball, and track and field. The first heavy-duty athlete I remember knowing by name was not a track athlete, it was Wilt Chamberlain, and that was because my older brother

George came home from college and started talking about him and showing me his photo in the paper. He was a big, strong, masculine black superstar, and I liked the way his name looked, even though I was pronouncing it wrong—Chom-ber-lane, I kept calling him. My tendency was to be the best I could be and not pattern myself after anyone I had seen or heard of. That is one reason my technique was different from everyone else's; I never wanted to copy anyone, and with my body structure, being so tall yet so quick, I don't think I ever could have.

Even as late as high school I didn't think of where my athletic abilities would take me. At best, I thought I could do what my brother George ended up doing. He ran at Lemoore, he ran in college, and then he went into the army. He got out of the fields, and he wore a uniform. That was what guided my dreams later, to wear a uniform and be someone in authority—a soldier or policeman or teacher. That's as far as I could think in high school, so I certainly never thought about it when I was still at Central Union.

As I advanced through the grades, I grew, and my athletic ability and performance grew with me. I was up to 6 foot 1 inch tall in seventh grade and nearly 6'3" in eighth grade, and even though I weighed only 150 pounds, I was strong. I built up some muscle working in those fields year-round. I never had to train; my training came in the fields. I was big and rangy and lanky; I had very good coordination, quick feet, and quick hands. I was getting better at all my sports. People marveled, saying, "That Smith kid is really good." I'd smile real wide, but I'd say to myself, "This is a lot easier than picking cotton or picking grapes."

The high school couldn't wait to get me; Mr. Focht made a point to tell Tuffy Burton, who coached track and field, basketball, and football at Lemoore High, about me. But people around the valley were already taking notice of me. Both nearby high schools, Lemoore and Hanford, were hoping I might end up with them. I thought, "Wow, somebody's noticing me, people are clapping their hands for me; this is great."

I was noticing a lot more than just my ability as I grew up. The concerns I had felt from the time I was in Texas and saw how white people treated my daddy and how we stayed separated by race, began to solidify and form a clear picture. The little things that people would say took on a different meaning. The times white kids would say that something smelled when you were in the room with them, making you think that being dark meant you were not clean. The way their straight, long, flowing hair was considered so pretty, not like the nappy hair you had, so that you wished your hair was straight like theirs. The way teachers gave the white kids the priorities and advantages and made you feel inferior, the way they smiled when they talked to those kids but walked past you with barely a word, the way you noticed how new and clean their clothes were, and especially the way that their mode of speaking was preferred over ours. It made it harder and harder for me to speak out in class, less likely that I would try to answer a question, less likely that I would ask a question even if I needed to know something; I would find it out on my own and ask the teacher only in a dire situation. I was ashamed of how my English sounded. It was never a drawback when I spoke at home; whatever way we needed to get our point across, we did, without fretting over its being proper.

The lesson I learned most, and it certainly wasn't something I wanted to learn, was how to be ashamed to be black. One day in fifth grade, my usual group and I were playing at the far end of a big field during recess, and the bell rang. Ernest said, "Last one in is a nigger baby," and I jammed, because I didn't want to be a nigger baby. Of course I beat everybody. No one said anything about what Ernest had said; I don't think anyone, except me, even thought about what he said, but I thought about it the rest of the day: he said nigger baby. That was a year after the incident where I was playing with a bunch of kids, with just the one other black girl with us, and I wouldn't say I'm from Africa because everybody would laugh, because no one wanted to be from a place like Africa, with the monkeys and wild animals and big, dark, big-lipped ugly people that didn't have the heritage Europeans had. Being white was desirable, being black was not. That is what society taught us at the time. Just like it taught us that being a nigger baby was something you didn't want to be. I didn't know any better.

As I put things into perspective, my interests in my classes shifted. I moved away from math and geometry and chemistry and got worse in them, but I gravitated toward social studies and history. Even though I wasn't a talker, I wanted to learn, to think, to exercise my mind, to find out the reasons for what I saw. I also began to realize that somehow, whether it was by learning or by running and playing ball, I had to go someplace away from where I was, away from the fields, away from chopping and picking and irrigating and trapping and hunting. It's what my father had said to me, it's what he said he would do if he had the opportunities for schooling that I had. A lot of these thoughts were unformed and unorganized, but I had seen a few other places, either out to Madera where we had relatives, or the places I traveled with Mr. Focht's teams. I even went to a square dance in the spring of my seventh-grade year; my partner was, again, one of the few black girls in class, Eleanor Jordan. It was a big annual dance at Hanford High School, which every grammar school in the county went to, and our school practiced religiously. Eleanor and I were great dancers, and we stood out in the crowd of 500 or 600 kids —not so much for our dancing, but because of our skin, and because I wore a light, pea-green shirt, a lot lighter than the dark-green shirt they had required us to wear. That was the only green shirt I had, though. The teachers weren't happy about that shirt, but none of them volunteered to buy me another one, either.

At first, it was good to be exposed to new places and things just because it was something other than the fields. Eventually, I realized that being in an environment like California meant being around more educated people than I had known before, seeing what other possibilities were out there for me, and learning that athletics meant more people wanted to know me. It was a while longer before I began to communicate with those people; at first I could only communicate through sports, but eventually I began to open up and show people that I was more than a guy who observed and smiled and was easy to get along with, that I was developing a brain to go with my muscles, and that I might not really have that much to smile about after all.

By the time I actually began at Lemoore High in the fall of 1959, I knew that whatever I accomplished there was going to bring me closer to securing a life away from the fields—and I sensed that both my body and mind could get me there.

Still, the shock of that first year at Lemoore reminds me of the one I felt when I began school in California after being pulled off that work bus. I was lost. The school was bigger, the bus taking us there was bigger, and there were more classrooms and more teachers and more fields and gyms and places you had to be. When that bell rang between classes, the place just exploded with activity for 10 minutes, then fell silent until the next bell. At least that's how it was for everyone else; for the first few weeks, I wandering around the hallways long after the bell rang, wondering where I was supposed to be, wondering if I was still on earth. For the first few weeks I didn't want to go because it all was too big for me. But I remembered that this was where I wanted to be, that I wanted to be where things were a big deal.

Then I started playing football, because it was the fall, and then played basketball in the winter and ran track in the spring, and sports made everything settle into place. In fact, everything settled in so much that I started getting recognition and accomplishing things in every sport from the beginning. I was probably a little better as a freshman than some of the seniors who got awards, and a few people told me so, but what could I do except smile and wait my turn? I still hadn't become someone who hoo-rahed about himself.

I got to know Coach Burton very well, because I pretty much had him the entire school year for one sport or another. He was a genuinely good person, one who would tear you up if you made him mad, but also someone who would smile at you and make you feel like a human being. I've tried to blend some of his personality into my coaching today. Some of it evolved in me without my noticing it right away. Bud Winter, my coach at San Jose State, had the greatest impact on me by far. In high school, I still hadn't developed my most efficient technique. I just tried to figure out a way on my own to make my tall, gangly body work best for me. Coach Burton didn't know the science and mechanics of running the way Coach Winter did, but then again, nobody did, much less a high school coach.

I shone in football as a receiver, taking all that punishment all day and all season long, and in basketball, where I could outjump everyone and outrun everyone on the fast break and where I was the school's all-time leading scorer when I left, and for a long time afterward. But it was on the track that I excelled. In the typical meet, I would compete in all the jumps, run everything from the 100 to the 400 and all the relays. Whenever my team needed points to win the overall title in a meet, I would enter an event, or Coach Burton would put me in. I was strong enough and in condition enough for all of them because of my work in the fields and because of the other sports I played. In fact, I got a lot of lift on my long jump and high jump from having had to pull my boots out of the mud on days I had to irrigate. In my junior year, I broke a meet long-jump record by going 24 feet 2 inches, and I rarely even practiced it. The record I broke had belonged to Rafer Johnson, who by that time had won an Olympic decathlon gold medal and who is also from the valley, from Kingsburg.

I had never planned much to run the 440 until one day in my junior year Coach Burton told me to run in it during a meet—one in which I was targeting my specialty, the 220, and had already competed in the shot put, which I rarely tried. I told him I had never run the 440, but he told me to run it anyway. I ran it as if it was the 220; about halfway through it, I couldn't even hear anyone else, that's how far ahead I was. Then, when I hit the backstretch, it felt like I was pulling the whole world behind me. I finished what I thought was a day and a half later—and everyone was congratulating me. I'd run a 47.7, the best in the nation that year. By my senior year I was running it in 47.3, nearly a half second faster.

The letters from the colleges began arriving at the end of my junior year, about 25 of them. They had seen my times, and many of them didn't know I was only a junior, the times were so good. They were better than the times of some of the athletes I recruit today. I was offered scholarships for all three sports. Among the schools that contacted me were Texas Southern (no way was I going back to Texas), Fresno State, Oregon State, Arizona State, and Hawaii. Those last three sounded too far away for me.

I narrowed it down to two schools: San Jose State and USC. San Jose State was willing to offer me a scholarship for football, basketball, and track, and I liked that proposition because I wanted to have a choice once I got there. USC wanted me pretty bad, though, and they brought me down for a visit in my senior year. I went on a double date to Disneyland, with a hurdler for the school, Theo Viltz, his girlfriend, and his sister. I stayed friends with Theo after that visit, but all of it was too much for a kid from the fields who still hardly had ever held a girl's hand.

I crossed off USC for other reasons; they wanted me to go to a junior college first, and I did not want to go to a junior college if I didn't have to. Plus, San Jose State, while it was far away, was close to Oakland, and my brother George and my sister Lucille both lived there; if I got in any trouble, especially financial, I could go to them for a little money, and that's what I did while I was there. And it was just far enough away so that I wouldn't be able to go back and get in the fields every weekend. So, San Jose was the place for me.

I ended up lettering all four years of high school in all three sports, 12 letters in all. I have all of them, as I said; I've moved so much since high school and college, and stuff has been in and out of trophy cases and on tables and hidden away and stored away and packed away, but I still have everything, even if I don't know exactly where each thing is. Several years ago I counted them all: 25 trophies, 85 medals, and 12 letters. I've even got belt buckles given to me at the West Coast Relays, which we received instead of plaques or trophies. I've got more belt buckles than I do belts.

While doing all of this and maintaining a respectable grade-point average—not great, around 2.2 or 2.3, good enough—I found time to sing in the choir, second tenor. Sally was in the choir with me when she was there. The Smiths never stopped singing. Also, I was voted vice president of the senior class. I knew I got that office because of my popularity, although, as I've said, I was not a bad student, just one who did not draw attention to myself in class. The class president had a 3.8, played quarterback and point guard, and brought about 30 books home with him every night, so I understand why he was president. A couple of times, though, I got to run a meeting in his absence, and at that time in Lemoore, for a black kid to be assuming the duties of senior class president was special. Black people still were not doing a lot in Lemoore at that time.

Believe me, this was not something I only came to notice on the victory stand, or when I arrived at San Jose State. I knew how Daddy was treated in the fields in Texas and in California, I knew how we went to one school and the white kids went to another in the early days, and I knew how those teachers and those kids acted and how they were treated compared to how my family and friends and I were, in and out of school. And while I was something of a celebrity in Lemoore at the time, I knew that when I was in stores or out in the streets, or putting up the letters in the message sign in front of Lemoore High (one of the duties of the vice president), I was followed, or stared at, or commented on, or even commented to. It was made very clear to me what I was supposed to do and what I was expected to do, and the best way to handle that limitation was to understand that and adhere to it. In hindsight, I realize that Lemoore was no different from the rest of America at that time, 1963, when I graduated. In reality, it was a mirror. And I have to admit that if I could turn back the clock and go back to that time, I would confront some people and ask them why they said certain things and reacted to me in certain ways.

In later years, I did go back; Daddy still lived there, and occasionally I would be invited back, and I made several trips back when I tried to get my youth foundation started. One time, I gave a speech there and said that Lemoore is not perfect, that there have been racist things done there, to me and to others, and that if I could have done something about it when it happened I would have. It is part of what the city is, I said. I will never forget that it is where I was from, but no one there should think it can't do better than it was doing. A lot of people were upset to hear that, especially from me; they thought (and some told me) that I had seemed so happy when I was there, because I was always smiling when I saw them. They felt betrayed somehow. Did I ever feel betrayed? Well, for all those years, my father picked their grapes and chopped their cotton and cleaned their children's classrooms and mowed their lawns and playgrounds, and that's how we were treated, like the janitor's kids, those dirty children from the fields, even when we were grown. The only time it ever was different was those few times I was on the track or the basketball court or football field. But they felt betrayed?

When graduation came—our class was 130—I was glad, but I was sad. The ceremony was my last hoo-rah at the school and in Lemoore; when my name was called and I walked across the stage, they named all the awards and read off all the places that had offered me scholarships. I enjoyed that. But it also was one of the emptiest times of my life, leaving my family forever. That's how it felt to me because I knew I probably would not come back to Lemoore very often; I'd go away and go to college and go on and move somewhere else and keep on going. Maybe I would come back as a teacher, one of my career goals—maybe even a doctor, although I really couldn't see that. If I was going to come back, I wanted to come back doing something for myself, instead of working for someone else. I'd done enough of that. In fact, in the summer before I went to San Jose, I worked those fields again.

I could at least look forward to living in a place in San Jose where, when it rained, the roof didn't leak.

The Biggest City I Had Ever Seen

4

I DIDN'T JUST DO FIELD WORK the summer before going away to San Jose State. I also scrubbed and waxed the floors at Central Union Elementary with my daddy. Once again, I was building up my body without ever going into a weight room or setting foot on a track: I had to move desks out of the way, big heavy wood-and-steel desks that weighed some 40 pounds not including the books in them, and run that big, heavy floor scrubber, stripping wax and applying new wax. But I wasn't doing it to get stronger, or because I loved waxing floors (or, for that matter, picking grapes or chopping cotton). I needed money for school. I had a full scholarship, but that meant, in cold, hard terms, $95 a month. Tuition was paid, and the $95 went to room and board and books. It didn't buy me clothes, didn't give me money to go to a show or to take a girl someplace. Every little bit I made that summer I put in the bank and hoped it would hold me throughout the school year.

Then again, I knew I wasn't going there to have a social life. I wasn't even really going to be a star athlete. I knew I wanted an education, which would keep me from scrubbing classroom floors and jumping in and out of raggedy pickup trucks to get me back and forth from the field for the rest of my life. My parents wanted the same thing. They couldn't tell me anything about what I was getting into; they just told me to go on ahead, get your education, do the best you can.

I just didn't know how much of an education I was in for. It started from the moment I arrived at San Jose State in August 1963. I flew there by myself, from the airport in Fresno, my first time ever flying. I was on a little prop plane, with my one lonely bag, big and gangly, wearing ankle-high jeans and old torn-up sneakers, with a real short haircut and no hair on my face and my ears sticking out—just a weird-looking young guy. When the group sent from the school to pick me up at the airport got a look at me, they started laughing. In fact, the very first one to start laughing was Harry Edwards—a senior at the time, a basketball player and track and field athlete, and confidant to the growing numbers of us at the school.

St. Saffold, my first and only roommate at San Jose State, was there with his girlfriend. I came to find out later that I couldn't have had a more perfect roommate if I had picked him out myself. Yes, that was his name, St.; his middle name is Samuel. He was St., and everyone started calling me T.S. He was a year ahead of me and played football and basketball. He also grew up in the fields, in Stockton, an hour or so north of Lemoore, still in central California but more in the direction of Oakland and Sacramento. He was an extremely gentle, nice man, and very quiet, much as I was, although not many people anywhere were as quiet at me. He also had that religious base, and we made a habit of going across campus to church every Sunday morning. We lived together for five years at San Jose State, until he graduated and went to play pro football. In those entire five years, we never had an argument, not once.

When we got back to campus from the airport, one of the assistant coaches met us, and he took me to see my dorm. That dorm was a big deal to me: it had running water, which was something I wasn't used to, even though it was a communal bathroom downstairs. But it was clean, and as I said, the roof didn't leak. That was one of the many new experiences, some big, some very subtle, I had to get used to. I had never slept on a mattress of that quality, that firmness, before. I had to get used to walking on cement, on pavement, from place to place. I also had to get used to living around a bunch of new people—different people, because with my large family, I had been around a lot of people all my life. And I had to get used to so many buildings and so many people so close by—including St. Our room was a box, really; you could step from one side of it to another in one big stride; at least I could, because I had such a long stride.

Don't get the wrong impression about San Jose. I had been to some good-sized cities when I competed in state meets in Fresno and Bakersfield, and USC and Oregon were bigger places than this campus. And San Jose was very rural then, not the way it has become since, when the technology boom came and millionaires moved in and turned the entire area into Silicon Valley. Back then, it was just another hot, dusty inland town. But it was a whole lot bigger than Lemoore, and I had never lived anyplace this big. Bigger and faster and busier and more congested. I felt more comfortable there than I would have at USC, but I still had to make sure I kept up.

It was big and strange enough that it made me feel homesick, not for the picking cotton or chopping cotton, but for the people I left behind at home. I knew them, I was familiar with them, they were all down there and I was up here.

One thing that did make me feel right at home, though, was the makeup of the student body. At that time, from what I can recall, on the entire campus of more than 20,000 students, there were around 20 blacks, definitely no more than 30. Nearly all of them were male; there were very few black females, very few female athletes, and, thus, practically no black female athletes; intercollegiate athletics were not open to women then the way they are today. Out of the entire black student population, about 95 percent were athletes. I was used to that proportion, though, from living and competing in Lemoore. The few black people who were there were working in the fields. I had been aware for a long time that in Lemoore, the blacks were over here and the whites were over there, owning things, working in town, telling us what to do in the fields. It was the same at San Jose State—this place where education and advancement in life were the goals, was a place where not many blacks were present. Unless we were there to run or play ball.

This was one of the first times I became aware that the conditions under which I grew up in Texas and California existed everywhere else. Information wasn't very advanced in Lemoore. News from the rest of the country and the world didn't always get that far, maybe as far as Hanford, but not always to us. We had a telephone, but I sure didn't use it much; neither did the rest of us, because phone calls cost money. We had the radio and we had TV, but we didn't get much on either of those. We were kind of behind the times, and that's how I arrived at San Jose. I was aware of things like *Brown v. Board of Education* and Rosa Parks, and I had that sense of how we were treated differently than whites because we were black, but I had no perspective on it other than what I saw from my Daddy and from my own experiences around Lemoore. My view on the system in which we lived? I had no view.

So, in my first two years in college I learned more than I did in my elementary and high school academic tenures combined. I was like a plant taken from a small pot and planted in a bigger pot; it blossoms, the roots grow, and as long as it gets fed and watered, it will keep growing. I took root in the bigger landscape and began to blossom, and I have not stopped.

Most of my newfound knowledge came when I began spending all my free time in the library, once I realized what being a student truly demanded of me. But before that time, the major portion of my growth in my freshman year was through athletics rather than academics. Part of the reason for that focus, as I said, was the fact that if you were a black person on campus at the time, the odds were overwhelming that you were an athlete. And part of it was the constant reminder that you were still in a minority, even on the track and court and playing fields.

I decided not to play football my freshman year, but I played basketball, for the freshman team, because at that time freshmen were not eligible for varsity play. One of the reasons I had picked San Jose State ahead of the others, in fact, was because it was more of a basketball school, and at the time I thought more about basketball than even track and field. I assumed that eventually I would join St. on the varsity the next year. The freshman coach was a man named Danny Gline; the varsity coach was Stu Inman, who coached at San Jose State for years and eventually got into pro basketball as an executive. In preseason practice, I was doing everything, dunking the ball left and right, hitting jump shots, driving with ease. Already, the fast break was no problem because I could outrun most of the guys on the team. I was All-World in practice.

Then came the first game. I knew I was good, I had come from high school with many commendations, and I could jump better than our 6-foot-10 center even though I was a forward; I just knew I was better than every one of the kids on that team. But Coach Gline started five white guys in that first game. He put me in about four or five minutes into the game, and I started every game the rest of the season. But that choice has always been interesting to me, why he started those five white kids, when he knew I was better than all five of them—at least three of them, since he did start two guards, which was not my position. Since he put me in the game right away, and since I started every game after that, why couldn't I have started that first game? I've always believed that he just was not going to have a black guy in the starting lineup for the opening game of the season. I believed it then and I believe it now. I finished the season as the high scorer and high rebounder on the freshman team. But I couldn't start that first game.

Off the court, my first year was spent getting my bearings—figuring out how to get around campus and around San Jose, getting used to my roommate, making room for basketball and books, and grasping what I had to do to get out of there with a degree. I had an advantage I had brought with me from the fields and from my recollections of Daddy mowing lawns and polishing floors: I was afraid not to go to class. I also had the motivation of the conditions of my scholarship: I essentially was on probation for my first year in school, meaning that I had to maintain a 2.0 grade-point average for the entire year in order to be renewed the remaining time I was there. That 2.0 was the most important number in my life that first year, more than my scoring average in basketball and my 400 time on the track.

Plus, I had a set of "had-to's" from my elementary and high school days, when I would be too bashful or embarrassed to speak up. I had to read the books, I had to listen in class, and I had to take an active part in class, not just show up, sit in the back, and keep my hand at my side. I had figured out early on that human beings gave the grades, and they gave them for participation more than anything. Harry Edwards spoke out demonstratively about that in later years, and I have found out the same thing as an instructor today: participation in class shows the teacher that the student is there to learn, and to be sure, some of the teachers had to be convinced.

So I made sure I went to my classes. I did not have time between classes to go back to the dorm, drop off the books from one class, and pick up the others, so I carried as many as six books around all day. I knew I stood out enough on campus already: I was black, I was an athlete, I was 6 foot 4 and 180 pounds, and since no one expected anybody like that to be an actual student, I stood out even more. And when I was in class, I made sure I spoke out. I was just getting into the habit of communicating clearly in class, and to these teachers my ideas seemed a little abstract, or unclear, or different from what they believed. I was nervous almost every second I was in those classes, nervous before and after the class, too, but nervous in class and nervous when it was time for me to speak, even if I raised my hand to give the answer I knew I had. But I put great effort into trying to portray the image that yes, I was interested, even though I was not what they were routinely seeing in their classrooms. This took a long time to accomplish, because I was still tremendously shy.

My study habits changed substantially as well. I had always had the principle imbedded in me that if you do your work to the maximum of your ability, something good will come from it, and that for every step you take, God will help you take two more. Even though our lives were in the fields, Mulla and Daddy stressed learning and church. Of course, I had to learn the balance of the two the hard way: one time in high school, I had a big test coming the next morning that I needed to study for, and Daddy was insisting that I come to the evening church service instead. When I insisted back—not too hard, of course, because that was a good reason to get the belt—that I had to study, Daddy told me that when the time came to take the test, just trust in God to move the pencil on the paper and provide the answers. So I went to church, and the next day, I sat there at my desk for an entire hour, waiting for God to start moving my pencil. When that hour was over and the sheet was blank, I realized that God wasn't going to move anything for me unless I moved it myself first. It taught me to rely on myself above all other persons, and then I could trust that God would intervene for me.

Those first two years of college, I studied like I never had before. If it took six hours to read one page, I realized, you take those six hours to read it. I burned the candle at both ends studying. Many a night I fell asleep in the middle of a paragraph and woke up an hour later on the same sentence, and I had to read it over again—an experience that taught me to stay awake. A lot of times I woke up the next morning unable to remember what I had studied the night before because I couldn't stay awake or alert. I went over chapters before class if I had to. And I discovered the library and resolved to know that place inside and out, as if it was my second home—which, not long after I got there, it became.

The first major I declared was music, because I had sung from the time I was small with my brothers and sisters. But I realized that meant a lot of sitting in front of a piano, and that was not for me, because I didn't enjoy sitting, and I didn't take to coordinating my hands on those little white keys. So I switched to my second major, physical education, because that's what I thought all athletes majored in. That was the pervasive notion: If you were a great athlete, then you major in what you're good in. Not to say it was not a difficult major; it required a number of science courses. But even though I had an interest in general science, I did not want to give the impression that all athletes in college give, that I was in a "dumb jock" major. That meant another major change, to physical science. That lasted a semester. I was close—I wanted the science, but not that type of science.

I found my true interest from the habit I had developed of staying in the library until it closed. I studied for my classes there, but the more I read, the more what I read took my interest to other areas, and the more it made me ask questions that led to still other topics and subjects. I came to realize that the perfect fit for me was social science —I believed that it engaged the physical and mental sides of me; I wanted to maximize both of those sides, and by understanding both, I would be able to better grasp the social system I lived in and find the best way to be viable within it. That is what my bachelor's degree is in, social science (today, it would be sociology).

Social science, or sociology, is the study of people and of social systems. It is closely tied to history, and I gravitated toward the history sections of the library. Each piece of new information led to another, and I just kept gobbling it up. It was great stuff. I found out so much more about the system than I had ever seen before.

I noticed that the histories in my textbooks never included black history, so I searched for that in the library as well. It was in sociology that I first read the United States Constitution and the Articles of Confederation, the foundations of the revolution that broke the colonies away from England and created a democratic system of government. I learned exactly what that original definition of "democracy" was, and what the ideals of a democracy were and the rights that system granted to its citizens. I read about the 13 colonies and about Plymouth Rock—and about the arrival of African slaves in Jamestown, how the slaves were systematically segmented before the ships even left Africa for America, how it was assured that they could not communicate with others in their own languages, and how they were further separated and families broken up when they landed here. Systematically, I emphasize—communication is such a basic part of a social system, and here these people were strengthening their own communications foundation by destroying another's. It was easy to trace exactly how one segment of society granted itself a set of rights and entitlements while denying an entirely separate segment another set—or, more accurately, none at all. There may have been ideals, but human beings took them and divided them among themselves, giving their own group power and the rest of the people none.

I began to pull it all together. I began to see why we were treated the way we were in Texas, and why we were treated the way we were when we came out to California, at the camp in Stratford. I pondered the image of equality America prides itself on, while noticing that I was clearly considered a second-class citizen in that country—that a blond, blue-eyed 14-year-old was allowed to do more in the system than I did. Why was this? I came to the conclusion that I was living according to what the past had produced, that history had dictated my place in society long before I was born. That was not the way I had been raised and taught, but that was how I was being forced to live.

This all made me listen even more than I usually did. I have always been quiet and had to force myself to express myself to remain a functional student. I continued my educational pattern, talking more than I had, but continuing to listen to everything around me. (I later heard the perfect saying about that: It is better to remain quiet and appear stupid, than to open your mouth and remove all doubt.) I would come across a lot of different people during the course of a typical day, which consisted for those first two years of studying, eating, training, going to class, going to church, over and over again. I had no car, so I was walking everywhere, stack of books in my arms, and I was opening different doors, seeing different classmates, seeing different instructors, and, in the course of circulating off campus, meeting the different people of San Jose. I watched their movements, caught the sights and smells, and heard what they said, and I learned more doing that than I ever would have by engaging them in conversation.

Meanwhile, they would see me, notice I didn't talk much, see me smiling, and form an opinion about me right off the bat. I like to smile just because that is who I am and that is how my family has always been. I also still had a need, from my first days, of wanting to be noticed when I was running, to be liked. I got over that feeling fast once I knew how far it would get me trying to be liked by everybody, but the instinct to smile remained. The sight of a black athlete on a college campus, though, with books under his arms, smiling, brought many an uninformed preconceived notion to a lot of minds. For one, they believe we're all a happy, grinning people anyway, despite the atrocities we routinely suffer. For another, they assume that as a black athlete, I have nothing to talk about other than how fast I run. For yet another, I'm probably putting up a front or putting on airs by showing off that stack of books. I filed all of this away with all the other enjoyable and enlightening lessons I was learning.

You must understand that my experiences were nothing out of the ordinary for college life in the early 1960s, in California or anywhere else. Being in a nonsouthern state and being in an atmosphere of higher learning did not bar American society's basic racist tendencies from infiltrating. Those attitudes were as prevalent at San Jose State as they were anywhere else at that time, and they were more overt than most people know. They showed themselves with fellow students, they showed themselves with instructors and coaches, they showed themselves with my white teammates. There were incidents that took place long before Mexico City, long before the Olympic Project for Human Rights was formed, within the athletic programs at San Jose State, which illuminated the problem and the desperate need for a solution.

But a lot of the problem stemmed from the fact that the whites on campus simply couldn't come to terms with this new black presence among them. White people thought nothing of walking up to any black person at San Jose State and asking, "What sport do you play?" never thinking it possibly could be an insult. For us to turn it around and question them back—"Because I'm black, you automatically think I'm an athlete?"—would intimidate the person who asked the original question. It also would lead to a discussion about how we were there to be educated, just as they were. As many times as I dealt with that, no one should be surprised at the field of study I chose. It was critical to me to not only develop myself from the neck down and the neck up, but to blend the two, to make what works from the neck up work to help me from the neck down, and vice versa.

But facing that every day created camaraderie among the black athletes that might not have been there had we simply been a group of black students, or simply athletes. We all developed a bond with each other. The number of football players was greater than that for any other sport, so our friendships tended to revolve around them. Track athletes would sometimes wander into the cafeteria when the football players were there, and we would get involved in their conversation, even if it was about something directly related to football. Several times I sat with St. Saffold, my roommate, and his teammates Charlie Harraway, Fred Heron, Cass Jackson, and some of the others. We all shared the same experiences dealing with the racism on campus. Consequently, we all took great pride in seeing each other, and every other black student there whether an athlete or not, walking across campus carrying a book. It was pride for us, and we knew it wounded white people a little more each time they saw it. They saw it as an insult, having to share their school with black mercenaries who, they assumed, were only brought in to bring San Jose State athletic glory. Now, I can't say that every black athlete there was dedicated to his studies—but I do know that our presence and the fact that we were aware of all of this, scared white people. I'm sure that then, just as it is now, when we all came together as a group to talk as we did in the cafeteria, white people thought we were plotting a revolt. They couldn't imagine that we were talking about the things they talked about: classes, professors, home, how we grew up, and life on campus, along with the social issues that affected all of us. And, a lot of times, nothing to do with sports at all.

I still had to keep up my end of the bargain in athletics. I played the entire basketball season as a freshman, then immediately went to run track. I didn't get a chance to train specifically for track, which involved different motion and muscles than basketball. I found the transition difficult, and it only got worse in my first meet as a collegian that spring, in Berkeley, a dual meet with Cal. I was still long jumping, and halfway down the runway in my very first attempt, I pulled my hamstring, fairly severely. I couldn't do anything else in that meet, and it took six weeks for that muscle to heal, costing me the next few meets as well. Then in May, at the West Coast Relays in Fresno—I had run in that meet in high school, and now I was in the collegiate competition—I reached the final of the 400, against a great runner, Dave Tobler from the army. I felt good and strong and in control of my faculties, and I ran a 46.5. It wasn't a great time, but I was a freshman coming off the first really serious injury of my life, and I caught and stayed with Dave Tobler for the final 80 meters. He finished with the same time, got the lean at the tape, and was awarded first place—but because of my time and the circumstances, I was named athlete of the year by the U.S.A. Track and Field Foundation.

The honor made things look promising for my sophomore year—but I had one more scary moment before I reached that year. A note arrived at my parents' house in Lemoore notifying me that I was being disqualified from school. According to them, I had fallen below a 2.0 average, and my scholarship was to be revoked because of it. My sister Sally called me and left an urgent message for me to call home. I went to a pay phone near my dorm, and Sally was crying into the phone and saying, "Tommie, you've got to go home, you didn't make it in college." I didn't know what she was talking about. She told me about the note. She was so upset because she had been my partner from the beginning, closer to me than anyone else in the family. I told her I would check it out and for her not to worry. I went to the admissions office and checked my entire grade report—and there was a blank space where one of my grades for the semester should have been. One of my instructors had forgotten to turn in my grade. As a professor today, I've had that happen, even with the grade sheets being computerized, so I can understand that you can slip up and omit one person while submitting a hundred or more grades for one class. They put the grade in place for me; it raised my average to 2.2, and I was back on scholarship.

My sophomore year followed another summer making a little spending money cleaning classrooms with Daddy. Now we were also working at the elementary schools on the air force base in Lemoore, so that meant even more pushing and moving and handling those big floor scrubbers. I came back strong again and ready to continue my athletic path, but not long afterward I came to a critical decision about that path. I was allowed to compete in any of the three sports stipulated in my scholarship; I had passed on football, and now I was no longer sure about basketball, which had always been my favorite. Playing on the varsity, though, was a struggle. I practiced with the team in the preseason, and I was still fast and could still outleap almost everyone there. But for some reason, I couldn't catch onto the plays. I would be in the wrong place or too far downcourt or any number of other things, so that when the ball got to where I was supposed to be, it went out of bounds because I wasn't there. I also wasn't fond of the physical punishment I was starting to take, the same reason I passed on football; the biggest problem was the gym, which was sunk about six feet below the surface with the bleachers above and with the walls only four or five feet behind the baskets. I kept banging into those walls every time I drove to the basket because I was moving so fast and couldn't stop quickly enough.

More than anything, though, I found out that track and field served me better than basketball, served what I wanted to do better. Track is more of an individual thing, whereas basketball, with five guys on the court, is more of a team thing. Track has a team, but the whole team doesn't run the 100-yard dash together. I could lend myself to do things better by myself than with a group of people. It came from being raised to depend on nobody besides yourself. I still don't like to depend on anybody else, although I have come to realize over the years that groups are often much stronger than individuals. I would be taught that lesson later in my sophomore year.

So before preseason practice ended, I went into Stu Inman's office and told him I had decided not to play basketball this year and that I wanted to make track my primary sport. I thought he was going to blow up at me, that he would say, "You've practiced with me all this time, you should stick with us now," and so on, but he didn't. Coach Inman said, "Okay, Tom, I understand," he shook my hand and told me to be sure to come by to see him whenever I wanted to, and that I was always welcome back if I changed my mind. That was the greatest thing in the world for me to see, that he viewed me as a person who was mature enough to make that decision and that he complimented me on making that decision.

I went to Bud Winter and told him I had talked to Stu Inman and said I'd be concentrating on track and field alone, that I was ready to start my early-season training and that there wouldn't be a repeat of last year, when I got injured trying to make the transition from one sport to the other. Coach Winter got a big smile on his face, he turned red as an apple, and he shook my hand and said, "Okay, Tom, let's start your training." I was a one-sport man from that moment on, and the sport was track and field.

Track season began in earnest in the second semester. By that time, even throughout the concentration on training and classes and church and scraping together money to eat and time to sleep, I began to grow interested in the opposite sex. Not that I hadn't been interested before; I had had what you would call a girlfriend in high school, the sister of the man my sister Sally eventually married. And I had noticed women on campus—how could you not? But I had too much to occupy my time already. Plus, when you have seven sisters as I did, do you really need an eighth woman in your life? So I began to date the first serious girlfriend in college, a young lady from Los Angeles named Valerie Yates. Valerie would have a profound impact on my life that very year.

However, my social history at San Jose State would not be complete without noting that, yes, I had an interest in white girls. That was not a small issue on a college campus like San Jose State in the 1960s. It was a no-no, for many different reasons, from the white side and the black side. But there was a young lady named Kathleen Johnson, whom everyone called Kit. She was blond with blue eyes and very smart, all A's and B's. I was grateful to get C's. She would actually help me with my books, which was heavy duty for a white person to do, male or female. We became good friends, but dating was out of the question, not just because of the social situation, but because I had too many other things to take up my time. But just walking down the street or across campus with her, riding in a car with her, and certainly holding hands with her were considered taboo.

At that time, two major mindsets were clashing: the belief that one of the primary traits of black athletes on college campuses was their lust for white women and the growing popularity of "Black Is Beautiful." It was just becoming a recognizable fact that white women did not have to be on the pedestal they had been placed on, that white wasn't always right and black wasn't always wrong, and that white wasn't automatically prettier than black. It was no longer an insult to be called "black," and that term was becoming more acceptable than "Negro." In fact, it was preferable to be as dark as possible, because the connotations of being too light were being turned upside down; now, James Brown was singing, "Say it loud, I'm black and I'm proud."

So, although Kit and I became very close, we never became a couple in society. We studied together, talked together, went to each other's apartments, even sat next to each other in class, but never went any more public than that. She and I were both bashful and neither of us tried to get noticed, but obviously we both stood out wherever we were, and when she was at a meet, you couldn't miss her even if you wanted to. The truth is, I was not the only athlete being seen with white females. We knew what it implied socially, and we knew that no one would believe anything else about us. Some of them didn't even care, but I knew that it wasn't good to be out and about together, so Kit and I hardly ever were.

I was glad to discover, of course, that not every white person on that campus had an evil mindset about the black athletes there. In my sophomore year, I became friends with a white student named Art Simburg, who remained a good friend and associate from then on. Art was a journalism major, and he wrote for the campus newspaper, the *Spartan Daily* (San Jose State's sports nickname was the Spartans). He was not an athlete, but he wrote about sports and he liked to come by the track and watch practice and get to know the members of the team. He was tall, kind of chubby, with dark hair, and he did not have a problem associating with black students on campus. He also was a natural hustler, in that he knew how to get his hands on things when he or someone else needed them. When he needed money—he didn't like getting money from home, although his family did have it—he would sell encyclopedias or something like that, door to door, which hardly anybody, if anyone at all, does anymore. That was how he was able to raise money to travel to meets.

In that way, Art got to know everybody on the team and felt totally at ease with us, even with Carlos, who used to give him guff the way he does with everybody. We got close to him and felt comfortable with this white boy who liked talking to these world-class black athletes. By the time he graduated, we were close enough that we hooked him up to be a representative for Puma, the shoe company, a perfect fit for him. In return, he was something close to being our agent; in fact, he almost became the official agent for several of us. He helped me feed my family later during my time at San Jose State; back when I was scuffling to make money for my first wife, Denise, and my first son, Kevin, before and after Mexico City, Art would talk Puma into sending shoes to us, to wear in competition. We'd get as many as 10 pairs at first, and we'd sell them for five dollars a pair— yes, that was the cost—which would buy enough Similac for Kevin for a week. Soon, Puma was sending up even more shoes, and we kept selling them, at a higher price. The thing was, I didn't run in Pumas; I wore Adidas. I liked Adidas and had set 10 world records by then while wearing them. I had never received a red cent from Adidas for doing it. Art took care of that: "Wear Pumas," he said, "and I'll make sure you get everything you need." So I started wearing them, and the money and shoes started flowing, and I said to myself, "This is all right. I could continue training and not have to worry about washing cars to support my wife and child." They took me to the factory in Germany and everything. I wore them for a year leading up to Mexico City so I could get used to them. I wore them when I won the gold medal, and they were sitting on the victory stand that night—I had taken them off, of course, as part of the silent protest. But it was important that I have them on the stand, because they helped me get there, during the race and long before. They were as important as the black glove and the black socks. And it was all because of Art stepping up for me.

Art was with me the first time I set a world record, and the first time I participated in a protest for civil rights. He was going to be the author of my book originally, right after Mexico City, around 1969 or '70. He lived with us for several months at the house on North 11th Street in San Jose, where we fixed up the back porch for him and where we sat every day for months talking about the book and several other things. But the book never got done. That was the first of many attempts to tell this story. Art, of course, was part of the story. We're still friends, and for years, until I retired and moved to Georgia, we lived near each other—but we don't talk or get together very often at all. It's my fault as much as anyone's. Carlos lives in southern California, too, and in the same way, we just see each other when we see each other.

Back in those days money was hard to come by, which was why Art was such a savior when his Puma deal came through. Otherwise, I had to fit work in among class and training, because the money given for scholarship barely covered the bare necessities. That was why I went back to Lemoore the first two summers in college. In the summers following my next two years in school, I worked for the Oakland public schools, in a job Coach Winter and some of the Spartan supporters found for me. It was the same kind of work I had done for Daddy in Lemoore: refinishing playgrounds, basketball courts, and tennis courts, hot work in the summer sun. I made seven dollars an hour. I didn't spend any of it on rent or anything; with the dorms closed on campus for the summer, I stayed either with my brother George or with my sister Lucille, both of whom lived in Oakland. I also was able to stay there when school let out for Christmas or for spring break. They were my saving grace. That was a big reason I chose San Jose State in the first place, because family was close by when I needed them.

I hung on to enough of what I earned to finally buy a car in the summer after my junior year. It was a little 1962 Volkswagen that I bought from Howard Blethen, who was principal at one of the schools in Oakland where I worked and was a Spartan Foundation member. He also was kind enough to give me work at his house, in his garden and backyard, more money I could put toward that car. Still, I only had money for enough gas to get around campus and back and forth to practice. If I wanted to go on a date, the gas money wasn't stretching that far.

It amazes me even now that I got by the way I did on the money I had. One reason I needed to have a couple of dollars to spare was that many times I didn't have a chance to eat at the cafeteria on campus; I would be coming in late from out of town after a meet, or I would have a late practice, or it would be a Sunday, and the cafeteria would be closed. I had to eat whatever I could get my hands on, corn chips or Zingers or Froot Loops. During the time I was accomplishing some of the greatest feats of my career, I was barely eating. I couldn't have gotten fat if I had tried; most of the time, my body was feeding on its reserves and making me even more lean than I was before. I got stronger, but I was not spending anything close to the proper time at the table.

I compare what I lived on then to what athletes in college get today. They don't get everything they are entitled to, but they get more than what we did, and in a lot of cases the athletes of my day laid the foundation for them to get what they can. They now can get endorsements, they can have jobs and receive money for things like speaking engagements, they can run professionally, they can compete professionally in one sport while remaining eligible in another, and the best in the world can now make millions. These are things we fought the collegiate sports governing body, the National Collegiate Athletic Association, as well as the AAU and the Olympic organizations, to get back then. I remember when I returned from my third year with the Cincinnati Bengals and asked the NCAA if I could run track again, because I had been a professional in football but not in track, and they said no—I was a professional now and could not become an amateur again, regardless of whether I was doing it in a different sport. I asked questions, I called my legislators, I went to the top of these organizations. I kept bugging and bugging people. Eventually, track stars were allowed to play pro football and continue to run track internationally, and Willie Gault, Renaldo Nehemiah, and others did so.

That success didn't do me any good, of course. Back when I held 11 world records, I never reaped the financial benefits of it. That is no surprise. We as black people, who were enslaved for more than two centuries and built this country, never received reparations, and we never will. I won't receive anything retroactively. I won't get a percentage of the endorsement contracts that are negotiated for the Olympic stars today and have been for the past decade or so. People tell me, "Well, Tommie, you did get compensated, with a free education." There was nothing free about that. I received an athletic scholarship, and I worked for every cent of it. What I put into it physically to perform for San Jose State and what I put into it academically to receive that degree—I don't believe to this day that I got back what I put into it. The fame was no reward for me; I was not someone who thought about becoming famous through running track. In fact, I tried to avoid that kind of notice; the achievement itself was more important to me than the fame that came from it.

So it still came down to compensation, and $95 a month and the opportunity to compete in the classroom with other students with fewer demands on their time and effort was not sufficient payment for what I gave. Yet I endured it and survived it because the alternative was the grape fields.

I was thankful, though, that I was going to be on scholarship for five years as long as I maintained that grade-point average and kept running track. The one exception to that promise was Vietnam. My sophomore year, 1964–65, was when Vietnam got really, really hot, and there was no guarantee anymore that college enrollment would keep you exempt from the draft. If your average dropped below 2.0 and you lost your academic privileges at your school, the army had every right to take you, and it wasn't long before grades and eligibility didn't matter at all if your number came up. That scared everybody back then, because we knew already that if we were drafted, we were going to Southeast Asia and that there was no guarantee that you'd come home—and that if you did come home and were not in a flag-draped box, you would bring all your faculties back with you.

I was not going to halt my education to go to Vietnam. It wasn't so much because I didn't want to go there—although I didn't—I just didn't want to think about doing it until I had achieved my primary goal, a degree. I had worked very hard to get where I was, and I didn't want anything to interrupt it, including a war that hadn't even been declared to bring democracy to someplace that didn't want it. Particularly when the very country exporting democracy hadn't even bothered extending it to its own citizens yet. Some things never change, do they, now that this country is doing the same thing today, and never really stopped doing it in between?

During the second semester of my junior year, I got the shocking news. My roommate St. ran into the room and told me, "You've been drafted!" I scowled at him hard and told him very firmly that there was no way I could go into the army while I was still trying to finish school. No, St. pointed out, it wasn't the army, it was the Los Angeles Rams. I've got to admit, it sounds funny now, but I wasn't laughing then. For one thing, I pointed out to him that I couldn't get drafted to play pro football either, not while I was still eligible to compete in college. As it turns out, I actually could have left school and played had I wanted to. But I made that decision quickly: it was far better for me to remain in school and complete my education and then take the potential riches of pro football—rather than play, get injured, and be unable to make that money or return to school. In all seriousness, too, it didn't worry me that I'd be playing football in the pros after having last played it in high school. If they wanted to pay me to do it, I would go willingly and happily.

Still, after the draft I was contacted by representatives from the business company operated by Jim Brown, the former NFL star. He wanted his company to act as my agents when it was time for me to play. I agreed to have him be my agent when I did leave college, and I signed a contract in which he would get 10 percent of the salary I got from the Rams. In exchange, he forwarded me a $2,000 advance, which I put in the bank, for safekeeping, and made sure not to spend a dime of it until I started making money in the pros. In later years— after Mexico City, to be exact—that arrangement and the advance from the legendary Jim Brown would reenter my life and teach me a lesson worth far more than $2,000.

The army did come calling soon after that. I immediately raced down to MacQuarrie Hall, one of the new student buildings on campus, where the ROTC office was. I signed up as quickly as I could. ROTC was the only way I could fulfill my military obligation and remain in school; while completing my studies, I would be taking ROTC classes and training to be an officer, and after graduation I would go into the service as a second lieutenant—and later than had I just gone in as a draftee. And I could bank my ROTC stipend to help make ends meet. The real price was that I had one more thing to occupy my time besides practice, meets, classes, and studying.

For the next two years, on ROTC days, once a week, class began at 6 A.M., an hour of marching and drilling and saluting and addressing the officers, in full uniform—hat, gloves, shirt, tie, coat, slacks, socks, shiny patent-leather shoes. We wore the uniform everywhere we went the rest of the day, including to my 7 A.M. class that day. That was a blessing in disguise for me, because I didn't have many clothes anyway, so that was one less set of clothes I had to worry about wearing to class. Besides, I liked wearing that uniform. I looked sharp, and I made sure I kept it all looking sharp, just as I had learned from my mother growing up in Texas.

I was a good soldier, followed all the rules and regulations, and said "Yes, sir" and "No, sir" when I had to. I even helped keep Art Simburg looking sharp; he had also joined, for the same reason, even though he wasn't an athlete and had a comfortable grade average. He wasn't taking any chances; not many students were, and we had five or six ROTC companies of 10 or 12 soldiers each by my senior year. I had to help Art tie his tie and tie his shoes properly just about every morning of class. I'd help him make sure his clothes didn't have lint and that his shoes shone. We'd leave from my apartment on the south side of campus, the tiny one-bedroom apartment St. and I now shared, to go to the class together. We also served together at Fort Knox, in Kentucky, in the summer of 1967—it was the last place I wanted to spend a summer, down south in the '60s, but the national championship meet had been in the south that year, and Art and I went straight from the meet to the base for the summer.

I have to admit, I was enjoying ROTC more than I ever thought I would. One of my goals as a youngster had been to be in the army, to have a position of responsibility and authority, and ROTC allowed me to do that. It also was a perfect fit for my disciplined nature. It even gave me a patriotic feeling for the first time, a sense that I was doing something truly American, that I was a vital part of the system. I definitely appreciated the chance it gave me to finish school; it all seemed to offer the best of all worlds, and I started to think that everything in my life was coming into order.

Of course, I was still learning about the real exercise of democracy in this country, and I had yet to learn and grasp how the black man was treated by his own armed services throughout history, the way he was segregated from his own comrades in war, and how he often fought with valor and died for his country yet never received credit or recognition and was treated like a subhuman when back on American soil, even when wearing his nation's uniform. I also had seen, by then, how America had treated Muhammad Ali when he opposed the war and refused induction, as a conscientious objector based on his religious beliefs. Had I been drafted, rather than join ROTC, I would have considered refusing to serve as well—but after seeing what they did to Ali, what chance did Tommie Smith have?

These thoughts ran through my head throughout that second year in ROTC. I knew that I was glad I never took these thoughts to my father. I knew that he would have said that I should go if called upon and do my best, just as he had told me when I left home to attend college. I don't think he would have understood how I treasured my education above all else, including serving this country in Vietnam. Serving would have made him and the family proud; they were proud of my being in ROTC, and they were patriots regardless of how America had treated us. So that was a topic I never discussed with them. Our beliefs in what we had to do to make this country better for all its people went in different directions. I tended to think that in a country that burns, bombs, and lynches its citizens as they march for their rights, fighting in another part of the world to instill that system elsewhere was not the way to go. If I were to lose my life for a cause, I wanted it to be a cause in this country, fighting for freedom here instead of somewhere else.

It was more of my nature to keep these kinds of thoughts to myself, even from my family members and closest friends. We would talk about them on campus at times, among ourselves, discuss the indignities we regularly suffered. Many of these discussions involved Harry Edwards, both before he left San Jose to obtain his master's degree and after he returned. Occasionally, we would engage the white students who carelessly unveiled their prejudiced views, challenging their assumptions and watching them either come to understanding or turn away in anger or fear.

But talking was one thing, doing was another, and my instinct still was neither to talk a lot nor to do anything that detracted from studying and running track. It was easier to do this than to step out and act. There were more than enough things happening outside the campus of San Jose State to remind me of what others were doing to make change. After a year and a half as a student and an athlete, I was aware of these things, but was not aware of the platform from which I could take action.

It was inevitable that I would find my platform, that my growing prowess on the track and my feelings about the situation in this country would converge to make an impact I had never imagined they could. That time came during my sophomore year, in the spring of 1965.

Run Before You Walk

B Y EARLY 1965, the latter part of my sophomore year at San Jose State, the idea of black empowerment was becoming popular, as awareness of a system that was not treating people equally grew. At the same time, my prowess as one of the best sprinters in the world was growing as well. Little did I know that the two forces would converge within me on a single spring weekend.

Already by that time, much had happened in the civil rights movement, particularly down South. The bus boycotts in Montgomery, sparked by the protest of Rosa Parks, had been years before. Dr. Martin Luther King had moved into prominence; the March on Washington had been less than two years earlier, and there had already been several nonviolent demonstrations, many of which had been met with violent resistance. One of the worst retaliations had already been perpetrated: the bombing of a church in Birmingham, Alabama, that killed four little girls as they prayed in Sunday school. The Freedom Rides had begun, and already many of the riders into the South had lost their lives. The Civil Rights Bill had been introduced by Lyndon Johnson. The march in Selma would take place later in that year. And early in that year, Malcolm X was assassinated. History tells us that 1965 was a milestone year in the movement. With everything that was happening, society was growing anxious about the change it was undergoing and about the people fighting for their rights as human beings, exercising the freedom of speech they had been denied but to which they were entitled.

Yet as a student and an athlete at San Jose State even at that time, I wasn't much in tune with what was going on, although I did know that things were going on. I certainly had no anticipation that I would be a civil rights activist or leader. One of my first memories of the movement was hearing about Rosa Parks, while I was still in grammar school at Central Union Elementary School. That was the first time, I believe, that I was very conscious at all about the rights of mankind and what was guaranteed to us—as I learned later, guaranteed by the Constitution of this nation. But by the time I arrived at San Jose State seven years later, I felt I could not spend much time on that effort. I was there on a scholarship to play basketball, football, and track, and I had received that because of my athletic achievements in high school. My scholarship came with conditions: I was under academic probation for that first year, and if I did not complete that year with a grade-point average of 2.0, a C average, or better, the scholarship would be taken away. Had I lost that scholarship, I would have been out of school, and that meant returning to the fields with my daddy in Lemoore, and I probably would have been there to this day.

In my first year, the 1963–64 academic year, I played basketball; that was how the seasons of competition went, basketball beginning in the fall semester, then track and field beginning in the spring. Football went on at the same time as both, with the season taking place in the fall and spring practice the following semester, and those demands eliminated football from my repertoire of athletics. Partly because I was not able to concentrate on both as I did in high school, and partly because I was not interested in getting banged up, suffering a major injury to my legs, and being unavailable for track, I decided after my first year to concentrate solely on track and field. I had made it through my probation period, but I still had to work my buns off to keep my GPA up to 2.0 or better. By then, I had learned that those grades, that education, that degree, was what held value; that was my path to improve my life, be more viable in the system, and be a better individual.

As I continued at college, however, I found that there was more on my mind than just bettering Tommie Smith. That feeling grew naturally as I became aware of the challenges of being a black athlete and student at that time and in that place. Being an individual thinker who would not wholly swallow another's ideas, who would be responsible for what one thought—that was rather difficult for me at that time. I had come from a background that I knew a lot about by my actions but knew little about mentally. I was not taught about black history, the contributions of my own people to society, by my family, and certainly not by my grammar schools in Texas or California or my high school in Lemoore. Like many black kids in my day, I was embarrassed to mention the continent of Africa while growing up because I thought it was demeaning; I thought the heritage of Africans was something that was smaller or less than that of the Americans. I was taught to work hard, but not to be proud. I don't think any time in my grammar school or high school years the word "pride" was part of anyone's vocabulary when talking to me. It was work, church, athletics, and school—and school was the most important for me and those around me, because succeeding in school facilitated participation in athletics, and participating in athletics was presented to me as my only avenue toward being viable in the system. It was not even presented to me as a path toward anything else, because even then it was not a sure thing that education could raise our standing in life. Our lives were the fields.

So I was at a minus entering college, where I was confronted with the knowledge I should have attained already, coming out of a system that had not been instrumental in the thought process, a system which was racist. I took it for granted I was supposed to work in the field, I took it for granted that I was supposed to sit in the back of the classroom, I took it for granted that I was subordinate. And these assumptions came from my not believing in myself, not believing that I was endowed with the mental strength or capacity to truly become a viable part of the system—not as an athlete, but as a human being. Regardless of the cycle Rosa Parks had broken for all of us years before, I was always in the back seat.

It all created a student, even as I entered college, who was reserved in many ways, as I have mentioned before—not someone eager to speak out, in class, in public, more willing to listen and not full of confidence in expressing myself or my thoughts. In spite of all of that, I was conscious of human rights, even if I did not have a name for them at the time, and even if I had everything to learn about them because of the emptiness of my background of formal learning. From growing up in Texas and, later, in dealing with the labor camps in which we lived when we first came to California, I knew there was a difference in the way people were treated according to color. I knew how I had grown up, how my family had lived, and how my father had kept us together and supported us under such adverse conditions. I had worked in somebody's fields somewhere almost as far back as I could remember. In a sense, because I had come to this point in my life with no knowledge or background in politics, I had a freedom that I didn't know I had. I began to ask questions, to myself and later out loud: "What does this all mean? Do I really have certain rights?" Those questions led me to do some research—I went to the library, I studied, and even in my bashful state I talked to people. I talked to my roommate a little bit about it, about the rights of people, about civil rights, about white people calling black people nigger, which was even more of a heavy-duty word then than it is now, because it was so commonplace, so routine—white people never hesitated to call you nigger this, nigger that. It took a while for me to learn that the word doesn't mean very much, and that it means even less once you know who you are, what you believe, and what your rights truly are. Otherwise, it's just something they call you.

As time went on at San Jose State I became more aware. I wanted to find out more about all this, so I could deal with it on both a realistic and an academic level—so I could talk about it from a base of education, rather than just from being a black man. It was my incredible fortune that San Jose, and the college, was one of the emerging centers of thought and activism about the rights of humans according to this nation's own Constitution. There were a number of San Jose State students who were highly motivated academicians and who were much more knowledgeable about the atrocities of the system than I was. Their presence and my own circumstances and growing awareness got me to reading and thinking and researching the history of this country: the slavery issue, the Constitution, everything that had to do with being a viable entity in the American system. This was even before I turned, finally, to sociology as my academic major. I was involved in lectures, speeches, conversations, activities in the classroom, and research in the library—trying to get my studies together, with a capital T, and doing what I could as an athlete to promote awareness of a system that was adhering too strongly, and for too long, to racist principles that completely conflicted with its own ideals.

Even then, I was more interested from the aspect of human rights, rather than civil rights or black power. I never was a Black Panther, although after the victory stand in Mexico City it was assumed that I was, and it is still assumed by many even today. I never focused solely on blacks to the extent that everything else was secondary; I did not want my participation to be about only one kind of people. I believed as I did even though most of what I had experienced, in the fields in Texas and in California, through Stratford and Central Union Elementary and Lemoore High, was with black people, my family and friends and others I grew up with. Even as I sought something higher for myself as a black man and for other blacks, I still sought it within a humanistic context, from the point of view that all were entitled to the rights many were denied. My goal was to involve myself, to use what I had, to create a better path for myself in college and for the other young black athletes who were coming up under me, and I could do that best by becoming grounded in the knowledge of these rights.

So at that point I was merely becoming aware of what was happening and what my role was in changing it and in educating myself. Was I marching in Montgomery? No. Was I marching in Lemoore, even? No. Now, earlier, as a student at Lemoore High, I did give a speech in Lemoore that was not very well accepted because I did mention the word "racism." That would not have meant much normally; had a farmer or a farmer's son marched around in the cotton fields or in the cornfields or through the grapevine—literally through the grapevine, not as the old saying—talking about the atrocities of the system, yelling and screaming at what needs to be done, nobody would have heard him, and if he had been heard, he wouldn't have gotten a response. But by then I was not just a farmer's son speaking about these things. I was the local star who had made it big in track and field, the student body vice president, and I normally had a smile on my face, as I often had when they saw me while I was growing up. Then I started speaking about the system and using that word, and that's when I became unpopular. Because of the smile on my face, people thought, "Well, he must be happy." When people smile, it's not necessarily happiness; it's just being cordial. I smiled, but I also spoke of the system and made it clear that I had a different idea of what freedom and the Constitution means than what others seem to want for other humans. That made people mad, and to them I became someone to fear, someone who was so against the system that I might pick up a gun and take their lives. That was the reaction we got everywhere, as black people and particularly black athletes who spoke out at that time, at San Jose and Lemoore and elsewhere, about the overall system that is infused with racism and the smaller systems, on college campuses and within athletics, that are small versions of the large systems. They heard it, and they thought we were ready to pick up something and hurt someone. All we were was concerned; we wanted to do something to heighten the awareness of a system that needed changing.

In reality, we could have taken the fight to its ultimate resolution had we truly wanted to, but we were acutely aware of what such actions would mean. It's one of the reasons I continue to emphasize my interest in the struggle as a human rights issue, not just black, not just civil rights. Even now, by just being black, no matter how you phrase your intent, people tend to put you in a category. You want reverse discrimination, or you're a radical or a militant or any other label that denotes negativity, when all you're really trying to do is create awareness of a system that needs change. Had we truly been radical or militant, we would have pointed out that in the Constitution itself, it says that if it does not serve the people, then the people should change it. That spells revolution. But that means war, as Malcolm X said, a complete overthrow of the system. We never said that, never said, "I'm a revolutionary," or, "I will revolt against this because I am black and am being denied what your very laws promise me." I am black, but we as blacks are not the only ones being denied. This, again, is why this is about human rights for me, and this is why what I did, and what we did, cannot be interpreted as radical or militant except by those bent on preserving a corrupt system at all costs.

I hope it's fairly clear that we were not interested in a violent solution. The students at San Jose State were simply interesting in increasing and spreading knowledge and making their voices known. That was when talk of a march in support of the people engaged in the fight for freedom, particularly down South, began to grow. I was fortunate to have grown close to many of the people who felt this concern deeply and believed a march to be an important step. Professor Harry Edwards, for one, had long noted that the masses had to become conscious of the system enslaving them. I had known Harry, of course, from his days as an athlete at San Jose State, who had spoken from the beginning about the injustices of the system. A march was important, he believed, to show that we are neither a violent people nor out to get recognition as militants. Our concern was to highlight a social system that does not treat its people equally, that guarantees in its own laws rights for all but in fact only grants those rights to a few, mainly whites in power more interested in maintaining that power than in allowing others to have it.

The other person I was close to with an interest in activism and awareness was the young woman to whom I was engaged at the time, although we later broke the engagement. Valerie Yates was from Los Angeles and had been exposed to a lot more things than those of us from smaller places like San Jose, and certainly more than someone from a place like Lemoore. She was a very good student, very literary, never at a loss for words and with great meaning in what she said. A lot of the women Valerie made friends with at San Jose State were socially aware of what was going on, and she not only wanted to be a part of changing the system, but also felt she had to be. She definitely was going to participate in this march.

But as I have said, I was developing my own thought processes and was learning to think on my own. I did a lot of thinking in the library or on the track, and as I did I began to truly grasp the convergence of the two, of my roles as an athlete and a student at that school. I may not have arrived with a wealth of knowledge about what was possible for me, but I was not a dumb student. In terms of absorbing what had been around me from Texas to Stratford to Central Union to high school to college, from working in the fields, playing all those sports and becoming a student, I knew a lot, more than I realized at the time. It had made up a portion of my personality. Plus, by that time, I was one of the top athletes in the world, and I do not exaggerate. I had turned my full athletic focus to track and field, and I had earned the accolades commensurate with my performance. I had one of the best coaches in the world, I ran for probably the fastest team in the world, and of all of them, I was the fastest. I had been injured participating in the long jump early in my freshman year, coming to track too soon after basketball season had ended, but once I healed, I came back and ran the 400 meters in 46.5 seconds, the best time in the nation that year, and that was not even my best event. Had I not been injured, I believe that as a freshman I could have run the 200 meters in the low 20s. I had considered that year more of a "Hello, track and field" year. Now, I considered myself a seasoned veteran. This year, I believed, and many others believed, including Coach Bud Winter, that I would be breaking world records sooner rather than later. In fact as the year went on, Coach Winter and I began to put plans in place to make a run at a record. When spring arrived and the season began, we aimed at a meet in mid-March, about a third of the way through the season, at San Jose State's track, in which I could attempt to break the world record for both the 200-meter dash and the 220-yard dash on a straightaway—a race that was rarely run, even then, with the 200 and 220 routinely run on a curve, as is any race today longer than 110 meters.

Meanwhile, though, I had spent the summer before that year back in Lemoore working with my father, both in the fields and in the schools in the district, helping him in his janitorial duties, cleaning classrooms, picking up the grounds, mowing the lawns, and running that floor-buffing machine all summer before returning to school to be a student and to fulfill this athletic destiny. Those forecasts for athletic glory could not spare me from my destiny in the fields or in a hot classroom.

But once I did return and get immersed in school, athletics, and my growing education about the system, I became more aware of my responsibility to involve myself in the changing of the system that was crumbling around me. More than many other students, by virtue of my position as a world-class athlete, I had something to contribute. I did have a personal stake in it, of course, as a black person, but as an athlete, I was aware of how we were perceived. Our power, responsibility, and influence, it was believed, were limited to the track, and by no means were we needed, or expected, to be viable anywhere else. The truth was quite the opposite, though: we were fast on the track, but we also had brains, and there was no reason we should not apply our brains and our influence to the equity of this system that we lived in—or, to be specific, the inequity.

That spring, the opportunity presented itself for me, and other athletes on campus, to join the fight and take up our responsibility, to use this unique platform for something besides enriching the athletic reputation of the San Jose State track and field team. The plans for the march began to take shape, and the particulars came together: in support of the people down South fighting (and dying) for freedom, and to show the community that we were willing to take a stand for justice as well, the students planned a march from the San Jose State campus to the main administration building in San Francisco, roughly 60 miles away, for the weekend of March 13 and 14, 1965. Leaders such as Harry Edwards spread plans for the march around campus by word of mouth. Everybody knew about it, and there was sure to be a huge turnout. The San Jose State athletes were going to be part of it as well. The whole demonstration was very well planned and well orchestrated by the older students, right down to the route of the march, where we would stop and rest for the night, how we would conduct ourselves, and to whom we would speak in San Francisco. There were even plans on how we would return to San Jose—we certainly weren't going to walk all the way back.

The march was the talk of the campus, and between my growing awareness of the system and of my own role as a world-renowned athlete, I knew I had to involve myself, to show my support for the fight. And if you've read this far, you probably know the conflict that arose: the march was to begin on the same day, a Saturday, as the meet in which I would attempt a world record for the first time.

There was no particular time when I said, "Okay, yes, I'm going to do this; I'm going to run the best I can and then I'm going to join the march." I think the decision came to me as people made their plans to march. I decided that I must sacrifice, and I don't mean sacrifice making money. We're talking about physical and mental sacrifice, to the point that one's life might be lost, especially when you're dealing with marches and the racist attitudes of people that were so devastating that you could lose your life in one step. Had the meet and the march not coincided, I would have left with a big group early that Saturday morning; I wanted to go with that group, but I chose to meet up with that group later in the day, then continue to San Francisco the next morning. You may be asking yourself, "Why not go with the big group and not run in that meet? That way you will be with the group the entire time." I didn't feel that way; as much of a responsibility as I felt to the marchers and to their cause, especially as one of the most famous athletes in the world, I had a responsibility to my team, my teammates, my coach, and my school to participate in that meet. If I had to jog to catch up with that group, I would. Thankfully, I didn't have to jog, and I did catch up with them.

I had to break that record first, and that effort would take all of my concentration. The conditions were thoroughly in my favor that day. It was a small meet, a triangular, between us, the College of the Pacific in Stockton, and Cal–Santa Barbara, schools that we regularly faced. Generally, our meets started in the early afternoon, around 1:30; as I recall this was no different, and the weather was good, as it usually is at that time of year in San Jose. The track at San Jose State, on the south end of campus near the other athletic facilities, was a good one, a good, hard surface, a cinder track, one of the better tracks around at the time. This was before the advent of artificial tracks such as the type used today at most major colleges and major competitions, but Coach Winter took care of it, manicured it well, made it conducive to fast times. Even the spikes we used at the time, rather long at a half to three-quarters of an inch, could penetrate the track even if it was hard. It was supple enough that even a body like mine, weighing in the neighborhood of 175 pounds at the time, would be able to push off and dig in at full force and full speed without breaking up the surface. It was perfect for what I was attempting that day, largely because Coach Winter had made sure it would be.

Coach Winter had also set up two finishing tapes for me to break, one at 200 meters and one at 220 yards, about nine feet further. For me, that represented one good stride, and would allow me to break both records at the same time, in virtually the same recorded time. He also opened the gates in the chute at the end of the lanes where the 200 on the straightaway ended; the race ran the full length of the track, through the chute, and actually to the outside of the track. Again, this race was rarely run, so this was a special case, and it was the only way to complete the race. Still, this was a recognized world record; both records were held by Dave Sime, who had set them in 1956, at 20 seconds flat. Coincidentally, my older brother George ran against Sime in that race, for the College of the Sequoias.

I was running in four events total that day; I also ran the 100-yard dash, winning it in 9.5 seconds, and a little before the 200 straightaway I had competed in the 4-by-100 relay, which we won in about 40.7 seconds. We also did well in the mile relay, so before I went to the start line for the record attempts, it had been a good day. I felt ready. As I've said, I had known throughout my sophomore season that I had a great race in me. In the blocks for the try at the record, I felt very good, no injuries, no hurts, no stiffness—only the thought that the big group was going out on the march that morning and I had to catch them later. But I had to block them out for the time I was running; I had to concentrate on my sprint form, because it is a science, and Coach Winter had coached and trained us diligently to understand and use the science to our benefit. Coach Winter did not have much to say to me beforehand. Bud Winter was not a guy with a lot of words; he was a good speaker, a humanitarian, and he had thoughts for people. Now, he dealt mostly with the past few weeks, the workouts we'd had, especially on the grass. We didn't have to go much over my sprinting form at that point; I knew it well: high knees, arm action, put them together, relaxation, foreleg reach, hand movement but no head movement—most of all, use your muscles to the maximum without tensing up. It was the form and technique I already had perfected and the one I used up until that final race in Mexico City.

I really did not think I would feel any different if I ran a good race or a world record that day; I just wanted to run the best race I possibly could. It was like tuning a fine car and putting it on the track to see how it performed, not necessarily running fast but using technique and seeing how it felt. Much as I later did in Mexico City— although that was largely because I was running with a pulled muscle —I planned to redline, pushing it as hard as I could push it without blowing it up, and not easing back and letting the second car beat me. And, as was part of my form, I knew when I had to compensate for exhausting my muscles, when to shift to different muscles or ligaments or tendons, when to bound instead of power, and when to shift to a slightly longer stride in order to rest a little more between strides.

I also had to employ an ankle flip, which is exactly what it sounds like: on every stride, those now-elongated strides, I flipped the ankle out and down to lengthen the stride to its maximum, bound off of it, flip it up again, and go into another stride. That way, my body still goes as fast as it can without either tensing up or slowing down. I knew that I had the ability to run faster than anyone else, but in order to set a world record, I had to put everything in place, from zero to 220 yards. I had to concentrate on each stride, not waste a fraction of a second; each stride had to be to its maximum. If you misstride once, your next stride would have to take up the slack for the last stride. No stride in that race could be weak because a tenth of a second lost, as small as that seems and as fast as that goes by, would eliminate the chance of a world record.

This particular race offered a big challenge. Because it was a straightaway race, coming out of the blocks wasn't as difficult as finishing the last 30 or 40 meters. It would be even more critical for me to use my form and technique because in that final stretch, without coming out of a turn, my muscles definitely would suffer oxygen debt. Changing my stride and shifting to other muscles was the only way to maintain my speed and output of power from those first 50 meters out of the blocks.

It helped me that my teammate Wayne Herman, one of the many 9.3 sprinters we had at San Jose State, was in this race. Wayne is a little guy, maybe 5 foot 6, and he really pulled me out well in races, both the 100 and the 200, because he was so good from the start, and if I didn't stay in contact with him early in the 100 meters he'd beat me. I'd worked on the starts early in the week and the weeks before with Bud Winter and went through the techniques of getting out fast, staying low, powering out, and using that throw hand to throw me outward and not pull me up straight. Now, when the gun sounded, I got out of the blocks well, not great. But I was out with Wayne, and I realized, "Uh-oh, I'm out with Wayne; I don't have 100 meters to go, I have 200 meters to go." Being out with him in the early part of the race gave me a better chance of running a faster race, and the first 70 meters of that race was faster than any 70 meters I had run in a 100 race before. I was cognizant of people in the stands as I went by; I didn't look up, but the stands were a blur to me, and I heard the oohs and aahhs as I went by, and they quickly faded as I moved past them. Of course I didn't stop to have tea or coffee because I didn't have time, but the crowd's response did give me a sense that I was moving fast. I was timed at 10.3 in the first 100 meters, and the world record for the 100 at that time was 10 flat, so I was on a great pace for the 200; the longer I ran in the 200 meters the faster I got, because of my leg power and my leg length. But the oxygen debt was going to get me at this distance, and it did, when I was about 170 or 180 yards down the track. I had to go to my techniques to elongate my stride, shift to other muscles, flip the ankle, and maintain the speed and power as my muscles got exhausted. I kept using those techniques even as I went through the gate, about 30 to 40 meters from the finish line—finish lines, actually. About five strides before I got to that gate, everything gave out, but I continued my stride and hit the first tape, then the second.

I knew I had run fast because Wayne ran a 20.5 and I was a good three steps ahead of him, in my strides. When I came to a stop and turned around, the timers were looking at their watches in amazement, as if to say, "My watch didn't start, or maybe my finger was a little slow." No, the fingers weren't slow; it was that the race was fast. Twenty flat, tying both records. Those were the first world records I had ever held. Eventually I would hold 11 simultaneously, which had never been done and has never been duplicated, and this is where it began.

I don't really think the magnitude of that race had as much of an effect on the spectators on hand as it had on Bud Winter and me, because we had been talking about it for a few weeks. Coach Winter hugged me, I got handshakes from teammates and the other competitors, and the press wanted to talk to me; they realized what had happened and wanted to make a big deal about it. To the crowd, it was just another good race, until they said it tied a world record. Then there was silence, because a world record was not an everyday occurrence, and that's how the crowd took it. As it set in, seconds, minutes, and hours after that, people realized, "My goodness, this day produced a world record. This guy is very good; we'll follow him throughout his career." And that's what happened. The funny thing was, there was not a big crowd that day. There were a lot of regular followers of San Jose State track, who were interested even in seeing a small triangular invitational meet. They knew all about Speed City and knew this year would be no different than the past, except possibly better. The rest of the crowd was students, some of them friends of mine—no relatives, however—and they were kind of awestruck at what they saw, not so much at the outcome or the fact that it was a world record, but at the speed passing the stands and the form Tommie Smith displayed.

The reason the crowd was not as big as it might have been, however, was pretty simple: many of the people who would have attended had gone on the march. The march was a lot more important to a lot of people than my running in a track meet, and I can certainly understand their reasoning. After all, that's where I was headed, too. My good friend Art Simburg was the only other person I knew that watched me at the meet and then went to the march; in fact, he was the one that drove me to meet the marchers that night. I don't believe Art actually marched with us, but he did take me to the marchers, and he was involved in the planning of that march, behind the scenes rather than directly. He was probably the best friend I had at that time, and is still a good friend, very innovative, with a lot of insight of what's going on.

So setting that world record wasn't a big shock or surprise to me; I had other things on my mind, namely, the march and the people that had gone out in the morning and would walk the entire way to San Francisco. This was not just a small march of 20 or 30 people; about 100 people went on this march. I did not think of it as history at the time, that I had tied a world record one day and gone on my first civil rights march the next. It was announced by one of the leaders of the group the next day; she told the crowd, "We have a celebrity in our midst, and we're glad to have him here because it certainly will help make this march notable to have someone in our midst such as Tommie Smith, who just set a world record yesterday at San Jose State." I felt good about it; I heard the people around me saying little things—"Oh my goodness, really, that's great"—and it made me a part of the world in its fight for human rights.

Joining the march after the meet was not all that difficult, because we had planned it well. Coach Winter knew about my plans but didn't say anything about them; he really didn't involve himself in the politics of the black athletes or black people unless he was asked to do so. He might occasionally ask of me, "How are you doing, Tom-Tom? Is there anything I can do for you?" I would say, "Nothing, Coach, I'm okay." It's not that I wouldn't seek help when I needed it, but in general I depended on no one but myself, and still do.

Yes, I did shower after the race, and Art picked me up in his Volkswagen and took me back to my dorm to get whatever I needed for the march, which wasn't much, maybe another shirt to wear the next day. I was dressed normally; I wore jogging shoes, which were easier to walk in than hard-soled street shoes, knowing I had to go 20 to 30 miles. I did not take anything else with me that would have been extra weight. "How about money?" you ask. What money? I didn't have any money. I didn't bring along any food or drink, either; I don't really remember eating anything, just drinking the water someone else had. My mind wasn't on eating, drinking, or reading a book, but on my survival on that particular march to San Francisco, and on getting back to San Jose.

The marchers had settled in for the night at a high-school gymnasium in Sunnyvale, about 35 or 40 miles south of San Francisco, a little more than halfway through the march. By the time Art and I arrived, it was nighttime, around 7 o'clock. I had to find the person whom I felt most free with, my fiancée, Valerie Yates; I knew she was in there with a group of mutual friends. But it was dark. It also was very quiet, because one thing we didn't want to do was disturb the peace; that would be a direct cause for the march to be broken up, if we were loud and unruly. The last thing we wanted to be was disruptive in any way, either by being violent, sloppy, or loud and unruly. I had a half a book of matches, and I started striking matches and looking all around that gym for familiar faces. I was walking very carefully around and through the mass of marchers resting on that floor; I certainly didn't want to make a scene and upset anybody by stepping on him or her while I was looking for Valerie. But I couldn't find her, and I was down to my last match. I struck it and kept looking and still couldn't find her—and as it was burning my finger I saw a face in the shadow, and it was her. I told her, "Valerie, I made it, and I did good in the meet," and so forth. She said, "Great! Rest, because we have to get up early in the morning to march from Sunnyvale into San Francisco; it's going to be a long march."

I sat there the rest of the night with her and the others. The marchers were mostly black, although there was a sprinkling of whites among them, most of whom I did not know, and since they were there with us I did not feel uncomfortable with them. I didn't say much; a few people did ask me questions, mainly about how the meet went and how the race went. That was how some of them found out I had tied a world record for the first time. I did know a lot of people on the march—besides the students, there were several athletes participating, and I knew them all well—and that made it easier on me the next day as I marched. As I had mentioned, it made it easier for them as well to know that I was marching with them after having tied the record. In all, it made it easier to start conversations, which had not been my strength. In terms of sleeping and bedding, there wasn't very much at all, a shirt, a coat, maybe a blanket to lie on or to put one's head down on; like me, the marchers had traveled as light as possible. Nothing about the accommodations was luxurious at all, but to me, it did not make a difference. If I had to sleep on the floor of a gymnasium, that was fine; it was clean, and though it was hard, I had slept on hard, much dirtier ground in the irrigation fields in Lemoore.

We got up early the next morning, cleaned up after ourselves, used the bathroom if we needed, and set out for San Francisco. We had to make it by the end of that day, and we did, but it was a long, hard march. We did not march on the freeway, which would have been the most direct way; we were not allowed to, so we had to take the back streets. Traffic was not as heavy on those roads, but cars did travel on them, and we did encounter white people who did not know what was going on, 100 people marching through their streets. So they called out from their cars, jeered us, called us niggers, called us all types of profanity, and a few threw objects at us, bottles and other things. There was never a major incident, though, and nobody got hurt. But I could not help thinking: why are these people doing this? All we're doing is marching to support the movement of people down South for human rights, exercising our constitutional freedom of speech. Little did I know that racism was so blatant and overt at that particular time; there was nothing stopping those people from being inhuman to us as we marched. The newspapers and television constantly carried news about our fight all over the nation for human rights, but here, in San Jose at this time, people didn't want to hear about it. They thought everything was fine—we white people work hard to get what we have, so they should work hard. But one cannot work hard if one can't get a job, if one can't get the opportunity others have. This was something those people were never aware of, especially in terms of us athletes. If they had known a world-record holder such as myself and a number of other athletes on scholarship at their nearby university were marching with these people, they would have been stunned. They thought everything was okay because we were running fast.

Was I scared? Scared to death. I had seen enough of what was going on down South to know that you don't jump out on the street to march and not lay something on the line, such as your life. Guns were just as potent in the 1960s as they are now. This danger was on my mind, and I know it was on the minds of the other marchers. I truly felt like a part of that group, even though I had joined them after it started. Even though I knew I had to run in my meet as they began their march, I could feel their presence as I was at the meet; I felt them moving, I felt them being harassed. In fact, I believe that really helped me in my race, knowing they were really doing something for humankind. It was my responsibility to do something for them, for humankind, to run a good race and then catch up with them.

But even as the marchers and I were fearful, we never let it slow us. We never let the name-calling and jeering and object-throwing provoke us. Martin Luther King's stand for nonviolence inspired us to march and to stay nonviolent ourselves; we did not, I repeat, did not carry sticks or guns or any kind of weapons to either defend ourselves or provoke anybody. Many of the athletes on the march served to keep the march running smoothly, organized and without disruption; a few marchers walked on the periphery to make sure we stayed on our route, remained orderly, and did not leave any trash or belongings along the way. We talked along the way, but in a quiet tone of voice out of respect for our surroundings. We were not there to make a scene, only to support the freedom marchers and the fight for systematic change. In all, it was one of the most organized functions I had ever taken part in. The group had remained strong and unified in the first leg from San Jose, and remained that way throughout that second day from Sunnyvale to San Francisco; its spirit was not broken by the long march, the fear of violence, or the actions of the passersby.

We finally got to San Francisco after about 12 good hours of straight marching, and believe it or not, the person we went to see, a black politician who was supposed to greet us and hear what we had to say, did not show up. Yep, that's what I said, did not show up. So we stood around, peacefully of course; a few white guys came out and said a few words, and pretty soon the group broke up and we got our respective rides back home to San Jose. Someone had arranged to have cars up there for us, ready to bring us back. It took me a while to get a ride back, and I don't remember with whom I rode back; all I remember was being grateful, because walking back to San Jose would have been a little too much, even for me, although the march itself had not been a very hard chore because of my physical condition for track and field. It wasn't nearly as hard for me to make that distance as for other people who were not in the physical condition I was in.

This was something big for Tommie Smith. It was the first time I had stood up with a group and said, "This system is not perfect, and it should be changed because the Constitution does not represent everybody equally." It also was my first act of involvement through athletics. It signified for me, for the first time, that being one of the best in the world in any activity obligated you to contribute. I have continued to believe that to this day. That's why I review myself almost on a daily basis about what am I doing—is it good, is it bad, is it according to the Constitution—because I want to follow the laws of this country, but when those laws don't represent you, then something has to be done. I found that out gradually during my sophomore year at San Jose State, and it frightened me to the point of being very active. I discovered that in terms of how society valued me, my world record was at the top and my growing up in Texas, in Stratford, and in Lemoore was at the bottom. I saw the good and the bad and knew I had to do my work in between, and I wouldn't find that connection without education. This march was part of my education; it matured me quite a bit to be with people who cared about human rights and believed in them so much. I talked more that one day that I did the whole next week, because I wanted to hear what people had to say in the march. Outside of that one time as a high school student vice president giving a speech that no one really wanted to hear, I had never done any civil rights things in Lemoore. Now, two years later, I was in a bigger city and with a bigger platform because of what I had accomplished.

Still, part of me believed at that time that I was just a person who was putting forth an effort like everyone else. We didn't stop to get newspapers during that march to see what Tommie Smith had done the day before. But when one of the leaders announced that I was participating in the march after tying the world record, I know it kind of helped some of the people continue. They recognized that running fast did nothing to keep you from being a second-class citizen, and that someone like myself was willing to take a stand for the rights of all people regardless of how fast they were, or if they could walk, as long as they had a brain.

I didn't realize it consciously at the time, but it was the first chapter of the library of Tommie Smith's activity on the track and off.

The Coach and the Professor

IT WAS NO COINCIDENCE that my day of running and protesting during my sophomore year at San Jose State involved both Bud Winter, my coach, and Professor Harry Edwards. It's also no coincidence that after having been a student of both men, I became both a coach and a teacher later in life. I learned from both of them, on the track and in the classroom and away from both locations; I incorporated their lessons and their ways of teaching them into my methods of instruction, so much so that one can see the traits of both men within me when I impart a lesson to others.

Anyone who has spent time with, or even around, strong personalities such as theirs could not help but be influenced heavily by them. At the same time, however, it probably was inevitable that those two personalities would clash, directly with each other in some ways, but also at a convenient and logical point of convergence—me. I had the distinction of being able to see close-up the similarities, differences, and conflicts in these two distinguished authorities in their fields.

I also got to see how their personalities affected me. In hindsight, something of a difference of opinion was bound to rise between me and Harry Edwards, and it did—just not until after my days at San Jose State had ended and I had gained some measure of experience and perspective. To this day, I respect Harry Edwards and always will, but the passage of time and the knowledge that comes from time led me to understand who he was and where he stood.

My respect and love for Coach Winter, meanwhile, will never fade, and he has been gone from us since 1985. The program he built at San Jose State, the one that became legend as Speed City, departed even before he did, a loss that had to break his heart long before the rest of him passed away.

To fully grasp the impact these two men had on me, though, one has to understand, again, who I was and what San Jose State was when I arrived as a freshman in 1963. Throughout my entire grammar school years, at least from the time I lived in California, I don't remember ever having a black teacher at Stratford Elementary, Central Union Elementary, or Lemoore High School. As I entered college, the one and only black teacher I had had was Ms. Carey at the segregated one-room schoolhouse next to the church and cemetery in east Texas. After that, I never had a black coach, a black instructor, or anyone. It's not something I thought about consciously until decades later, but for my entire life before I entered college, I knew almost nothing of black figures of authority by personal experience. The closest thing were the straw bosses whom the white owner had put in charge of my daddy and us and the other workers in the fields, someone to control us while he was out of sight, staying cool and not getting his hands dirty.

Obviously, back then no one thought enough of black people to allow them to teach their own children in school; allowing them to oversee each other while they were picking grapes and chopping cotton was as much as those white people could envision. I must have known this instinctively as I was growing up; remember, when I was dreaming of what I would be when I grew up, I always dreamed of positions of authority: soldier, teacher, or policeman.

I also had never had a black coach during all those years, dating back to my first coach at Central Union, Mr. Focht. I was on practically every team in every sport imaginable, lettering in every sport every year, and never once did I have a black coach. I was part of an endless procession of poor black kids looking up to a white coach, someone we had almost nothing in common with, someone who had more say in our lives and fates than we did. That trend continued in college, with white coaches on the freshman basketball team and, of course, Coach Winter in track from then on.

The big upset in the order of things came in the classroom. Professor Harry Edwards was the first black instructor I had ever had. As he was a student when I first arrived, as well as part of the group that met me at the airport when I brought my country self in from Lemoore, he got to know me before Coach Winter did, and I got to know him.

The very first impression I had of Harry Edwards was that he was a very dynamic person. He was dynamic in stature, first of all—he stood about 6 foot 8 and weighed about 255 or 260 pounds at the time. He towered over me even at my size. He was a senior when I arrived as a freshman, and, while he had competed in the field events for the track team earlier, by this time he was strictly a basketball player. He played on the varsity with my soon-to-be roommate, St. Saffold, who was a sophomore. I know he wasn't very impressed with me on first sight—as I said, he laughed when he saw me and my clothes—and I'm not sure if he was impressed with me in the early days when we were getting to know each other, either.

But I was impressed with him, from the beginning; after our initial meeting on the way from the airport to campus, I thought, "This is a very smart person; what is he doing playing basketball?" That shows you what kind of knowledge and perceptions I had brought with me from my environment in Texas and in Lemoore. I was conditioned from the field and from being around Daddy's bosses, thinking that black people can only do certain things: run fast, jump high, speak only in a deep Southern drawl that almost sounds like cockney English (that's how much the language is mangled), laugh and guffaw, scratch and shuffle.

Harry defied those images I had. He was one of the smartest students on campus, athletic or not; he definitely was the smartest athlete I had ever met. Seldom had I ever seen an athlete on his level in terms of his motivation and his balance between athletics and academics. I don't even think his coaches knew how advanced he was—that he was majoring in sociology, a far more stable field of study than what most athletes at that time chose, and that he was carrying such a high grade-point average (a 4.0), or that he intended to get postgraduate degrees and make his name off the field instead of on.

Harry was a true academician, and I became more impressed the more I was around him. It was significant that I got to truly know him in an academic setting, rather than an athletic setting. He lived off campus in his senior year, but he was good friends with St., and when he came by our dorm room to talk, a crowd would gather in the room or the hallway. Again, he likely wasn't terribly impressed with me on first sight, because I would much rather listen than talk—but he did notice that I was always on time, that I was astute, and that I spent a lot of time either in my room or in the library, studying. Plus, my being a listener appealed to him and fit his personality. Harry Edwards was very verbal, still is very verbal, and he loves to be heard. That wasn't a problem with me; if Harry hadn't done any of the talking, there never would have been any conversation. St. and I talked a lot, don't get me wrong—but we also agreed with each other often, and when we didn't, we'd hash it out quickly and reach an agreement and move on. That's why we remained friends and why we spent probably 80 percent of our time around each other while we were students there.

Harry had a lot more to say than I did, and I'm not ashamed of it now. I learned a lot from him, and Harry learned a lot from me, and we both learned a lot from St. and he learned from us. It was a great educational experience between three black athletes who were also students, all of whom went on to earn degrees beyond San Jose State: we all earned master's, and Harry obtained his doctorate.

The most prevalent topic, of course, was the black athlete's plight on the college campus—how black athletes could, and must, survive and prosper academically in an environment that discourages, even resents, their doing anything besides performing for the university's benefit. One way or another, wherever Harry would run into me, St., or any collection of black athletes, the conversation would turn that way no matter what direction it had headed in. We could all be in our dorm room in Allen Hall shooting the you-know-what about any-thing else, and Harry would come in and talk and crack jokes with the rest of us—but his jokes always had a deeper meaning and sent a different message. He'd talk about people he encountered in class and around campus, about the way they carried themselves and the things they said that made them sound so oblivious to what was going on around them, and about the comments they would make that were so inaccurate that Harry couldn't help but correct them, in a way that would make fun of the person who said it.

The punch line, most of the time, was the way that the white stu-dents believed that they themselves were the educated, intelligent, per-ceptive ones, and believed that the black athletes were there only to run, compete, and entertain—but, in fact, the black student-athletes were carrying a burden on the field and in the classroom that their white counterparts could never fathom. Harry Edwards would say these things and make these points in ways that would make us all laugh, and make sure that we listened and learned while we were enjoying it.

As I grew up on that campus, I began to understand how and why Harry talked the way he did. He was thinking and talking about civil rights at a time when most of us were vaguely aware of them but didn't grasp their connection to our lives as athletes and students on our campus. In the way his mind functioned, he was a bit above the students at that college, black and white, athlete and regular student. He was far above me, because he was a senior and had a stature on campus that I was still far from attaining. The fact that academics came first for him made me realize that regardless of what I or anyone else thought about my status as an athlete, I also had prowess in the field of academics. Just like him, I would not be at San Jose State on a scholarship without it. He used to tell me, "If you couldn't talk, you wouldn't be running here. But you can't eat running, so don't look at running as a technique to get you through life. You're smart enough to know you're running fast, so use that." I had not realized that; running wasn't going to be my way to make a living, but what I did with my mind while I was running at this school would do that for me. Harry Edwards is the one who brought that to light for me.

I continued to learn more about Harry as he spent more time with me and St. The two of us would come back to our dorm from church on Sunday, and Harry would drop by and talk. I got more comfortable around him as that freshman year wore on and the details of his life and personality emerged. Harry grew up in poverty, as did St. and I, and had a lot of brothers and sisters just as we did, but he grew up in a much different way: he was from East St. Louis, Illinois, a destitute slum of a Midwestern city, the opposite of the rural life that St. and I had known in California. In his own books, he has told the tales of how he grew up there and how he broke free of that life. He used his mind, his athletic ability, and his size to pull himself up by his bootstraps and to make sure nobody would pull him down, especially verbally. He made sure he was a force to be reckoned with in every way, and he made sure he had something to say and that he'd say what was on his mind, no matter what the subject was. If the subject was athletics, he absolutely made sure he was heard. He was an advocate for us; he fought the notions and perceptions and preconceptions about black athletes and students that no one else had fought at the time.

I saw him fight this fight from the beginning, and from the beginning he was instrumental in my coming of age in my early college years. I didn't always agree with him, but I always came prepared to defend my argument through my inclination to study and research. As I absorbed all this, I learned from him what it really meant to be a student in that time and in that place. I would have to go to class every day, no matter how tired or sick I was. I had to compete in the classroom the same way I did on the track and the court. I had to deal with different types of adversity, and no matter how smart I thought I was, I was going to come across something along the way I didn't think I could handle, but I had to treat it as a test and overcome it the same way I did in when I met some sort of athletic obstacle. I had to put in the time, had to study, had to get that book I needed.

And I had to communicate—for me, the biggest obstacle of all, because it went against everything I had known as a student back in Lemoore. No more sitting in the back of the class hoping I wouldn't be noticed and have to answer too many questions. I had already begun doing that in college, and it came up in one of our many conversations in the dorm, as well as in the cafeteria with the other athletes. One must be up front to be seen, Harry insisted, because one has to be seen to be heard and believed. That was exactly what I didn't want, to be seen. But it was what I had to do now.

That subject gave me still another reason to believe that Harry didn't think much of me as a freshman. Had I thought through it more, I might have realized that he wasn't only talking just because he liked to talk—which was true enough—but because he sincerely thought talking to me was going to help me. I learned as I got to know him that he was genuine in how he presented himself and in how he reached out to us. He recognized that I responded to him, even if it wasn't always verbally.

Our conversations evolved and grew more involved as time went on. Harry's studies were in sociology, and it was just a matter of time before the structure of the system in which we operated became a topic of our discussions. Until then, I had never spent much time thinking about the system itself; my concern was how to get along in the system, and that was a concern shared by most nonwhite people I knew—what we had to do within the system to get by, to make a buck, to feed our families.

Harry brought a different perspective. It was up to us, he said, to understand how the system is constructed, the rules and regulations that govern us, and our place in the system. Most important, he said, we have to take more of a stand on how it affects us, to use those rules to our advantage instead of letting them take advantage of us. Nowhere, he said, is this need more obvious than in our situation, as highly visible athletes with measurable impact on society, and as black students in a place where we are not numerous, welcome, or encouraged.

Harry is the person who taught me the lesson about Jesse Owens. As far as I knew, from what I had learned as a student and as a sprinter who idolized him, the great Jesse Owens became great because he showed the world how wrong Nazism and Hitler were, right to Hitler's face in the 1936 Olympics in Berlin, with his four gold medals and four world records. America latched onto that story, because it proved that the American way was better than the Nazi way, that freedom would win over tyranny, that Hitler was rotten and so was everything he stood for, especially his beliefs about a master race. But Jesse Owens, that black man, still returned to this country as a second-class citizen, unable to eat in certain restaurants or hold certain jobs, and reduced to racing horses to earn money. That's history; we can talk about that until this time next century, and that fact doesn't change any more than the others do. But that sure isn't something that is taught to the children when the story of Jesse Owens is told. The story white people do tell about him might fit him neatly into their system, but just because they say it's true, that it is the entire story, doesn't mean it is. And in the long run, Jesse Owens' athletic supremacy did him no good when measured against his black skin in this society.

That was one of the facts that Harry would drop into a conversation that would leave my mouth hanging wide open. It was a fact being delivered by a black athlete at San Jose State who nobody (even me, in my ignorance when we first met) thought could be such an academician. We began to believe that if he could do it, so could we, and there probably were others before him who could have, and there definitely will be others after us who can. Harry proved that while he might be a case that's special, he was not a special case; with the right tools and associations, and with the knowledge that, as usual, we would have to work a lot harder than the white athletes to gain, we would become what he was, or even exceed it.

Of course, in the mid-1960s this was not the way people wanted to hear black people talking. To challenge the system that way—even by just talking about it—was being negative. That definitely had not changed by 1968 in Mexico City. Back in the early days at San Jose State, that made Harry Edwards dangerous. "Militant" was the word used to describe him. Not "intelligent" or "provocative" or "revolutionary," all of which he was. He was telling white America what it didn't want to hear, and didn't want others to hear, about itself. He also didn't care who liked him or disliked him as long as the truth was told, a trait not everybody had, but which comes in handy for a man whose thoughts and deeds are as contrary to what society is used to hearing and seeing as his were.

Harry Edwards definitely was a man who understood the value of talking, in every way. He still understands it. His lessons sank in with me, and eventually I developed into a man who could think for himself and express himself on his own. Of the reasons why we have gone our separate ways in the years since 1968, that would be the biggest. What Harry Edwards was talking about wasn't always exactly what Tommie Smith was thinking, and more often than not Harry Edwards was talking about, and for the benefit of, Harry Edwards. That's the way it should have been, and the more I understood that, the more I understood him and acted accordingly. It's how he always should be regarded.

Even back then, Harry was smart enough to realize that as long as he talked, he would stay out of trouble. That's not very hard to understand or contradictory. There was also money to be made in being a platform of social awareness and understanding; among the benefits of being a sociologist is understanding that aspect of society. He is not, and never was, afraid to say something that might be wrong, because it's not so much what you say but how you say it.

A lot of this became evident to me after he had graduated from San Jose State, gone to Cornell to earn his masters, and returned to San Jose State to teach. I had gone on to participate in the march to San Francisco, which he'd helped organize on a trip back—and, in his absence, grown even more into manhood. I had learned along the way that as much as I had learned from Harry, I did not want to become Harry. I'd met him when I was a teenager, and now I was in my 20s, and by the time he had returned from Cornell I had developed into a personality of my own. It was time for me to make my own decisions, stand on my own two feet. To be honest, I had come to that conclusion even before he returned. He had pretty much disappeared to go east before I realized he had; there hadn't been any emotional goodbyes, which was fine for both of us because we both came from big families and didn't spend a lot of time getting emotional about being apart from them.

When he returned, we both were headed on different paths toward the pinnacles of our careers, mine on the track and his in the classroom. His involvement in athletics and the athletes' connection to the system—particularly the system of higher education and intercollegiate sports—was growing. My visibility as an athlete was peaking, and I was coming to terms with how I, in my position, could make an impact on the system that had its own ideas about my value in it. I took one of the first classes he taught at San Jose State, on social mobility, which ended up being extremely popular, forced into a lecture hall because of the enrollment, and attended by quite a few white students.

The 1968 Olympics were still a good two years away, and we had never spoken specifically about any plans to make a statement in 1968 before he'd left and come back. We only knew, as our careers progressed at San Jose State, that the time was coming for us to take that stand, to create the platform we had always talked about. I had held up my end of the bargain by becoming a student in every sense, doing my studying, attending classes no matter how hard it might be to make every one, and speaking my mind more often. My hunger —actually, my addiction—for knowledge had led me to grasp all history, American and black history, and I finally grasped what Harry had said about the lengths to which white America went to control its slaves and ex-slaves and maintain the system: keep them ignorant, and keep them from communicating. I no longer was ignorant, and I had begun to communicate.

Yet overriding all the knowledge I had taken from Harry was the knowledge that I was my own man. I believe Harry has always understood that as well. It's the rest of the world that seems to struggle with it. Harry faced his own obstacles and challenges, but he did not face the ones Tommie Smith, and John Carlos, faced as the time grew close for the Olympics. He was not going to run for us, he was not going to make up our minds about whether to run, and he was not going to be the one taking that stand on that platform when the time came. For all that he did to plant the seeds of the protest in Mexico City, because of his idea for a boycott of those Games, he was not the man on the victory stand that night, nor the man who told us what to do when John and I got there. As everyone surely knows by now, Harry Edwards was not in Mexico City for those Games; as he stayed home to steer clear of the death threats he received, we faced the threats on our lives in person, on the track and on that stand. A lot transpired from the time we met at the San Jose airport at the start of my freshman year to the time I climbed onto that stand, but what remains a fact is that I was up there alone. The world might believe that this was Harry Edwards' Olympic protest, but the facts say different.

That is who Harry is, and that is fine. He simply is capable of saying something and then not acting to follow it up. What got between us more than the situation in Mexico City was a promise that he made to me and John—that he would start a college fund for each of our firstborn children. He made this pledge way back in 1967, when John and I were still students at San Jose State. Harry was teaching, and he was lecturing around the country. I had no money whatsoever, and he was well aware of that fact. John and I would not have even made it to that critical meeting about the possible boycott in 1967 had we not ridden in the back of Harry's truck from San Jose to Los Angeles the night before.

By the time of the Games, I had a son, Kevin, and John had a daughter, Kimmy. The Games came and went, we all struggled with our lives in the aftermath, and as we did, there was no college fund from Harry. He moved on to teach at Cal-Berkeley, wrote books, and eventually started consulting with professional sports teams and entire leagues, and those college funds never were started. We weren't looking for them necessarily, and we know that he had his own family and his own life, but he made that promise when we were committing ourselves to taking that stand that he had encouraged so much over the years, when we were setting ourselves up for the sacrifice we knew was coming. Harry moved on, and he forgot about the promise he had made to Tommie Smith and John Carlos.

If you say you're going to do something and then can't, or you change your mind, at least tell the person you changed your mind. That's about the only thing I truly hold Harry to that he said he'd do and then didn't. If he did not want to come to Mexico City, he had his reasons. This was a promise, though. What he has become over the years came from his use of prominent athletes to make his point —Tommie Smith and John Carlos in particular. You can say that he doesn't owe us anything, but he could take more interest in us now than he has. But there never has been money in doing things for us, the way there is for what he's done over the years.

One thing Harry has repeated over the years is that we all become captains of our own ship. It became true as we grew into our own personalities and made our own decisions later in life. For that reason, I can't get into the name-calling that some have turned to where Harry is concerned. He's not a dog. He is a politician, and that role has served him well. It just has made him different than what he was when he was a sociologist. Primarily, by becoming engaged in the politics of the system he once encouraged others to challenge, he has become one of the people now that we talked about then, part of the system we had challenged.

The other accusation heard about Harry is that he's an opportunist. John has called him that publicly several times, and our former San Jose teammates and Olympic teammates have done the same. Well, everybody's an opportunist, and Harry is only one of them. He's a person who has always tried to better himself, as I see it, and if you want to call that being an opportunist, go ahead. But to me, an opportunist is someone who really doesn't care about another person; he just wants to increase the bulk in his back pocket, or just cares about some political issue that has no relevance to anybody but himself. Nobody can say that about Harry Edwards. Opportunists treat people like they're dogs; or they treat people exactly how they themselves would never want to be treated. Again, we have our differences, and we do not speak regularly now—and he was not part of that initial ceremony for the statue to John and me—but I cannot say that Harry was an opportunist.

It's ironic that Harry is now stuck with that description, since it's the same criticism he once made of Coach Winter. It was one of the many disagreements between us about Coach Winter, a parting of minds that went back to when Harry threw the discus for Coach Winter before I ever arrived on campus. The roots also reached to Harry's beliefs about the roles of coaches in the athletic realm, on campus, and elsewhere, in which the coaches at the time were uniformly white and the players increasingly black.

I always could understand how Harry could come to the conclusion that Coach Winter was an opportunist, instead of a great coach (the conclusion I very quickly came to). I think all coaches who really believe in what they are doing have a real opportunistic streak in them. Human beings by nature don't just do something for nothing; they are not going to do Work (with a capital W) without wanting, somewhere down the line, to get compensated for it. Harry's point was that white coaches are in the business for one reason, to win; they need black athletes to win, so they will bring them in under whatever circumstances they can and by any means (including reaping the rewards of the black coaches who brought those athletes along, then not rewarding them by promoting them to their own level) to keep winning.

I did not buy it at first, but the facts proved it. Eventually every great white coach had to admit the truth, from Woody Hayes at Ohio State to Bear Bryant at Alabama in the heart of Dixie. You can't even hold black athletes back from the positions once denied them, the positions of control such as quarterback and center. Getting actual coaching jobs, of course, came long afterward.

That reasoning still implied that the white coach was nothing more than a manipulator who used up black athletes for his own gain only and was not actually imparting anything of value to them. That's how Harry saw most coaches, and he warned all of us at San Jose to watch out for white coaches in general because of the gap in social experience and awareness between us and them. Bud Winter, to Harry, was, at the very least, no different from anyone else. Harry was not the only person, definitely not the only black athlete at San Jose State, who thought that way about Coach Winter, that he was at heart a conniver, an opportunist concerned only with using his black talent to further his own goals. Again, it's one's definition of an opportunist. To me, opportunists take advantage of others and abuse that advantage to the point of hurting the other person. Bud Winter never hurt me; nothing he did ever hurt me.

Harry dealt with Coach Winter on a different level than I dealt with Coach Winter. Harry was not one to let anyone besides himself dictate anything to him. At the time he was competing for Coach Winter, he was an athlete determined to take his own future in his hands. He was also going to come at anyone he encountered from an academic point of view, reaching into his bag of words in order to communicate on any level, whether it's a street level or presidential level, or on the level of any sport you could think of. He definitely was of a mind to deal with Coach Winter from the perspective of a black athlete challenging what was believed to be true about a white coach's ideas being superior to a black person's, on any subject. I can't say whether this was anything he ever expressed directly to Coach Winter, and I feel sure that Coach Winter didn't express much on the topic to him, because he was a man of few words. I think if they had spoken more, they would have had a better understanding of each other.

I dealt with Bud on a coach-athlete level, not on a black-white level. I listened to him, just as I had listened to Harry. I actually was closer to Bud than to Harry; Bud was my coach, and as the athlete, I questioned very little of what he did in practice because I felt he had more knowledge than I did about track and field. I listened and worked. This could be because of my background of working in the fields and listening to the white man in the fields, and I didn't do badly in the fields. I didn't do badly in school once I tried to accomplish what I was supposed to accomplish in the textbooks. I was a follower, I tried to make people happy, and I tried to do everything I possibly could to make it easy for other people.

I also formed my own opinions on people at that point. They had to make themselves unpopular with me, and I gave them chances to do so by, again, listening and letting them prove themselves. That came partly from Harry, but it also came from my deciding that Bud had things that he could teach me, and that there were things that I needed to learn from him that I would not learn anywhere else. The input from both men made me a better person, yet I didn't let either of them sway my way of thinking. I created a personality of my own that I could live with by taking suggestions, modifying some, and deleting others. So there are parts of both of them in me, as a man, as a teacher, and as a coach. But just as I am not a creation of Harry Edwards, I am not a creation of Bud Winter. That's why when I would hear Harry talk about Bud, I'd look at him with a smile—a small smile or a big smile, knowing that Harry was reading me for a response, because he wanted to get a response and wanted to know if what he said had been accepted. That was my response: I had heard him, but I had not accepted it.

For me, accepting Bud was easy. He was one of the greatest persons I have ever met in terms of minding the business that he knew most about, which was track and field. He was a lot of different things: in his own way he was a statesman, a politician, a coach, and of course a husband and a father.

Bud was the reason I met Harry Edwards so soon upon arriving as a freshman; he was the one who asked him and St. and the others to meet me at the airport. I met Coach Winter soon after I got to campus. My first thought was that he was a simple person: a simple look about him, simple clothes, simple talk, and he smiled. I could relate to that. I thought: if this is what college is all about, hell, I can handle this. Once I had spent some time there and saw how everybody else was, I started to wonder how he could be such a nice person. I was used to coaches yelling and screaming all the time, yet here was a quiet man with a happy laugh who made you feel like you were somebody instead of a shadow following him.

What made Coach Winter appeal to me in the beginning was that he was such a total person. Despite the fact that we were different colors, he gave me the feeling that I was great, from the first day. How can a poor, little, skinny kid from the cotton fields of Texas and the grape fields of central California be great? Well, he wasn't just looking at where I was from, but at the production in high school, and that's what he was looking for. Others might have found him impersonal, irrational, even selfish, but the traits I saw in him, to me, were what made the people around him feel that they were great. I had seen the other coaches on campus, particularly my basketball coach, whom I was ready to get away from by the end of that freshman season. Nothing they had ever done had made me feel as if I were great.

Already by then, I was condensing the sports for which I'd earned a scholarship down to one. I had eliminated football quickly. I had seen what my partners in football had gone through. I also knew that San Jose State had a reputation for its wide receivers busting up their knees or backs or Achilles tendons or whatever. When I got there, most of the wide receivers on the team were injured, and I knew I didn't want to get into the routine of going to the trainer every day. I had spent enough time getting hit hard by the biggest guy on the other team every day in high school. I also saw all the yelling and screaming coaches were doing. And I figured, why not choose a sport in which I could be just as good or better, without the constant threat of injury, and in which I could become world class without having to rely on 20 or 30 other guys to get me there. So as much as they pleaded with me, I never put on the uniform there. It was not the end of my football career, I was stunned to discover years later, but I couldn't have foreseen the circumstances that would get me into a uniform.

My one and only basketball season ended not long before track season began, which is how I ended up injuring my hamstring. I had been surprised that Coach Winter had not approached me during basketball season and had stayed out of Coach Gline's way; at least I think he did. He seemed to mind his own business and did not mind anyone else's business. He was willing to let me do what I had to do. It was partly his way of letting me become a total person with my own mind. Even when he got me for track season, he minded his own business, even when that business was me. I had to learn the drills quickly, and I knew there were times I did them wrong, and he always made me feel that it was okay, that I just had to keep trying to get it right, saying it in a way that made me feel I would get it right.

When I got injured at that meet in Berkeley, I felt Bud's eyes on me, and I felt that I had hurt him as much as I'd hurt myself by getting injured. But the only concern he expressed was in me getting healthy again, and that's all he would let me concentrate on. He had me work with a great trainer, Lindsy McLean, who was the trainer for the San Francisco 49ers back then and through their Super Bowl years in the 1980s and '90s. You could see then why he was such a part of their family for years: he was a nice guy, quiet, with a dry sense of humor, and he knew his job and was very meticulous and professional. His job was to get me back on the track, and he did it, and he made it easy for me to work with him. I learned then that no matter what you think about the job a trainer does, no matter what his goal, you do not fight the person who is trying to heal you.

It was another indication of how Bud treated you. It was difficult for me that year to think he was real. I was sure I knew how he could create and maintain such a great program year after year. As I've said, not every one of his athletes has felt the way I did about him. One of the things some disliked about him was the way he used scholarships to build a great team; he would take one scholarship and cut it into two partial scholarships, so that one scholarship might pay for tuition and books, but not room and board, and another might only pay for room and board but not tuition. I received a full scholarship, and at times it didn't feel as if it was enough, so I know how a partial scholarship can be inadequate. I don't necessarily admire that in a coach, but that is one way to build a team, and he built a great team that way. I understand it even more now after having been a college coach myself, dealing with budgets and recruiting and limits.

And I proved that my full scholarship was worth it. I always knew that I could go to Coach Winter if I needed anything outside of my scholarship, and I'm sure that he might grant it to me and not to someone else who wasn't as productive for him as I was. But he kept out of trouble with that, and he built a tremendous team that way. For my part, I recognized that I was there to get an education and to participate in track and field, not to fight Coach Winter over something. Regardless of his tactics, he collected world-class track athletes there and sustained a great program.

When I later became a coach, I was able to put my studies in sociology to use in educating youngsters about the mind and body coming together to maximize their talent, to make them whole people. This is what Coach Winter was doing all along with me before I could put a name to it. The things that he said and taught stuck in my mind even before I realized in the classroom how to put those ideas into practice. Getting maximum usage of the muscles without tensing up—that's putting the mind to work to help the body. Keeping the body relaxed through the mind is what he had in mind when he advocated always being in prime physical shape, being prompt, using correct posture and form, breathing, understanding the body. Track, according to Bud, was the mainstay of a clear mind. He was in favor of keeping the mind clear, and he was open-minded about how to accomplish that.

My infamous shades were a perfect example. As I ran, I kept my eyes focused and relaxed, just as Bud taught me. I wore sunglasses in most of my races, especially those in the daytime. I didn't want to squint, because I wanted to have a very loose face, as he taught me. Nor did I want anything to distract me; the shades let me look out but did not let people look in. That attitude partially was a remnant of being a bashful kid and not wanting people to see my face. The one thing I never wore shades to do was to make me look cool. They were as much part of my uniform as my jockstrap or shorts; I sometimes put them on before my jockstrap, and sometimes after the race I jumped in the shower with my shades still around my neck because I'd forgotten they were there. I wore Polaroids, because it advertised at the time that they could keep certain rays out of your eyes; they were also light plastic and not heavy at all. They cost all of $1.98 then, and it took me 18 days to save up the money to buy them. I took great care of them because replacing them wouldn't be easy. I secured them around my head with rubber bands, not any sort of expensive, loud-colored glasses holder from the sporting goods store. Those cost money; I got rubber bands from the campus athletic office. They became my trademark, the representative of my personality, yet when people told me how cool they thought I was with the shades, or that they thought I was trying to put on airs about being the fastest man in the world, I looked at them as if they were crazy. An example of why that was not the reason: in Mexico City, in the 200-meter final and on the victory stand, I did not wear the shades, because the race was run at night.

Bud never, and I mean never, mentioned anything to me about wearing shades. He knew me pretty well by then, and he knew I was a very modest person, very quiet, and he knew that anything I had to wear I wore as a technique of relaxation and performance, and not to set a fad or be cool. If my coach felt comfortable and secure about my wearing them and never questioned me, everyone else should react the same way, I felt. Thus, I never gave a damn what anyone thought about my shades.

Coach Winter's personality emanated calm and poise. The fact that he never really yelled or screamed or got mad had a much more positive effect than did the craziness other coaches gave off. The most he would ever do in a meet was jump jubilantly and allow a big smile when something great happened. He never came off like a cheerleader, even though he was very encouraging—he was so smooth, so quiet, so consoling. He would say, "Come on, Tom-Tom," and that would be about it. You would have to work to find a reason to get mad at him. Some did, but it was difficult for me. He used kindness to destroy anything that might be negative. The fact that other athletes did get mad at him impressed me about him even more as a coach, because of the way he dealt with so many individuals and mindsets, knowing he could not please everybody, especially not temperamental sprinters. In my mind, the man did a great job.

Coach Winter truly had an open-door policy, and you could go into his office on personal matters. Even before you had a chance to talk to him, he might ask you about your family, your personal life, whether there was anything he could do to help out. Even if there was a problem and there was nothing he could do, at least you left his office thinking, "Hey, the guy really cares."

That kindness extended toward making us part of his immediate family. His wife had pledged to make a pineapple upside-down cake for anyone who broke a world record. For a while, I was the only one she made the cakes for, because not many others were running world records besides me at that time. She still owes me about six of them, God rest her soul. She must have known something, though, because sometimes that was the only thing I had to eat. I would share it with my roommate St. I don't know if he liked them, and I never could figure out the whole upside-down cake thing myself. All I know is that it was good, especially when it was all I had.

I can't recall ever doing anything to make Coach Winter mad, on the track or off. You might simply say that I did not want to do anything to him that I wouldn't want done to me if I were coach. I know that even more now that I have been a coach. In turn, I don't think he ever did anything to take advantage of me or of the other athletes, although obviously some of those other athletes might disagree. Those descriptions of being an opportunist never applied to Coach Winter as far as I ever knew. Even during my last few years at San Jose State, when I was collecting world records and he asked me to run in several events at a meet, I always agreed. For one thing, he was relying on me for leadership, and both he and I knew that the younger athletes looked up to me. For another, after growing up working in the fields 12 hours a day and going to school in between trips to the fields, running four events in one lousy track meet was nothing for me. He liked the fact that he could rely on me.

Of course, I am living proof that his coaching and teaching techniques worked. So are the other sprinters he produced over the years; he taught them all the same way, and he used us as examples of how to run. The science of sprinting, he called it; I had always felt there was a science to it, even when I was running in high school, but competing under him put it into perspective. He wrote books about it, including *Jet Start*, his technique of coming out of the block; my picture was on the cover, as an example of someone whose body frame demanded that I get off to the best start possible. After that, one of my nicknames was Tommie Jet. Coach Winter also made a series of films of us to show others, in the clinics he conducted around the world and in his own practices, how we trained and practiced his lessons. He got us all to listen, and the results were phenomenal. San Jose State was known as Speed City long before I arrived, long before John Carlos and Lee Evans arrived, and it kept that name long after we left.

In fact, one of the first people I met when I arrived on campus was Ray Norton, the most celebrated San Jose sprinter ever up to that point, holder of all the significant school records, the man who went to the 1960 Olympics in Rome (although he was unable to win the gold in any of his events, through a number of bizarre and controversial circumstances, none of which made him any less of a legendary sprinter). In turn, before I was through at San Jose State, I would have met or competed with Hal Davis, Bobby Poynter, Ronnie Ray Smith, Sam Davis, Kirk Clayton, Wayne Herman, Maurice Compton, and of course John Carlos and Lee Evans—and I could go on and on. Many of them stayed in coaching or went into teaching or other educational fields, in high school or college. Every once in a while at a big track meet, such as the West Coast Relays, a number of us would run into each other. Or we would see somebody that we had not met personally but who we knew had gone through the Speed City program. We'd see more than one, in fact, and we'd say, "There's another Bud product . . . there's another Bud product . . ."

We all carried his teachings on to the generation that we taught about track and field. It amazes me to this day that I ran so well and felt so good about going so fast. That was due to Bud Winter's type of training, his ability to humanely make one feel that one has a right to know how to sprint, and then to show you how to do it to the best of your ability. You owed something to your ability, but you were owed something from it as well.

This was an important lesson to me at the time, and just as important today, for a couple of reasons. It appealed to the religious upbringing I'd had; I always thanked my Creator for delivering up to me the materials to run that fast: my legs, my mind, muscles, and so forth. I didn't think I had done it by myself, but I did believe that these gifts were to be used. On the other hand, I had heard, and still hear, so much about how "natural" I was as a runner. One of my favorite descriptions I have heard about my running style is that it was like pouring oil onto glass, it was so smooth. But it was not as if I rolled out of bed one morning, jumped on the track, and ran fast. Just the opposite—I rolled out of bed, jumped on the track, and fell over my own feet. I was a skinny kid with long legs, and it took quite a bit of work to put all this form together and run at a speed of almost 30 miles an hour. Running was my craft, my profession, and my art. It had to be for me to get as much out of my body as I possibly could, running as fast as I was running. It took quite a bit of thought and preparation and going back to the drawing board before I could create the Tommie Smith style of running.

And it was my style of running, and mine alone. It was built from the lessons Bud Winter taught me, just as my personality off the track was shaped by Harry Edwards but was not a carbon copy. They both laid the groundwork for me to become a freethinking individual. Two men distinct and separate from each other, and in opposition to each other in many ways, influenced my life well beyond the time I spent as a student and athlete at San Jose State.

Above: On a European trip, I was asked to pose in a cage with a big cat. Comparison, you know!

Right: Some people thought I wore sunglasses to look cool, but to me they were just part of my uniform.

Speed City—the track team at San Jose State. *Standing, left to right:* Kirk Clayton, Jerry Williams, Sam Davis, Billy Gaines, Lee Evans, Bob Griffin, Frank Slaton. *Kneeling, left to right:* myself, Ronnie Ray Smith, John Carlos.

On the San Jose State track in 1967, showing my characteristic long stride—nine feet or more.

The finish line of the 200 meters at the Mexico City Olympics in 1968. When I knew I had won, I raised my arms in elation. Peter Norman, not visible here, edged John Carlos for the silver medal.

On the victory stand in Mexico City, moments after John Carlos and I made our famous gesture during the national anthem.

The day after the Mexico City race, I explained the symbolism of the silent gesture in an ABC interview with Howard Cosell.

The silent gesture in bronze and ceramic: the unveiling of the sculpture at San Jose State University, October 2005. The statue portrays John Carlos and me on the victory stand in 1968. The place of the silver-medal winner, Peter Norman, is vacant so that viewers can fill the space themselves.

The athletes and the artist. Sculptor Rigo23, who created the statue at San Jose State, is flanked by the three medal winners: myself (left), John Carlos, and Peter Norman.

Accepting my doctoral degree at San Jose State in 2005.

A country boy's travels

Above: With my father and brother Ernie in Lemoore, California, in 1999.
Below: At St. Peter's, Vatican City.

Facing page, top: The 1999 inductees of the Bay Area Sports Hall of Fame. Next to me are Joe Montana, Ronnie Lott, and Gordy Soltau.
Facing page, bottom: My wife Delois and myself with John and Charlene Carlos in 2004.

One of my proudest moments: my sons Anthony (center) and Kevin join me at
my induction into the Bay Area Sports Hall of Fame in 1999.

Linked Forever

JOHN CARLOS AND I RAN TOGETHER on the same team only twice in our lives. The second time was on the Olympic team in Mexico City. The first was not at San Jose State, because we were together at school for one academic year, 1966–67, and that was the year after John transferred from East Texas State University in Commerce, Texas. Then and now, NCAA rules dictate that a transfer has to complete a full academic year before becoming eligible to compete at his new school. If not for that rule, San Jose State would have had Tommie Smith, Lee Evans, and John Carlos on the same team, the same track, together. Can you imagine Carlos, Evans, and Smith on the mile relay? I don't want to be disrespectful, but we could have gotten a person in a wheelchair for the fourth leg and still broken a world record. Even though we never had a chance to team up that way, we knew Carlos was a force to be reckoned with later.

We all did run together during the summer, for the Santa Clara Valley Youth Village track club in San Jose. I had been running for them in the summer since I'd arrived at school as a freshman in 1963; Lee joined later and then John. We were too good for that club. It had been all white until we track runners arrived and made it world class. The officials who ran Santa Clara Valley Youth Village couldn't stand the pressure of black athletes representing them. The victory stand in Mexico City, along with the involvement of all of us in the Olympic Project for Human Rights, was the last straw. That year, they shut down the track club and started a swim club—and began sending their white athletes to the Olympics in the place of their black athletes. I had thought that I was the only one who believed that Santa Clara Valley Youth Village did it that way for that reason, until I heard John say the same thing at one of the panels the day we were honored on San Jose State's campus in 2003.

So there were, still are, and always will be similarities between the two of us, in the way that we think. But we were very different from the beginning, too, from the way we grew up to the personality we both developed. I first met him in the latter part of my junior year, when he came from East Texas State to visit campus, when he was considering transferring. I didn't know much about John; Lee Evans and Coach Winter wanted me to talk to him about coming here and tell him how badly we needed him in order to give us one of the best relay teams at any college. Lee was more of a recruiter than I was; that wasn't my personality, and I was too busy concentrating on other things, like my studies and training and ROTC and, at the time, my girlfriend Valerie (although it was about this time that she began to exit the picture and Denise was entering it). So I didn't have a lot to say to John Carlos, or time to spend with him, when he visited.

Even then, though, John had a lot to say. The one thing I truly remember about his first visit was that he was a big guy, and he talked loud and a lot. He was very verbose. He said a lot of things that didn't make a lot of sense, and then a lot of things that did make sense. You just had to pick through them for the things that made sense. It's a good thing that I listen so well. When John did arrive at San Jose State for good, even though he moved in different circles and made other friends, he did spent a lot of time with me and Lee, and among the three of us the chemistry was very good. Lee was the funniest one of the group, and he provided a lot of the laughter; John, because he talked so much, provided a lot of tension; and I was just there to listen and laugh and, if I injected something, inject it quietly. I was more into producing on the track and letting that speak for me; Lee saw that trait and called me "Sneaky," because I never broadcast what I was going to do, what I had done, or what anyone had said to or about me.

Lee and I had a natural connection because we grew up in the same area of California, and we had both made names for ourselves the past few years in San Jose. John was from Harlem, and he walked and talked and carried himself like he was from Harlem. But together, the three of us were a sight to see. We were at the same school and we hung out together, and when we were on the track no one in the world could beat us in any event we wanted to run. That's a chemistry you don't find today; it was unsurpassed by any threesome in track since then, at least as far as I've ever seen.

So the relationship between John Carlos and me was close, but it wasn't a relationship where one of us could not do without the other, either on the team or in society alone. We practiced together, we ate together, we hurt together, we talked about each other, and sometimes we got mad at each other for some reason, but it wore off—it's no different than two buddies on a team that hung out together. If there was one aspect that set us all apart, John, Lee, and I, it was academics. I was more concerned with getting out of college than with running a world record. I think Lee was second in terms of education being important to him; his priority was taking care of his family, because he was married then, to Linda, and had a child. John was a close third—actually, a distant third. I'm glad that he is teaching and into education now, but he never got his degree, and once you don't get your BA out of college, it's third on your list no matter how you look at it. I was not there just to be there, just to run; I was there to get out of school and get my degree. I don't think John thought that way. Maybe he did, but I know he did not receive his degree from San Jose State, and he has not thought it was very important to get it.

When we were at San Jose State that day for our tribute, he talked about not getting his degree and said, several times, I am not an educated man. He said it to show that the degree doesn't make a difference to him and that he does not worry about his standing in life changing because he does or doesn't have that degree. It hurt me to hear him say that, at that time and place. I realize that a lot of kids out there don't have their degrees, but it should not be said that it's okay not to have it. The reasons they don't have it should be dealt with. We're fighting to educate our youth, and for a guy acclaimed around the world the way Carlos is, to leave it up to other people to say he is not educated, it just doesn't follow suit. He should fight to defend his reason for not being educated, for not having a chance to be educated. Instead, he was saying, "Look at where I am now, the same place I would be if I had gotten an education." To me, it sounded like he was putting down education, like it was not important enough for him to get one, like he was pushing not getting an education.

But that's the 'Los. That's Carlos. I still respect him as John Carlos.

All this is important not because John Carlos had a different outlook on education than me. It's not even important just because it's part of his belief that honors and awards—and victories and gold medals—mean more to me than they ever will to him, his way to justify where I am and where he is. This is important because so many people believe one of two things about John Carlos and Tommie Smith: that we were and are bosom buddies because of what we did on the victory stand, or that we are distant enemies who have no relationship and never want anything to do with each other. Neither one is true.

People say to me all the time, "Why don't you hang with him? You're brothers, you're married." Those people don't understand our differences. I don't like to hang with Carlos, and Carlos doesn't like to hang with me for the same reason. I'm too quiet, I do things with an aura of quiet, and he's not quiet; he does things with a burst of verbal energy. So we cannot be together because we're both so hardheaded in our own ways of life. We choose to stay apart in our lives. If something happens where we're both supposed to be together, I'm professional. But the 'Los is the 'Los.

But we never were in a state of mind where we could never be together, which is what so many people believe. Those people say, "We've got to get you two together, you two need to be together, you need to end this and get together." A lot of people can't understand why he and I never did a book together or tried to do a movie of our lives together. There's no getting John Carlos and Tommie Smith together, because we were never apart. People who think they can get us together because we were on the victory stand together have the wrong idea of friendship. We probably will never be in a venture together, and that's just the nature of the two of us. If it was John, Lee, and I, or if it was John and Kirk Clayton, whom he was much closer to on the San Jose State team, or John and Jerry Williams, whom he talks to a lot and stays in touch with, that would be different. But with John and Tommie, there is too much water under the bridge—what he said about me and what I said about him.

Some of it is just two versions of the same story. Everybody wants to know who came up with the idea for what we did on the victory stand, who brought the gloves, and who wore what, and I say one thing and he says another. I've told my story about it. My wife Denise, while shopping in Mexico City with John's wife Kim, had bought the gloves and the socks. I was wearing the socks—all the black track and field athletes wore them—and I had the pair of gloves with me at the stadium. When I crossed the finish line in the 200, all I felt was, it was done, like Jesus being on the cross and saying, "It is finished." That is why when I hit the tape you could see the genuine smile on my face, but when my hands came down, I realized where I was, what I had done, and what was going to be for me the rest of the time at the Games. I had no idea what would happen after the race in terms of social speaking, but I knew in my own mind, before I even got to the victory stand, that if they thought that race was something, they should wait to hear what I had to say, what I'd been wanting to say, and what they'd been wanting to hear for over a year. I had the gloves, but even then I didn't know what I was going to do with them. I was thinking about wearing both gloves, but what good would that do? That was when I talked to John about wearing one of the gloves, told him that I was going to do something with the glove on, and to just follow my lead when I got up there. Then I thought about turning around on the victory stand, but I didn't know if that was right, either.

Then, all of a sudden, on my way toward the stand, I decided, why not represent the flag with pride, but do it with a black accent, and add some prayer? So that's what it was. If you look at me, you'll see it was done in military style, the way I turned from facing the man who presented me with the medal to facing the flag. It was a military turn; I was in ROTC, so I knew the move. Then it was fist up, a movement of conviction. My head was down because I was praying. When it was over, I did another military turn and stepped down. I struck the perfect sharp, straight presentation. I wasn't going to do any haphazard move. People expected us to go up there and hoo-rah, get loud, slap hands, or something. We did it with pride, and we wanted it to represent everybody without making a statement for anybody, just a silent gesture for anyone to interpret their way. In a way, the gesture I made represented my father, for all the times he worked those fields and endured everything he did, who didn't speak much and was very quiet but let his actions speak for him. He was who I thought about during that time and in the years afterward, when the pressure on me for what I did was so great, when that pressure along with the love for humanity that drove me to do it was so strong that I didn't know how I would survive it. I wanted the gesture to represent him, I wanted it to embody that pride and love for what America is supposed to be. With those two gloves, we were able to do it all.

John tells everybody that he came up with the idea for the gloves, and that he got the idea for the raised fist from a poster he'd seen on the wall of his friend Kirk Clayton before we ever got to Mexico City. He says that he had the idea to roll up our pants legs, to take off our shoes, and to wear beads around our necks. If he wants to say that, that's fine. He's said a lot of things; he's said that he helped Bob Beamon, our Olympic teammate, train for his record-breaking long jump at the Games. John sees things differently. Everybody sees things differently. He also says that his head was up and his fist cocked a little because he was watching out for someone trying to kill us and wanted to be ready—and I had thought the same thing, that someone would end it for both of us right there on the stand, before the anthem was over. So that's something he said that I believe.

But John has also said, over and over again through the years, that he let me win the race because a gold medal meant more to me than it did to him, and that he had decided this back in Lake Tahoe at the trials, when he won the 200-meter qualifier in what would have been a world record, except for the record being voided because his spikes were ruled illegal.

Specifically, this is what he said in his own book, *Why?*

> The race don't mean shit to me. I talked to Tommy [sic] about making a statement after the race, and he agreed. When he agreed to assist me, the race became secondary. I knew how much the gold medal meant to Tommy, and I wanted to see his dream come true. I felt that a silver medal would be fine with me as long as I get a chance to make a statement. If the medal meant everything to Tommy, he can have the medal. I need him to watch my back and I watch his while we make a statement on the victory stand.

And this:

> I led the race for the first 130 meters to allow everybody to know that
> I had the ability to win the race if I wanted to do so. But I chose not
> to. I shut down my jets to auto pilot around the 140-meter mark. I
> looked to my left to see if I could see Tommy coming. I did, but it
> seemed like he was struggling to make the lead. I looked back, and
> I yelled, "Come on Tommy, and quit bullshitting if you want to
> win this race."

That will break up a friendship right there. That could cause me
to go find John and kick his ass. I could question whether we believed
in the same things in Mexico City; I don't know any more. But I rise
higher than that; I don't go there. When the book first came out, I
would not read it. My wife Delois read it, but I didn't have to. I know
what's in it because I have heard it from him for years. I know a lot
of the stuff is not true, and I don't mean "not in the spirit of truth"—
I mean, not true. John knows it's not true, I know it's not true, Lee
knows it's not true. But it's in that book, and I'm not going to go out
in the street and tell people, John says this and that. Let him handle
that. That's why I wanted this book out. The other times I could
have written this book, it wasn't my time, it wasn't the right time.

John has done his book, and now I've done mine. Harry has done
his. We all have our own stories, and we all have our ideas of what is
the truth. I know that I was a world record holder; I know I was a gold
medalist. Whether it means a lot to them or not, that's how the system indicates greatness: who came first, not who came fifth or third
or second. But John Carlos wants to say I won only because he let me
win. Well, you can't do that. That's like beating your child to death
and then saying you did it because he was too loud. Or like stealing
money and saying it's all right because it was yours in the first place.
Or burning your house down because you have an extra match. Or
beating your wife because she is a woman. Saying he let me win for
a reason like that is saying he beat himself. Why would he do that?
He let me win? John, you can't do that.

But that is how he talks, and that is why we can't talk and we can't
come together because I didn't want to talk about the same things he

wanted to talk about. He talks that Harlem talk, saying that tangible things like medals—and, as he said, college degrees—don't mean much to him, so that's his reason to let me win. But I oppose the idea of letting someone win, especially in this contest. That's fraudulent; you don't go into a contest and let someone else win. You can go to jail for that. Look at what was at stake. Why would one jeopardize his personality or his freedom of speech by saying he let the world record holder do something, and the world record holder is now the world record holder. I don't understand the rationale. He does.

Basically, he's in denial. I believe that he believes what he says. That's the sad thing. It gives credence to a very stupid thing. It doesn't make him look good. He's supposed to be a competitor. I really like the guy, but as long as he keeps separating us by saying things like that, I can't agree with him and I can only talk to him so much, because I'm the one he's talking about negatively.

If you look at the race in Lake Tahoe, the Olympic trials qualifier, and talk about someone who could have let someone else win, you'll see that I had no chance to beat John Carlos that day, and I had very little intention of even making the team. I had just gotten back from Germany, I had diarrhea, I wasn't stretching, I wasn't forceful—I was just running because I was Tommie Smith and I was supposed to run. Even in my lethargy I still took second place with a 19.9, the fastest I'd ever run. But Carlos couldn't have been beaten that day, not by me or anyone. It was Carlos's day. It would have been his world record, but we told him not to wear those shoes because they weren't ratified by the USOC, the IOC, anybody, anywhere—and not only did he wear them, but Lee wore them too. Carlos ran a 19.7, the fastest ever, but the world record was out. And why did they do it? For the money, the Puma money. I'm glad they had money, because I sure didn't have any. But it cost John Carlos a world record, and when I won in Mexico City, I was the one with the world record, even though it wasn't as fast as his time in Tahoe. My record lasted 11 years.

John is right when he says that winning the race was important to me. I couldn't even think of losing the race; sometimes the thought entered my mind and I just shunned it. That first stride could have stopped me from winning, but it didn't. John turns that around and says in his talks that, well, he and Tommie are different; Tommie likes his trophies and medals, but as long as John Carlos has his heart and his family and his right frame of mind, he doesn't need the other things, and he has given his medals and trophies away. What message is he conveying there? What is he saying about me?

But this is John. You know whose voice was heard most in the days after the victory stand, who was the one giving the most interviews, making statements on behalf of the Olympic Project for Human Rights, and being what he usually is, loud and verbose. When he talks about it today, he's emotional about how it all happened in Mexico City, and how nobody owes him anything, and he's just who he is, and he acted from his heart, and his love for people drove him, and he would have died to protect that—just some really heavy shit. It sounds so good, I want to applaud sometimes. Yet as everybody knows by now, and Lee has said it several times as well, Carlos was not involved with the technical meetings, the preparations, for the proposed boycott. I didn't see him at the meetings. But he was the spokesman in Mexico City and when we returned home and when the topic came up anywhere at any time. When we were at San Jose State in 2003, who did all the talking? When he gets in front of a microphone, he goes. I just sit there, and the people ask me, "Mr. Smith, what do you think?" And I talk very briefly, I keep it short, and I'm gone, and he comes in and he talks.

That has always been Carlos's *modus operandi.* I have no hate for him because he does that; I just know he does that. He was also correct in saying that we had each other's back in Mexico City; his strength was where I did not have strength, because I was not one to talk, and still am not. I think I was his strength at times, and he was my strength at times. If we were on different sides of the river, I was the crossing over, and he was the crossing back; he'd jump on my back crossing over and I'd jump on his crossing back. I believed in him then, and I still believe in John Carlos.

But as much and as well as he can talk, there are some things he can't talk about—being the gold medalist, because no matter what he says, he was the bronze medalist, and he cannot talk about winning, except to tell that story about how he let me win. When that time comes, he has to either contact me or do it without me, and he can't do as much without me (for example, make as much money) as he could with me. He can't do a whole lot without the gold medalist. They're not going to want him without me, but I can do things without him. In a way, I'm held responsible for his actions and his movements. I've been told that many times, as I've said, including by John's current wife, Charlene: that it is my responsibility to get the two of us together so we can make the most money possible. Yet I also know that John Carlos doesn't want to be in a place where he is not the one in control—as Harry Edwards said, captain of his own ship. When Carlos needs me, I don't automatically do what he wants. He can do his own thinking and talking and has his own mind, but it does not get him as far as it could if I were included in whatever function he has in mind. The truth is, I went years without doing these things because I was into my work; in fact, I recognize that I hid in my work for a long time, wherever I was. It wasn't about money; finances have their place, but they don't have a big place for me. I'm doing okay after all this; I won't starve tomorrow. There is money to be made now as I travel, speak, and lecture and as I write this book, but this is more about continuing to educate and to be educated.

John has endured a lot in his life. His wife, Kim, committed suicide about 10 years after Mexico City, and I know it had to do with the strain of what happened because it helped bring my first marriage to an end. He raised his three children to be good, strong young people. I was glad to see he has found happiness again with his wife Charlene. His health was not good when we came back to San Jose State in 2003; he almost didn't come in that day, and he withstood the entire day and night of ceremonies through the pain of those kidney stones. I understand what it's like to feel like you don't know if you'll make it this far.

I just don't want to jump on his back anymore, and I don't want him to jump on my back. We both have families, wives, and children. All those years when we both lived in southern California, we probably lived no more than an hour and a half apart. Our wives would do things to try to bring us together, and back when I first began working on this book we almost had something in place for us both to be at my house. I can understand their wanting that because they have not known us for as long as Carlos and I have known each other. I'd love to go to his house and have him come over to our house.

We've discussed doing it, but it has never happened. Those who have said that 1968 "married" us—and even John said that once—are wrong. Our lives are separate; I respect his life and he respects mine. I'm there if some occasion brings us together, like the honors we have been receiving at San Jose State. But I don't like to be so dependent on another person that I can't move without him. That's where a "marriage" is good for John; because of his personality, it helps him if I go everywhere he goes.

I cannot be mad at John for the things he has said in the years after Mexico City, not after he was one of the ones who wanted to do something and not find a reason against doing it. I couldn't be mad at the athletes who decided, at the meeting before we left for Mexico City, that they could not boycott, could not get involved in a protest, and would let others follow their own conscience. A couple of guys said, "Hell no, I'm not doing it; I want to make some money after this race." We had a couple of guys in the army who said, "I can't do this shit; I'll get court-martialed." Some of them said, "I'm happy in life; I don't need to do this." And there were some of us who said, "We've got to look further than just us." Some of them replied with: "That was the wrong thing to say; who else matters? Who's going to make me some money?" We decided that it wasn't going to happen, and that each athlete would do what he thought he should according to how we felt—and we decided it very calmly, quietly, and without a lot of negative talk. Ralph Boston, the leader of the meeting, made it clear how we would conduct ourselves, saying, "Okay, we're not mad at each other, because that's what the Man wants. If you go out there yelling and cussing at each other and acting unhappy, they have won the battle and we would have destroyed ourselves, like we do most of the time." John never put anybody else down. He spoke his piece in that meeting, as I did, and he agreed that no one was going to put anyone else down for making his own mind up. He took a stand as well, joining in our gesture on the victory stand. If I couldn't hate those others, how could I hate him?

Yet John is still John. He will talk, he will antagonize, he loves stirring things up. It was a source of pride for both of us that it was a white man, a white student, Erik Grotz, who started the whole campaign to bring us back to campus and honor us with the statue.

Carlos was asked about that at a classroom panel discussion that day, and he said, in effect, that Erik must understand how it's going to affect him, or he might not know yet how it will affect him—but because he is associating himself with us and what we did, it will probably ruin his life. That got a nervous laugh out of the audience, and I said, "Oh my God, don't scare this kid." He bit off a lot, maybe more than he anticipated. He has had to answer a lot of questions and had been put on the spot to explain his plan and his motivation. But 'Los, being 'Los, put him in the spotlight unexpectedly later that very day when he grabbed the kid and put him between us during that TV interview during the barbecue. That was a little bit too much for Carlos to do to him, but that's Carlos. The more you resist him, the more he'll fight to embarrass you; that's what makes him look good. I was telling him, "Let him go, don't put this young kid to the forefront like this." The interviewer, Lloyd LaCuesta, who interviewed us back in 1968 when we first returned from Mexico City, was actually pissed off at Carlos for doing that, and the two of them had words—they came out friendly, but they did have words. That was him getting attention for himself. You can imagine him out on a track, after he'd just won a race, with people up in the stands giving him accolades, soaking it all in. That's positive attention, but he doesn't care if he gets negative attention that might touch other people, or all the other people, as long as he gets the attention. He is a positive person, but he will use negativity to make himself heard. The idea he had about bringing Erik into the interview was a good one—and he could have done it differently. He could have invited Erik up there, even escorted him up there. He could have said, "I would understand if you don't want to come, but Tommie and I would love it if you came up and sat between us." The kid might have wanted to come up. Instead, he was yanking and pulling him up there, yelling, "Come on, come on." He'll embarrass you and not mind at all, because it doesn't embarrass him.

Most people won't even notice something like that when John Carlos does it in a place like that. It always looks very normal, very comfortable when we are together in a setting like that. No one knows that we didn't have a college life together unless we say so, and we rarely are asked. I think that he has something against me that I don't understand, when I hear or see the things he says about Mexico City and about me. What I have against John is nothing; I still respect him. If we were not as close as some think we were supposed to have been, or if we were not as close as Lee and I were, that is normal even for two people on the same team and at the same school. What tied John and me together was the race in Mexico City—the only thing. He goes his way in life, and I go mine. But when we're together, we've got to be professional, and we are. That's how people see us, tied together as two black athletes on the victory stand who had the same idea in mind and acted it out. We don't hate each other; we just won't hang out together and probably never will. That's just the nature of John Carlos and Tommie Smith.

But in the times we've been together, no one has ever asked John Carlos, "Did you let Tommie Smith win that race?" I hope somebody does. I'd love to be there when he answers it.

No Gold, No Glove

D ICK GREGORY, the nightclub comic then coming into his own as an activist, had talked about black athletes boycotting the Olympics as far back as the 1960 Games in Rome. The talk surfaced again in 1964. I don't remember much about it. I do remember believing, after the freshman year I had at San Jose State, that I was ready to compete in the Games in Tokyo. I knew it from my very first meet as a freshman, when I ran a 20.7 in the 200 and ran a good leg in the 4-by-100-meter relay. I smiled internally and said, "Okay world, I'm ready, here I am." I got injured later, but I came back by the end of the season, ran a 46.5 400, and was named an All-American.

That time was also good enough to qualify me for the Olympic trials in the summer of 1964. That is, I qualified to go to the prequalifying meet at Rutgers University in New Jersey, which would qualify me for the actual trials later in New York. Still, that sounds simple enough, until you realize that back then, if you competed in the summer, you could not compete for your school. That summer was the first time I ran for the Santa Clara Valley Youth Village track club. But the club did nothing for me to send me to the qualifying meet— no travel money, no travel arrangements, no coaching or administrative help, none of the things athletes have to be able to take for granted in a competition like that. At that point, not only had I never traveled from the West Coast, I had barely been away from San Jose since arriving on campus, and the trip to college had been the furthest I'd been from Lemoore since I had arrived from Texas.

My old teacher and coach, Mr. Focht, stepped in and got the city of Lemoore to raise money for me to go. That was only the beginning of my problems: when I landed at the airport in New Jersey, I didn't even know how to get to Rutgers. I asked around and finally figured out where I was supposed to go and where the athletes were supposed to stay—but didn't know where or how I was to eat. I got to the meet the next day, and still ran a 47.3, third in my heat, to get me into the final to qualify for New York. There were some big names in that race, Dave Tobler and Adolph Plummer, but regardless of how big the names were, everyone in that race was older than me. More important, everybody else there had a coach who could tell them the time and place of the final race, because the race was not listed in the program. There would be one general announcement on the PA system just before the race, and we were to be on the starting line and ready to go when the time came. I was told all this at the finish line of my heat, but I had no one to help me, and already on a scale of 1 to 10 of being afraid, I was about a 9¾. There was chaos on the track and people running all around. With all that confusion, I just wanted to hear the announcement, and I needed to rest. I went up a little hill near the track and sat under a tree, tired and hungry.

Apparently, I nodded off. I don't know for sure. I do recall hearing my name being called to the starting line. I jumped up to run toward the track, and on my way there, the gun sounded. That was the end of my freshman track season, not to mention the end of my chance to go to the 1964 Olympics. It was the first time I had ever missed a race. I wasn't embarrassed, and I was too tired and nervous and hungry to be angry. Tommie Smith was not a big enough name back then for anyone to come looking for me. I just left the track, packed up and left the meet, went back to the airport, and found a flight back to California. I went back to Lemoore and helped my father scrub floors in the classrooms again. I didn't make any vows to avenge what happened, because as far as I was concerned, what kept me from running was the fact that I was completely alone there, with no help, no representation, and no support from a coach or from my club, support that would have made it easy for me to make it to that qualifying race.

With that experience behind me, I came back to school in the fall of 1964 a seasoned veteran. I had three more years, and I had one of the best coaches in the world in Bud Winter and one of the best teams in the world, already dubbed Speed City, with so many superior sprinters that if you couldn't run a 9.3 in the 100, you weren't going to cut it. Our 4-by-100 relay team, which went on to set records, consisted of all 9.3 sprinters or better. Even with all that surrounding me (unlike my Rutgers experience), I still found myself hustling to eat properly, rushing to the cafeteria after returning to campus from a weekend meet, and getting by on whatever I could get out of the snack machines if I didn't get back on time.

I had no time for anything else besides academics and athletics. In my junior year I briefly pledged Omega Psi Phi, a black fraternity. One day I showed up six minutes late to the house after I had stayed a little bit longer at practice, and I was told that if I was late again, they would have to use the Omega Psi Phi board—a paddle—on me. I was a man who honored my commitments, but I told them, "I have one father, and he is in Lemoore, and he is the only person who lays a hand on me, and whoever else tries to won't ever lay another hand on me." Then I walked out and never came back. It was becoming clearer every day that Tommie Smith, and nobody else, could be counted on to take care of Tommie Smith.

My sophomore year was when I set my first world records, in the 220-yard/200-meter straightaway; that same day, I won the 100-yard dash in 9.5 seconds. The records began to pile up in my junior and senior year, but already in my sophomore year Coach Winter was relying on me to compete in several events and to win some meets almost single-handedly. I ran every distance from the 100 to 400, ran the 4-by-100 and 4-by-400 relays, and was still long-jumping as a junior, going 25 feet 11 inches at a meet at San Jose State that year. That was just a half-inch less than I had gone in my freshman year. My 400 times kept dropping as well, but it was as much of a favorite of mine then as it was when I was in high school. It was too long for me, but I wanted to help my team out, and it also made me stronger for the 200, so I ran the 400 not for time or to be world class, but for strength and conditioning for the 200.

That had always been my best event, from the time I ran a 21.0 as a freshman and barely got nosed out in my return from the hamstring injury. Of the 11 simultaneous world records I once held, four were at the 200-meter or 220-yard distances, on the straightaway and on the curve. I kept lowering the 220 mark until I did a 19.5 late in my junior year, 1966. After having missed the NCAA championships when I was a junior, I set a national record in the 1967 meet as a senior, at 20.2 seconds.

I also teamed up for some of the great relays of that time; teams I ran on held outdoor and indoor records in the 1,600-meter, the one-mile, the 880, and the 800 meters. I think most sprinters will agree that relays are the most fun to run; there is a camaraderie of four people preparing to win, negotiating a win, looking good in unison, and then feeling the ecstasy together, instead of individually. I will never forget the 4-by-400 race at the Los Angeles Coliseum in 1967, at a meet that was supposed to be the United States against the Soviet Union until the USSR team pulled out at the last second. My San Jose State teammate Lee Evans ran the second leg, and I ran the third; Bob Frey of UCLA led off, and Theron Lewis of Texas Southern anchored. Lee made that record happen, because he ran the second leg in 44.5 seconds, the fastest 400 meters ever run to that point, relay or not, and handed me a huge lead along with the baton. People went crazy when they announced his time—they let out a huge "aaaahhhhh," which I heard, but didn't know why. They kept making noise because I ran the third leg in 43.8, beating Lee's mark. Lewis finished it up to get us under the three-minute barrier, the first relay team ever to do that.

People still come up to me to talk about an indoor relay in San Francisco, at the Cow Palace, in my senior year. I was the anchor, Lee was third, and the first two legs for San Jose State were Bob Talmadge and Ken Shackelford, two white guys. Like I said, and as Wayne Herman had already proven, everybody at San Jose State was fast. I was only a few strides ahead when I got the baton, and I knew I was going to have trouble negotiating turns on the shorter indoor track with my long build. The other runner had shorter legs and was much better built for indoor. You could hear people in the stands muttering, "San Jose State's finally going to lose." I took off, and the turn got there really fast. We were running on boards, literally, wood with lane markers painted on. The only way I would make the turn was by hook-sliding as if I was going into second base, so that's what I did, and I got 30 or 40 splinters in my leg doing it. I scraped skin off my left leg, and blood was flying alongside me down the track. I felt faint as I crossed the finish line, but we destroyed the second-place team, and everyone swarmed around me, jumping up and down, Lee Evans and Coach Winter. Suddenly my legs went out from under me. I think I passed out from the loss of blood. They took me to the training room and put alcohol on the leg; I still have the scar, and I can still feel the burning of that alcohol on my scabbed leg. That same four-some later went to the West Coast Relays and set the 4-by-220 relay world record.

That same indoor season, in a meet in Oakland, I ran the anchor on the 440 relay, had to come from way behind when I got the baton, and caught and passed the other runner in no time. I couldn't believe I had moved that fast on those boards. That's another meet that friends and spectators remind me of a lot; they swear that's the fastest I've ever run, anywhere at any time. That definitely was the sickest I had ever felt after running, physically sick, including Mexico City.

Individually, my best indoor race was at the Mason-Dixon Games in my senior year, at Louisville, Kentucky—the 440, twice around on a new 200-yard track, which I won in a world-record 46.2 seconds. The picture of that race that hung on my office wall for years at Santa Monica College showed me seemingly running away from seven white men—they were the race timers, they were the only people close to me, and they wore expressions of awe. I remember I really didn't want to be there; I had spent the previous summer at a base in Kentucky in my ROTC duties, and the last thing I wanted to do was be back in that state. The plane home couldn't take off soon enough. But Coach Winter wanted me to go, and it was worth it. I found out later than only one other man up to then, Jamaica's Herb McKenley, had ever held the 440 indoor and outdoor records at the same time.

Without question, though, the race most everybody remembers during my college years was the 400 against Lee Evans, my teammate, at San Jose State, in May of my senior year. I've been calling Lee my "teammate," but he was more than a teammate, and more than a partner in the Olympic Project for Human Rights. I have always believed that I saw him when we were both in high school, out in the grape fields in central California. I was in Lemoore and he grew up in Fresno, and he picked in the fields just as I did, and I remember a time my family and I were picking in a field somewhere between Lemoore and Fresno; I can even remember the location of the field. I remember a little guy picking with his family and just watching me. Later when we knew each other, we told stories from picking in the fields, and he said he thought he saw me! So I've always thought we were destined to meet on the track.

Lee is a couple of years younger than me, and came to State as a junior, when I was a senior, after he had spent a year at San Jose City College. He was shorter and thicker and more powerful as a runner, with a style that probably is the exact opposite of my own, even more different from mine than John Carlos's was. I was built for the 200 and 400, while he was perfect for the 400 and 800; he had that kind of tenacity, that kind of form, that kind of strength. My form was a bit more refined than his, mainly because I had mastered Bud Winter's high knees and long strides longer than he had. He had a more raw stride and raw strength. We were the perfect contrasts.

I had heard about him before he came to San Jose State; we were both the talk of the city, and on many weekends he would run in the morning, when City College held its meets, and I would run in the afternoon when State held its meets. Word would come out that Lee ran, say, a 45.5 in the morning and set a national and meet record, and in the afternoon I would go out and run a 45.1. That left him in my shadow a little bit, and I don't know how it made him feel, but he had a reason to work even harder to make sure I didn't put water on his fire every weekend. There definitely was a rivalry before we ever became teammates.

The one time we had met in a race, in a Pacific Coast AAU meet in Sacramento when I was a junior and he was a sophomore at City, was in the 220, where I already held the world record, and I won in 20.1 seconds. I still didn't pass him until about 80 meters from the finish, and he finished in 20.5. We talked about it years later, and he told me what he was thinking during the race: "Man, I had heard of the high knees when I was in junior college, but I had never experienced your high knees. I went into the backstretch and I was moving; I thought no one would ever catch me. No one had ever done it before. Then I saw a knee out of the corner of my eye, and the next thing I saw was your butt; you had gone by me in one stride." It meant a lot to me to hear him recognize my accomplishment and verbalize on the technique of that race.

Once he came to San Jose State, we ran our separate events, because we did not want to be rivals on the same team, and Coach

Winter did not want it either; he would only do it if he had a particular goal in mind besides getting points to win a meet. For example,
he set up that first 220 race my sophomore year when I got my first
record. But, finally, just before my final season was about to end,
Bud set up a race at San Jose State, basically a farewell race for me.
It was an all-comers meet, but his real reason was to get either me
or Lee the 400-meter/440-yard world record. I didn't want to run it,
and neither did Lee, because we were friends and did not want the
animosity we had to have to run our best, did not want to be enemies
even for that amount of time. But we went ahead and did, and when
we prepared for the race that day, I could not believe how many people showed up to watch: at a track that held about 400 fans at best,
about 5,000 came, packing the stands, sitting in trees and on fences,
standing on top of cars, sitting on top of buildings, and hanging out
of windows nearby. Nobody even paid attention to the events before
that, only the 400 at the end of the day. When the starter said, "On
your marks," you could hear a pin drop.

As I was in the blocks, I decided I didn't want to do this, so I told
Lee, "I don't want to run this race, so I'm gonna come out a little
bit fast and then grab my leg and pull up lame." He kind of looked
at me with those empty eyes and kind of nodded positively, I thought
—but when the gun sounded, and I ran five strides and looked up
expecting to see Lee ease up, I saw Lee running full speed, wide
open. I thought, "Oh my goodness, we weren't supposed to run
this hard," then I got kind of insulted, and I went after him. By the
time I got to the backstretch, all I saw of Lee was his elbows and his
heels. I got hit in the face with the dirt from the cleats of the runners
ahead of me, and as you know, I wasn't used to having anything
but clear air and space in front of me. I decided that this wouldn't do,
and in the middle of the second turn I caught him. I passed him as
we headed to the straightaway. It was my speed against his endurance
now. My technique made the difference, my stride and my high knees.
My speed proved more positive for me than his endurance did for
him. I won and was timed in 44.5 for 400 meters and 44.8 for 440
yards. Bud wanted world records, and he got them.

That 400 record lasted until Mexico City in 1968, when Lee blew
it away in the final with a 43.8. Some say that was even more impres-

sive than my 200 record, and the pressure he bore while running it might have been as great as the pressure when I ran my race. He certainly was under great pressure on the victory stand. Lee and I were linked as runners, friends, and members of the Olympic Project for Human Rights more than John Carlos and I.

By then, pretty much everybody in America knew who I was, and to an extent who Lee was. Our race got a lot of attention, including a story in *Sports Illustrated*. The week before, though, I had been the cover story for the magazine. Me, a full cover, not a picture with two or three other people, but a full-body shot of me running. It was big being on the cover of anything, like *Track and Field News* when I was a freshman, but it was especially big to be on the cover of *Sports Illustrated*. When the magazine first asked me to do it, I talked to Coach Winter about it, and he said he thought it was a great idea. The photographer came and said he would spend an entire day with me and take about 300 to 400 shots of me—and, as it turned out, the one that was used, a full-body shot of me in my gold warm-ups coming out of the blocks on the San Jose State track, was the first one he took in the morning. I still have some of the other photos he took, including me running in the water down at the Santa Cruz beach.

Frank Deford, the writer of the article, drove us around all day in the car he'd rented for the trip, a Mustang Shelby, black with a big yellow stripe down the center. I wanted to ask him to let me drive it, but even though I was a big deal with all my world records, I didn't want to portray myself as a fool, so I never asked him. If I ever see Frank to this day, I'll tell him that I wished I had asked him. Frank was a very nice, personable guy who asked very good questions and wrote what I still think is one of the best stories ever written about me, and definitely one of the best written about me in those years. I felt obligated to answer all the questions he had for me, which is something that unfortunately was not the case with many journalists I dealt with later, who taught me that sometimes it's better to hold back or not talk at all because of the way they portrayed me.

It was an honor for me to get that cover story. It had been a long time coming, but it was finally paying off—after being out in the cotton fields in the backwoods of Texas, spending those 12 hours in 108-degree weather down in Lemoore, now the rewards were starting to roll in. The whole country was learning about Tommie Smith, and they now had to believe what they were hearing; a lot of people back then really didn't think someone could possibly be running as fast as me and thought Bud Winter was lying about it. People on the East Coast who had never seen me suddenly started taking notice, and magazines and newspapers and television stations started to call me. Before that cover story, there were writers and stations overseas that showed more interest in me than the ones in my own country. I was lucky if I got a little write-up, and I mean little, in the *San Jose Mercury*.

The article covered everything that was important in my life, such as my family, my days in the fields, and the importance I put on academics. The one aspect that it did not address was my awareness of what was around me, what I had learned in my classes, from my listening and learning and communicating amid my surroundings on the track and in society. That was definitely addressed later by the newspapers and magazines. I knew how much more there was to my life and my future than running. The whole world became interested in the life they knew after that *Sports Illustrated* story. That meant that the platform formed by my visibility was under construction.

As influential as Harry Edwards had been, two other instructors at San Jose State had the most direct impact on me: Drs. Bruce Oglivie, a sociologist, and Thomas Tutko, a sports psychologist. They have become known around the world since my time at the school. More important to me, they both made me feel intelligent, relevant, and important in terms of what I could contribute beyond athletics. Most of what I was saying in their classes had substance; the problem, they knew, was pushing myself to speak. They gave me the confidence to speak and showed me the power of what I said.

One time in my junior year, when a particular parable he was teaching got me to come to his office for some explanation, Dr. Oglivie pointed out that I never said much, and that I ought to start. I asked why, and he told me: "You're somebody. You're a great athlete, you're a good looking kid, you'll go somewhere in life, and people need to hear what you have to say." I remember him vividly, sitting back calmly in his chair, with his gray hair at his temples, just talking to me. Dr. Tutko's office was next door; he was fairly new at the school, and I didn't know much about him, but Dr. Oglivie brought me over to him, and we talked. When we all were done talking, I was leaning hard toward finally choosing a major, social science. The idea of making myself heard through my status as an athlete began to come together even more than before.

By that time, I had a lot to say. I had seen and heard enough about the system and where it was demanding that I fit in—but I also saw that there was a path for me to become viable within that system and to affect it from within. I knew how much it shook people up to see me, a black man obviously on campus solely to add to its athletic glory, carrying books everywhere and spending so much time in the library. Those people weren't willing to remove me from the hole they had placed me in and couldn't realize that they, in fact, were the ones in a hole and were stubbornly fighting to stay in it by keeping me in the one they thought I was in. They could not acknowledge that I not only understood the rules and laws that govern this system, but that I knew they were not being upheld equally as they were intended, and were actually being used against us. Not only did I have that knowledge, but I was gaining a means to act on it, a way that would be remembered far more than my time in the 100.

As my last year of track eligibility ended, I wanted nothing more than to get out of college, get my degree and my teaching certificate, get a job, and be prepared to support a family—by then I was a father, and I was engaged to Kevin's mother, Denise Paschal. Money wasn't even the most important thing; I wanted to be capable of living the life I was entitled to in the system. Mexico City was more than a year away, and I wasn't far removed at all from not having a decent place to live. But who would I be if I was not active in making sure that I would have that viable place in society once my running days were over? There was no way I was going to just be thankful I was in college on a scholarship, and sit and keep my mouth shut and be sure I don't make my coach or instructors mad.

By then, Harry Edwards and Ken Noel—another instructor at San Jose State and another athlete—had already circulated the idea of a boycott of the 1968 Games. Meetings had already been held, before I had started attending and before it was even known as the Olympic Project for Human Rights. Word had spread to other athletes on other campuses, to other prospective Olympians, and then to the public. The issues at stake were well known. Apartheid was still the rule in South Africa, and the country was still banned from international competition. Muhammad Ali's fight with the government over being drafted had already begun. Demands to hire black coaches to go along with all these black athletes on campuses were growing. There were athletic organizations that were still all white, including the New York Athletic Club, host of one of the most prestigious amateur meets every year at Madison Square Garden.

And there was the housing issue at San Jose State. As far back as my junior year, it was apparent to me and every other black athlete on campus that it was next to impossible to get an apartment in San Jose. Even though my roommate St. and I did get an apartment off campus, I'm sure that the athletic department had some control over it, since it was only 100 meters from the gym on the south side of campus. Every other attempt to rent an apartment did nothing but show the overt racist tendencies in that city. The black athletes who did not get apartments were housed in a motel near campus.

One time, I saw a "For Rent" sign on the lawn of a house right down the street from where I lived, so I walked up to the front door, and as I did, I saw some curtains close. I knocked on the door, long and hard, got no answer, and finally left. A light popped into my head, and I asked a white girl I knew in one of my classes to help me out. She went and knocked on the door, the door flew open, she asked about the apartment, and the landlady said, yes, we do have one available. My friend left, and I walked up again—and the curtains closed again, and no one answered the door.

We knew our white teammates never had to go through this, that the landlords opened the doors to them, and that the fraternity houses welcomed them. It was another example of how we were not being treated the same as them, even though we now made up 50 percent of the teams on campus. Things needed to change, we knew —and Harry came up with a strategy to get things to change and to make sure the large number of us were heard loud and clear: he proposed a peaceful protest by students and players at the first home football game of the 1967 season, against the University of Texas at El Paso.

That caused an absolute panic on campus and, as it turned out, all over the state. For one thing, word got out somehow that local Black Panthers and other groups planned to be more disruptive than Harry had planned. I don't know where that came from, but it scared everybody to death. The president of the school, Dr. Robert Clark, heard what Harry was saying and admitted that it all had to be changed—but he also was afraid of a race riot at the game no matter what he did. So he canceled the game outright. He got the school and the city to open up their housing policies, so it was a victory for our cause.

The loudest critic of the cancellation was none other than the actor elected governor the year before, Ronald Reagan, who called for Dr. Clark to resign and thought he should have just crushed the protest and played the game instead of submitting to a "policy of appeasement." Reagan had a lot of support, and a year later those supporters did their best to get the state to halt funding to San Jose State because of what we did in Mexico City, and the fact that Dr. Clark did not join in condemning us and calling us ungrateful Communist sympathizers. Yet at that same time, not long after Mexico City, the black San Jose State football players, angry at treatment by their white head coach, walked out of a practice and threatened to boycott a game against Brigham Young University, an ideal target for a boycott because the Mormon Church, which ran the school, had even stronger racist tendencies than San Jose State, or any other school. By then, the black athletes were used to making points.

But the cancellation of that football game put action behind the few scattered words about an Olympics protest. Some of those words had come from me, just before the controversy over the game stirred up. In early September, I ran in the World University Games in Tokyo, won the 200, and was second in the 100. When the meet was over, a reporter from Japan asked me directly about the possibility of a boycott. Other nations, of course, were more aware of the racial prejudices in the United States than we were in our own country, so it took someone from another country to bring the topic up. So I told him yes, it was being discussed and considered. Nobody had told me to talk about it; it was the truth, and I was not going to hide it.

That got around the world and back to America quickly. When I got home, I was swamped with requests to respond—actually, to take it back and apologize. I issued a statement through the athletic office. It wasn't what people wanted to hear. It read, in part:

> I have not made any precise open appeals to Black athletes to boycott the Games. I, as an individual, cannot tell another Black competitor that it is his duty to forget a goal he has sought for himself in this field. . . . My conception of the greatest amateur athletic achievement is to win a Gold medal in the Olympic Games. From now until the Games, the events which occur in our society will probably influence the decision of many Black athletes. Hopefully, a boycott of the Games never will be needed to bring about necessary changes in our country. But, if a boycott is deemed appropriate, then I believe most of the Black athletes will act in unison.

I didn't know that for certain, because a boycott was still only an idea at that point. We knew something had to be done because of the ways we were being treated in this country, the bombings, the assassinations, and the water hoses and police dogs in the South. We knew how we had been treated right there in San Jose when we tried to rent an apartment or eat in certain restaurants or tried to be students instead of just fast niggers running for school glory. We also knew that others around us were doing something, marching, wearing Afros and African clothes, giving black handshakes, and singing, "I'm black and I'm proud." But even then, as college students trying to survive day to day, we didn't know how instrumental we could be for change. The interview in Tokyo woke us all up. We were known around the world, and it hung on everything we did, because we were on the brink of a world record in every race we ran, and we were going to be interviewed every time we ran. When we spoke, it caused a commotion everywhere. So now, we ran fast so that we could be heard.

We didn't have real solutions then, just a lot of hypothetical solutions, and even then we weren't sure when to talk and how much, because we were thinking about getting the white man mad and not getting invited back to run. It became more obvious that reporters were asking us not just about the race we ran, but also about some incident involving race relations, hoping to get a reaction that would make a story for them. We began to really reach down for statements that would make our point but also be generic and not alienate us from the world. I don't know how my comments in Tokyo or my statements afterward sounded, but that's what was on my mind. I also knew I had grown a lot and become a lot more knowledgeable about the world since I'd arrived on campus in 1963, and since I first tried to make the Olympic team a year later. Now, people cared where I was and what I did, and I could communicate my thoughts.

All the talk about boycotting Mexico City, which had dated back to the discussions about protesting the football game, didn't become formalized until October 1967, when we finally officially met and put together what later was called the Olympic Project for Human Rights (OPHR). Again, human rights, not civil rights, nothing to do with the Panthers or Black Power—all humanity, even those who denied us ours. Harry led the meeting; Lee and I were there. It was the first meeting on the subject I had attended. Harry had talked to me throughout the years about social issues, but the stage was much bigger now. What he had said about the responsibility of the most visible athletes was coming to life in front of me. I was the big athlete on campus, the record breaker, the name known around the world—the Chairman of the Board, I called myself. If something as big as a boycott of the Olympic Games could start on that very campus within the circle of black athletes and I wasn't taking part in it, then their platform would have been very weak. Harry knew that even better than I did, because he's no dummy. My presence was going to make the boycott go, just as my presence at that march to San Francisco had given it momentum. When I realized that, I made a point to understand the platform so I could communicate it; Harry was going to be a spokesman, but the athletes would need to be eloquent, since there was no other academician involved in the leadership.

Some people had the impression that I was pushed into the movement. I wasn't pushed, and it wasn't a situation where someone made me get involved. It was more one of them making me understand the need for my involvement. I could have said, "No, I don't want to get involved; I want to go on and get me a job and make good money and not be bothered." But with how I had lived and what I had seen, knowing that I never wanted any other black person to live the way

I had lived, I had to get involved, and the way to get involved was to use the thing I knew how to do best.

In November, the athletes interested in the OPHR went to Los Angeles, to a national black youth conference, to discuss whether a boycott was viable. Martin Luther King was one of the speakers there; so was Huey Newton. Harry drove his pickup truck down from San Jose, and Lee, John, and I and our wives rode in the back of the pickup, all the way from the driveway of my house on North 11th Street to the meeting place in Los Angeles. We drove at night, and anyone who knows central California knows that in November it's not warm and balmy at night. But we had to go at night because we were scared that someone would try to kill us before we got there. So we froze in the back for 300 miles, and at a rest stop near LA, Harry came back and said, "Damn, it's cold back here. Why don't you guys turn on the fire?" He had gas stoves in the back that we could have lit. We didn't know.

At the meeting, I stayed in the back, just listening, once again. There were about 200 people there, and Harry and Dr. King and Huey Newton spoke, and John was so moved by it all that he spoke, too. I was fine with listening, because I kept thinking that with all that black talent and intelligence in one room, anybody with a big gun could have taken us all out in one shot.

Lew Alcindor was there, along with Mike Warren and the other brothers from the UCLA basketball team, which had just won the championship and was about to try for another. My name was nothing compared to his as far as nationwide fame was concerned. The funny thing is, while there never was a boycott, and I was the one standing in Mexico City taking the heat, Lew Alcindor and the other basketball players actually did boycott the Games. That's the only way I can look at it. Alcindor and those guys never intended to try out for the Olympic basketball team. Part of the reasoning was that had they been directly involved in an Olympics protest, it would have destroyed their careers—their pro careers would have been tampered with. Now, I don't believe that, because they were that good; imagine someone trying to stop Lew Alcindor from playing professional ball. I know it wasn't that he didn't want to get involved in the OPHR, but like me, he wasn't verbose enough to make the kind of statement John and I made. He just decided to stay home. I've always thought about that, why Lew and the others did not go. There were two sides to it. The OPHR was such a valid cause that they were afraid of what would happen if they supported it, so they used boycotting the Games as their way of supporting it. It allowed them to say they agreed with the cause, but staying home helped them as well.

It turned out right for them, because since then you've never heard of Alcindor and the basketball players going through what I went through. I don't have anything negative to say about them, and I'll never criticize them for not being there. To me, Lew Alcindor has always done and said just enough for people to remain positively interested in him. When he took the step to change his name to Kareem Abdul-Jabbar, denouncing his slave name, he shook a lot of people up, but he claimed that his religion backed him up, and no one could tell him he was wrong for adhering to his beliefs, as Muhammad Ali had. I thought no one could tell me I was wrong for my beliefs, and my statement had been silent—yet I doubt very seriously that there have ever been as many questions about Lew Alcindor changing his name as there were for me doing what I did on the victory stand. Again, I cannot criticize; he boycotted in support of the OPHR. The project was a double-edged sword for everybody.

Nobody, competing or not, boycotting or not, could relate to how much hate mail and death threats those of us most deeply involved were receiving. I started getting them as soon as my comments in Tokyo had gone public, and they really have not ever stopped, even when I stayed away from the spotlight. They came during the planning of the protest and during both sets of Olympic trials, and they continued in Mexico City. They came to San Jose State, eventually they came to my home in San Jose, and they went to my parents' house in Lemoore. Of course, there was never a return address. But we got called everything. We were racists ourselves; we needed to be shot, hung, sent back to Africa (sometimes, fake airplane tickets were included—that was a little amusing); we were never going to live to run in Mexico City; we had only 48 hours to live; and we were only niggers living in the white man's land. I hate that I can recite everything, but I remember it.

You knew what kind of intellects you were dealing with, and you knew there were going to be people who would object to anything you were trying to do. But it hurt to know there were human beings who would say those things to other innocent human beings. And it hurt to realize where society really placed you. When you were running fast and keeping your mouth shut, people loved you to death, I said to myself. Now that you're smart enough to realize what the system is like and that you have the power to bring about change, this is how they show their love.

I had to live in fear every time I went on the track, every time I went to class, every time I went home, hoping my house wouldn't be blown up or the windows shot up while my wife and son were inside. I would get knocks on the door and nobody would be there, or there would be a rap on the window or a phone call with no one at the other end, or someone shouting from the street. I wouldn't tell Denise, because she had enough on her mind, but I would quietly get up and take a walk outside to check. This went on for months.

People, including Coach Winter, would tell me to ignore the problem, because the ones sending the threats were just angry and they weren't trying to hurt anybody. I appreciated the advice, but it didn't help; it was easy for them to say, as the ones not being targeted. Harry would tell me to just protect myself, to never strike first but to strike back if they do and make sure they don't strike a second time. I was ready to do that, because I knew he was getting threats, too. In fact, I sent him most of the threats that came to me, and I never saw them again. I don't have many of the original threats and hate mail; I either sent them to Harry, or they were lost when a man I had loaned them to, during a previous film project about my life, had them repossessed from the storage facility they were in. I don't know what ever happened to them; if I had known then I would be writing a book, I would have saved all of them to show off here. But I don't have to see them to remember them. Harry, John, Lee, and a few others were the only ones I could talk to about them. For the most part, I was on my own.

But we continued to meet. Because of the New York Athletic Club's exclusionary, racist practices, we staged a boycott at their meet at Madison Square Garden that nearly shut down the event. Even the Soviet athletes refused to attend once we informed them of what we were doing and the reason we did it. Only a couple of black athletes attended, and the few fans who showed up didn't know how to react to them. That only increased the hate toward us, but it achieved results. Not long after that, the International Olympic Committee changed its mind about allowing South Africa into the 1968 Games.

The black athletes competed in the first Olympic trials in Los Angeles, which were kind of a diversion by the United State Olympic Committee to make sure the real trials in Lake Tahoe were not disrupted by a protest or a bunch of controversy. The officials put it out that the trials were in Tahoe to prepare us for the altitude in Mexico City, but that wasn't the only reason. We met in Tahoe as well, once the team was selected, and by then the USOC in their negativity and stupidity was doing everything they could think of to stop any boycott. They spread a rumor that we were sending threatening letters to all the black athletes to get them to agree to a boycott. The truth was, we were the ones getting letters from the USOC, saying that if anyone embarrasses, or thinks about embarrassing, the United States in Mexico City, he (it was directed at the men) would be immediately sent home—and that if anyone even talked about a boycott before the Games, we would be kicked off the team and not even be allowed to go.

That was undoubtedly an Avery Brundage production, since he was behind just about every institution in the sports hierarchy we were fighting against. He was an American, but he wasn't in charge of the USOC; he headed the entire IOC. I don't think I ever knowingly had direct contact with him. As far as I was concerned, Avery Brundage was just another racist white man. Nothing I heard ever changed my mind about it—the bald head, the glasses, the mumbling about us "boys," the fact that the club he belonged to in San Diego kept black folks out of it just the way the NYAC did. He thought white was it. Harry Edwards has called him "our version of Bull Connor." I say he was our Hitler. This is a man who called Jesse Owens, an acknowledged American hero who had beaten the real Hitler 30 years earlier, "a fine boy"—and then sent Owens to us in Mexico City, to see what we were up to and then to talk some sense into us after the victory stand. This is a man who defended his position against our proposed protest by saying that politics did not belong in the Olympics, no matter how many flags he saw flying and national anthems he heard playing. He thought he could just ignore the politics of it when it did not suit him, and get everyone to believe him just because he said so.

A lot of the athletes directed their rage at Brundage; in Mexico City some of them vowed not to shake hands with him when he awarded them their medals. But he meant nothing to me; just to support my teammates, I briefly thought about wearing the black gloves when I shook his hand on the stand. The funny thing was that Avery Brundage did not award John and me our medals; the honor was passed on to someone else, which tells you that they suspected something was up. As for his threats while we were in Tahoe, we replied with a letter of our own, telling them that they, in reality, were threatening us, and that they didn't have any proof that we were even discussing a boycott.

That statement was completely true, because the final decision to boycott or not did not come until we met in Denver after the trials in Lake Tahoe, when we were to be measured for our uniforms and make final arrangements for Mexico City. The meeting was very organized and very well run and moderated by Ralph Boston, the long jumper and sprinter who was a gold medalist from 1964. Harry was not there; John, Lee, and I were there, but not to lead, just to participate like everybody else. We discussed everything that had gone on in the past year and a half, and we found out what everybody knew about the Olympic Project for Human Rights and what they didn't know. This is when we decided that we would not boycott as a group, but that each athlete would do what he individually felt was necessary in the fight.

We came to this conclusion because there were so many brothers who decided they had too much on the line, and so many others who really couldn't make up their mind what they thought was the right thing to do. Some of them, including two of our best sprinters, Charlie Greene and Mel Pender, said they could not boycott because they were in the military—in fact, were running under the military's banner, on their money and support—and they feared being court-martialed or dishonorably discharged for committing an un-American act. I wasn't in the army, but I was still in ROTC trying to become a second lieutenant just in case they tried to send me to Vietnam, and even though they technically couldn't have court-martialed me, they could have pushed it to the brink. But that was those athletes' decision.

A lot of the other younger brothers were worried about their professional sports contracts—much like Lew Alcindor and the basketball players—and one track athlete had already signed a pro football contract. Some had other business interests they wanted to start or continue after the Olympics. And a lot of them were expecting to get endorsements from their Olympic participation, and they didn't want any protest to spoil their chance at the almighty dollar. From the beginning, Jimmie Hines, who went on to set the 100-meter world record in Mexico City, wanted nothing to do with it. To this day he denounces the whole thing, says that I did what I did without the input of the rest of the team—which is what we had decided to do in that meeting—and that I cost him money, me individually, by association. Every once in a while, I see an interview with him where he blames me for not becoming a superstar after Mexico City. Honestly, I don't have time for that lack of intellect. If he thinks that John Carlos and Tommie Smith messed his career up, then he didn't have one anyway. Jimmie Hines has always been like that, and he's not going to change. He has his own business and takes young kids places and helps them out, and that's great, but I wish he'd grow up and stop thinking that I ruined his future. He doesn't even have the intelligence to understand that it was the white man and the system he created that controls his money, not Tommie Smith.

Then there were the athletes in the South who couldn't understand how these guys on the West Coast thought they could pull something like this off. Charlie Scott, the basketball player from the University of North Carolina, was the first black player ever at that school, and he believed that if he had ever talked about the OPHR, he would have been thrown off the team, and probably lynched. He wasn't there for protest, he was there to play basketball and get an education, so he wasn't going to say anything. To me, that sounds like prison.

Last, some did not want to do anything because they did not believe there was anything wrong. That's what I call stupid. But overall, I was proud of the men at that meeting. There was more to the proposed Olympic boycott than black athletes jumping up and making problems; we were a thinking team. Most people on the team did want to know what it was about. Some of them were real young—the youngest was a high jumper named Reynaldo Brown who was 18—and even they were listening and speaking their minds. Reynaldo did not want to risk his future and potentially lose money; I gave him five dollars to go get a haircut and look good in his uniform. Still, I couldn't tell them how their minds should lead them. All in all, almost everybody paid attention, some understood—but only a few did something. Those who did gave up part of their lives to make this gesture, so we could do some good, and so we would not second-guess ourselves later and say, "Maybe I should have." We did what we did, and it has held up for so long because we were the first, and because we knew what it might mean to our lives.

Sitting now in retrospect, I don't think it could have happened better any other way. I was happy the black athletes chose to compete. If they had chosen to boycott, I would have gone with the masses. But the way it turned out worked, because in reality I was the cause of it happening—me, Lee, John, Harry Edwards, we were the hub of that wheel, and a lot of the athletes didn't even want to be any of the spokes; they thought they might be crushed once that wheel started rolling. Nobody that wasn't supposed to be in the hub was in the hub. We still involved as many black athletes as we could, and plenty of the white athletes as well. In the final analysis, the Olympic Project for Human Rights succeeded.

Once we got to Mexico City, the athletes met one more time. Someone who was not there at any meetings, or anything else, was significant: Harry Edwards. He took someone's advice not to come because his life was in danger. We didn't even need him in Mexico City to speak for us—he just could have been there physically with us. This was a bigger, more important gathering than the ones we had in San Jose, in Lake Tahoe, in Denver, any of them. If nothing else, anyone who believes Harry was the instrument that steered us onto the victory stand is wrong.

His presence would have been felt when we met, two different times, with a figure no one had anticipated having an impact there: Jesse Owens, who was working for the USOC as what they called an "athlete's representative." That was the role he played when he spoke to the entire United States team before the Games began. I was at the edge of my seat as he talked about 1936 and how his mouth had been so dry before his races he was spitting cotton, and that his proudest moment was when he had stood for the national anthem, because it represented freedom. That made me relax; I was there because I believed the exact same thing, and I was feeling the same thing. I felt as if my daddy would have made that kind of speech to me.

But then, Jesse attended our meeting the day after John and I were on the victory stand, a meeting to which all the athletes were invited but which ended being almost all black in attendance, except for Harold Connolly, the hammer thrower and my roommate in the Olympic Village, and the members of the U.S. rowing team, all from Harvard, who later were threatened with expulsion just for voicing support for us. We knew why Jesse was there, and we were right: not only did he try to tell the white athletes to leave so he could talk to us alone—a move we all rejected—but he also tried to get information out of us about whether the black athletes had any other protest plans, to take back to the USOC. We did not tell him anything. He got really upset, and he started crying and asking, "How can you do this? I'm the person who's responsible for you being here now. How can you do this to another black brother?" We applauded him and tried to treat him with respect, but we tore him down verbally after he left. The whole experience hurt him badly, which he made clear in his later books. Years later, I thought about the talks he had both times; I got his address in Arizona from a friend who knew him, and I wrote him a letter to tell him the pride I had in him and what he represented, and to thank him for being who he was. I don't know if he ever received the letter; three weeks later, he died.

Nothing Jesse Owens said, nothing Harry Edwards could have said, could have changed what I faced once the competition in Mexico City began. The weight was all on me now. There was no way I could lose. If I had lost, I would have lost everything, and the whole year and a half that we had talked would have been in vain because I wouldn't have been able to do what I did. I think that if the positions had been reversed, if John had won the gold medal and I had finished third, with our personalities, the result and the aftermath wouldn't have been a lot different—he would have done a lot of talking, and that's what he did anyway. But without finishing first, I had no way of saying what I meant so that people would understand; no one would have listened, and I would have been relegated to oblivion. No, it could have been worse: I would have been laughed at, told, "See, nigger, you went and didn't do anything; you should have kept your black mouth shut."

No one will ever know what anyone else would have done as a protest, if someone else had decided to act on the victory stand first. What Smith and Carlos did was so strong that no one else could top it. We put out a message to be seen, not heard. We said nothing, but as they say, a picture is worth a thousand words, except that in this case it was a thousand things to think about. The gloves were something to think about; the socks were something to think about. It was the silent gesture heard 'round the world. Everyone has a different interpretation of it, and I get asked about it all the time. I'm writing this book to clear it up once and for all. You don't have to ask me anymore.

Avery Brundage threatened to kick the whole Olympic team out if anyone else did what we did, but what he didn't realize was that no one else had to do it. It was done; the whole world got the idea, period. That's why Lee got in so much trouble, because when he won his gold medal two days later, the day we were told to leave, people back in San Jose thought he should have stuck his hand to the sky or turned his back or not shown up or something. Lee didn't have to do anything; we had made our stand, and it couldn't have been portrayed any stronger than that. I really pity Lee, because when he got back to San Jose, people jumped on him—"Why didn't you do anything?" Wait a minute, Lee said, I wore my tam on the stand, and I took my tam off when the national anthem was playing indicating I respected the flag, and I had two other dudes with me up there, from the East Coast, and they didn't understand things the way we did. I guess that's why I like Lee so much now; he stood up under the pressure, I mean stood under it, and though he didn't have a chance to do what John Carlos and Tommie Smith did, he stood behind us with his life. You talk about a friend—there aren't many others like

Lee. And I know Lee had hard times after that, the same as if he had raised his fist on the stand himself.

Lee is working on a book to tell his story at the same time I am. Harry has his story, and John has his story, and they've told theirs. Mine happens to be the story of the gold medalist in all of this, and there are things I did in this that they could not have, and things I can say about this that no one else can. I'm not belittling what they wrote; it's that this is my story. I respect them, just as I hope they respect me and what I say.

This entire effort is important to the understanding of the man on the victory stand that night in Mexico City—why he was there, why he is where he is now, and where people who saw the silent gesture think he should be. Where I went after stepping down from the stand, then, should not be a surprise to anyone.

Paying the Price

9

THE FIRST QUESTION out of most people's mouths to me, when they talk about Mexico City, is: "How did you feel when they took your medal?" I can't answer it, because John Carlos and I were not stupid enough to listen to the USOC, travel over to their office, and hand over those medals. They did ask for them, the next day, but of course we did not go, and each of us has his medal at this very moment.

The next question usually is: "How did it feel when they threw you out of the Olympic Village?" Well, technically, that didn't happen, either. The day after the silent protest, we moved out of the Village and into the El Diplomatico Hotel, where our wives were staying. We had planned to get out of the Village after our races anyway; we had already moved our stuff out the day of the 200-meter final. Had we still been entered in any other races, the rules said that we had to stay in the Village, and we didn't want to make our race illegal by not staying in the Village. We were covering every possible angle. Once our races were done, we could move out. The U.S. team did not need Carlos in the 4-by-100 relay because he was the fifth-fastest guy there, and they did not need me in the 4-by-400 relay. So we were finished. I came back to my room in the Village the next day, Thursday, picked up my last few things, a jockstrap, uniform, shoes, bags—and on the way out, the press was waiting. They got me. There's a picture of me from that day that went around the world, of me coming out of the village in a gray shirt and carrying that one bag.

The interview that most people remember, the one with Howard Cosell on ABC, took place immediately after the protest; that was when I explained exactly what the symbols on the victory stand meant. I told him the following.

My raised right hand stood for the power in black America. Carlos's left hand stood for the unity of black America. Together, they formed an arch of unity and power. The black scarf around my neck stood for black pride. The black socks with no shoes stood for black poverty in racist America. The totality of our effort was the regaining of black dignity.

The interview that very few in the United States have seen took place on Thursday; it was done by the BBC at the hotel. I wish I knew where the tape of that interview ended up; it has circulated over the years from my first wife, to my second wife, to a group of people who had planned to do a movie about me, and it's disappeared since then. What I remember most is that when they called me, I told them I didn't want to do it, that I was tired, and that if they gave me a thousand dollars I'd do it—just drawing a phenomenal sum out of my head, knowing it wasn't going to happen. They said, "Okay." Shocked, I said, "Okay what?" "Okay," they said, "we'll give you $1,000 for an exclusive."

John and I were in adjoining rooms with a door in between, and we got together and talked about it—and said yes. While we were waiting for the BBC people to come to the hotel, the phone rang; it was the USOC, asking us to come back to the Village to meet with them. The more I think about this now, the more I wish I had gone, to see what they would have done. But I said no, we were finished, we had no more races to run, and my leg was still hurting. They were adamant, so I passed the phone to John. All I heard was "motherfuck" this and "motherfuck" that, and then he hung up. So I figured that was the last time we'd be talking to them.

When the phone rang again, I thought it was the USOC again—but it was the BBC. We went downstairs, and the BBC had it all set up in a nice room, but a dark one. They talked to us for 20 or 25 minutes, gave us the money, and they were done. I was almost scared to take it. Twenty-five minutes and $1,000—that would pay rent for five months, buy Similac, and put gas in my car. We were happy. Then, when we got back upstairs, the BBC called again, asking if they could do the interview over again because something didn't take the first time. For that $1,000, it wasn't too much to ask from us.

The next day, Friday, was the day the USOC officially took our visas away and told us we had to be out of Mexico within 48 hours.

That afternoon, we went to the stadium, and Cosell interviewed me again, in the press box. While we were talking, the stadium got real quiet. I knew they couldn't hear my answers to Howard, so I looked up, and Bob Beamon was on the runway, rocking, ready to take off. We both stopped to watch, and as he took off, I said, "Oh my God, the man is flying." When he hit the board, it was like he was free, and he just kept going and going; when he landed, I jumped up because I knew it was a great leap. I still get chills thinking about that scene—him falling to the track on his knees, crying, holding on to Ralph Boston, our teammate, and the officials just looking at the pit, trying to calculate the distance and finally having to get a steel measuring tape, because their automatic viewer only registered up to 28 feet. When they announced "8.90 meters," no one was really sure what it meant, but they knew it was longer than anyone had ever gone. It was 29 feet 2½ inches. On the victory stand, Bob Beamon took off his shoes and rolled up the legs of his warm-up pants as a show of support for us, and Ralph Boston, who won the bronze, stood barefoot.

That leap was the last record from 1968 to fall. The track and field team set 10 world records, with the black men and women setting seven of them. It was the strongest Olympic team ever sent. It was so strong, two world-record holders did not even run in their events; I did not run in the 400, and Carlos did not run in the 100. But mention '68 to anyone who watched, and there's one thing they remember.

They don't even remember Lee Evans' record in the 400 meters on the same day we were told to leave and the same day Bob Beamon made his record jump, or Lee's performance with the 4-by-400 relay team that set another world record. Some people remember them on the victory stand, because they didn't make a silent protest the way John and I did—because, as I said, it already was done, and nobody else had to do it. They also don't remember that John and I had to talk Lee into not going home himself, once he heard that we were being sent home. John and I and Coach Winter had to calm Lee down, make sure he stayed, and make sure he concentrated on winning.

As we prepared to return from Mexico City, I had a good idea about the reception we were going to get back in the United States. There weren't many people who even believed in the concept of what we did, much less what we did itself. What bothered people was where it was done, how it was done, and most important, who it was done by—young dummies, black athletes who had not graduated from college. I was coming back to finish college and to support my wife and my son. Actually, Denise was going to support us, because I couldn't work; I had to start right back up and get my teaching certificate. Besides, at that point I didn't have had a job to return to.

Two weeks before the Games, when it was obvious how involved I was in the Olympic Project for Human Rights—even though no one knew exactly what anyone would do—I had been fired by North American Pontiac, down the street from our house in San Jose. The staff had told me that they didn't like the idea that I might do something embarrassing or insulting at the Games, and that if I was going to do anything like that then I shouldn't bother coming back there when the Games were over. I had begun to be afraid for my life while working there, so in that sense it wasn't bad for me to be let go.

The staff was really happy with me before that, though; they had been the ones hanging banners on the front of the dealership, telling customers to come inside and meet the future Olympian. I was washing the new cars out in the back, but when a customer came in wanting to meet me, I changed out of those wet, soapy work clothes and into a jacket and tie and came to the front. Little Johnny and Mary and Susie came in many times to see Tommie Smith, and I'd tell them, "Okay, kids, run fast like me and tell your dad to buy you track shoes." As soon as I was finished, I had to go back outside and do those wheels. I even had people buying cars from that place because of me; people came in there because of me. Lee Evans and Martin McGrady, a heavy-duty quarter-miler and half-miler on the indoor circuit, both bought their first cars at that place, a couple of GTOs, through me. I never got a commission, though, because I didn't have a dealer's license. I wasn't even allowed to drive the cars—although I did, because I had access out back to the keys; I would take this black 1966 Chevelle and sit way down in the seat. It was the only way I could get to and from work. They never noticed because I was so far down their chain; if I had ever been pulled over by the police, I would have gone to jail. That was how I lived: a world record holder, busy pleasing people at my own expense, hoping no one would notice that the car I was driving to and from work so I could feed my family didn't belong to me.

And that was before Mexico City. Nobody was lining up to help Tommie Smith once I got back. I knew there would be opposition when I landed back in the United States; I just didn't know how strong. And once I found out how strong and I started calling for help, all I got was toxic fumes.

We left Mexico City on Sunday and flew into Los Angeles, and as we were landing I looked out of the window and I saw all the cameras and lights. Denise and I both wondered, what's going on out there? We didn't realize it was for us until we got off the plane. The long flight from Mexico City had kind of calmed me down, but when I saw all of that, I quickly got mad again. It started as soon as we got off the plane: "Are you Tommie Smith? What did you mean by the fist in the air? Are you a racist? What are you going to do now? Nobody likes you." What am I supposed to say to all that? "Yeah, I'm a racist, I'm a Black Panther. Now give me some money so I can feed my son." They might have wanted to hear about what a racist I am, but they didn't want to hear about me needing to feed my 21-year-old wife and my six-month-old son.

That was just the beginning. When our connecting flight landed in San Jose, there was nobody to meet us at the airport, no security, nothing. I thought we might have gotten a little protection there. The newspaper guys had those big old cameras, big enough to knock you down if they hit you, and they knocked our wives around and almost beat them down to the ground trying to get to us. The only friendly face we saw was a writer for the black newspaper in San Francisco, Huel Washington, who got us into his car and drove us home.

It was obvious as soon as we returned to campus that it was going to turn its back on us. Everybody wanted to hear what we had to say, of course, and we spoke at a rally on campus, set up by the black student union, a few days after coming back. But the attitude that made John and me believe for decades later that we would never be welcomed back warmly or with honor was already in place. The one important exception was Dr. Robert Clark, the president, who had listened to Harry Edwards the year before and helped end the segregation in campus housing. On the day that John and I were ordered to leave Mexico City, he had issued a statement.

> We at San Jose State College are proud of the achievements of Tommie Smith and John Carlos in the Olympic Games. All Americans should be proud of their achievements.
>
> In addition to the pride in the accomplishments of these athletes, I think we all should question the ambiguous moralistic posturing of the American Olympic Committee when they condemn our athletes after the U.S. Olympic Team refuses to dip the American flag during the opening Games ceremonies when all other nations do so in respect to the host nation.
>
> Millions of Americans must have seen Tommie Smith on television, as I did, explaining the symbolism of his and John Carlos's gestures, which have caused their expulsion from the Olympics. His explanation was calm and rational; his sincerity unquestioned. The message he conveyed should be of real concern to all Americans.
>
> I regret that our treatment of our Black athletes has been such to prompt them to feel they must use the Olympic Games to communicate their real concern for the conditions of Blacks in America. Our own minority people should be able to be heard here at home, rather than needing an international setting to gain attention for their cause.
>
> I hope that their gesture will be interpreted properly. They do not return home in disgrace, but as the honorable young men they are, dedicated to the cause of justice for the Black people in our society.

I'm sure Dr. Clark had some thoughts about how and where it had been done, but he chose to dwell on the positive and leave it to others to speak negatively. That's why he was criticized, because he saw only the positive. He took a lot of heat. Alumni claimed that they would stop contributing to the school and said they were ashamed to be associated with him. Others demanded that he resign or be fired and promised to vote against an initiative that would have given $15 million of state money to fix up the campus. One writer said he hoped Dr. Clark would "contract a long-term cancer very soon." He was vilified for supporting us "niggers," "boys," "riffraff," "Communists," and "baboons." The hatred came from all over California—

including Lemoore—and from as far away as South Carolina. It's all in a collection of Dr. Clark's papers at the Martin Luther King Library at San Jose State.

I missed a few days of classes after returning to campus, but taking time off, like a semester, was out of the question. When I did have to take classes, I took them at night, because those who hated me, what I had done, and what I had stood for had too much of a chance to get me during the day. I was not going to give anybody that opportunity. One class, meanwhile, I never had to worry about again; I was asked to leave the ROTC program, and I was given an honorable discharge.

I was not about to drop out of San Jose State. If I had to, I would have gone to a junior college. I would have done something to finish school, as far as I had gotten by then; I just know I didn't want to go back to Lemoore and pick cotton, chop cotton, and cut grapes. That's what they expected from me. When I did go back there, it was to teach.

I taught during that final semester because of a stipulation at the time that came with receiving a social sciences degree at a California state college. Anybody becoming a teacher in the state had to be a student teacher for one semester. The student had the choice of assignments, and I chose Central Union Elementary School in Lemoore, the school I graduated from, the school whose floors my father had cleaned and waxed and whose lawns he had cut for so many years. I know that they thought I would be back cleaning classrooms just like my father; in fact, some of the teachers, when they saw me in the hallways that semester, asked me if I had come back to work for Mr. Smith the way I used to. No, I told them, I'm a teacher here. It blew their minds. Look, they said, Mr. Smith's boy is back, with a new walk, a new talk, and an education. And they appreciated it; Central Union was so short on teachers that I got a classroom of my own and didn't have to assist anybody. I did my semester, and it was the last requirement for my degree. But I never walked down the aisle in a cap and gown to receive it; there were no midyear graduation ceremonies back then, and by the time graduation time in 1969 came around, I was already in Cincinnati playing professional football. They mailed me my degree.

It was a very scary year. I had no money, period. The year before I went to Mexico City, when I was training for the Olympics and working, I had bought the house that Denise and I were renting, for $150 a month, on North 11th Street in San Jose. The man who had owned the house, a very nice old man who lived on the other side of town, decided that he didn't have a need for it any more and that his children didn't want it, so he'd sell it to us for $35,000. The man at Bank of America knew my name and decided that he was all right with what I was doing and why. He said that even though we did not have any collateral, he agreed that it was a good property at a good price and gave us the loan. It was a blessing. But when I got back from Mexico City without a job, I still had house payments to make and a baby to feed. I swept up streets, did anything I could to stay alive, and I borrowed on the house and got myself in over my head.

I knew already that what Harry Edwards had said was true: I could not eat speed. I could not have made a living running track; the USOC had banned me from Olympic, international, and national competition. Coach Winter had tried to enter me and Carlos, who at least could still run for San Jose State, in meets in Canada, but nothing ever came of it. Even if I could have been allowed to run, I could not have made enough to live in the system as it operated at the time, whether meet organizers offered per diems or, if they wanted you badly enough, gave money under the table. Track and field at the highest level has been professional for years, with athletes able to get appearance money and endorsements in the millions. Back then, if you got enough to pay rent once in a while or to put in the bank, and got some shoes or T-shirts from a shoe company, you were lucky. I wore Adidas while I was at San Jose State and set most of my world records wearing their shoe, but I got almost nothing from them for doing it. My college friend Art Simburg helped get a deal with Puma, which is the shoe I wore in Mexico City, and which was the shoe that sat next to me in my stocking feet on the victory stand. But I did not get much from them either, not until years later when Puma tried to market a shoe around me, called the TS 19.8, which was just a poorly made shoe that never sold well. I had to write to Puma years later, while I was coaching at Oberlin College, and ask whether I was owed any royalties from that shoe; I was sent about $700, and that was it.

Besides, if you were black, you were not getting paid as much for competition as the white stars were, including the other 1968 Olympians, like Bob Seagren, the pole-vault gold medalist. We were getting pennies or nothing compared to them. Maybe I didn't have the right representation, but it was more likely I wasn't the right color; either way, I missed that boat.

After the silent protest, though, there was never a chance that I would earn anything from track and field. Just as important, I never would know how fast I could have become. I was 24 years old in Mexico City, and I was running 28 miles an hour then. I would have just turned 28 by the time of the 1972 Olympics in Munich, and everyone has seen what runners like Carl Lewis and Michael Johnson have done as they have matured. I knew kinesiology and biology, I knew what hard work was, and I knew what it took to be the greatest—the greatest I could be, not the greatest I could be according to someone else. I also had that incentive my father had given me all those years ago, that if I ever stopped winning, I would be back in the grape fields with my brothers and sisters the next day. I had run 19.8 in the 200 in 1968, and I know I could have eventually run an 18.7. No one has ever broken 19 seconds in the 200, but I know I could have done it back then had I continued to run.

Yet with all the components of the system lined up against me, punishing me for the sin I committed against their values and beliefs, the treatment I received from black folks hurt even worse. I was looking up to them for support, but I found out that there were more blacks than whites who didn't want anything to do with me.

I had already found out what the priorities of my own Olympic teammates had been when we discussed whether to boycott or make some sort of statement in our meeting in Denver before the Games, and I have seen and heard many of those teammates dissociate themselves from John and me ever since. I also was on hand to see America embrace another big, strong black athletic hero a few days after it condemned us on the victory stand. To this day, all I can do is laugh when I think of George Foreman; I laugh whenever anybody asks me about him and his little flag-waving act in Mexico City a few days after the silent protest.

Not long ago, a radio station asked me to come on the air for an interview, right after George Foreman had done one. I went on, and I was very respectful to George when I talked about him. The interviewers kept avoiding asking a direct question about him, beating around the bush, and I finally said, "What you really want to know is how I feel about George Foreman's flag. George Foreman did what he felt was necessary. George Foreman had pressures on him that made mine look even bigger." By that, I mean that George succumbed to the pressure put on him by the system, and if he succumbed, I must have been under even greater pressure, and I managed to withstand it.

But George never had a chance to resist that pressure. It's not his fault. He was an easy guy to convince about their side of it, because he wasn't smart enough to understand the obvious. He was just a young kid trying to make it, 19 years old, five years younger than I was, uneducated, in and out of jail, a thug and a thief. He thought that by allowing him to fight for his country at the Olympics, America had done him a favor. He felt he had to thank America. At least that's how he put it, and keeps on putting it. His coach at the Olympics, Pappy Gault, was one of those Jesse Owens types, from the old school, a big believer in the idea that we have to prove to the white man that we're worthy of him before we can get that money from him. So while we were all talking about using the Olympic stage to make a statement about the system, Pappy Gault was telling everybody that his fighters weren't going for any of "that demonstration stuff." And when George won his bout for the gold medal, Pappy stuck those two flags in his hands, and George paraded around the ring waving those flags, and America ate it up.

When I saw that, I was very bitter, very angry; I thought he was doing it to minimize the effect of what we had just done on the victory stand, which is what it did. But I don't even know if he knew it at the time. I believe he realized it later and came up with an alibi for what he did. When he is interviewed about it, he says that he didn't realize the magnitude of Smith and Carlos, and when he got back home, at every party he went to, there were Smith and Carlos on everyone's wall—not him, who knocked out a Russian for the gold medal, but Smith and Carlos. Now, he says, he has to live with seeing pictures of his dancing around with those flags, and everyone thinks he's a white-man lover.

It's a cute story, but the truth is that then and now, George Foreman has played every role they've wanted him to, including the big brute who was going to knock out Ali. And Ali just stepped all over him, didn't he? Boy, I just smiled during that fight. I didn't even hoorah, I just smiled. Ali whipped him so bad, I even felt sorry for him. Now you see him, and he still tells everybody he's the All-American story, rising from a criminal life to become heavyweight champion and then a millionaire selling grills. He did what Pappy Gault wanted, he did what white America wanted, he did what those people who persecuted Ali wanted, and now he sells himself as someone America can embrace and cuddle and love. That's a person with a weak mind. He's so nonchalant now about what he did, just the way Carlos is about letting me win that race. Carlos believes it, and George Foreman believes he didn't do anything averse, that he only did what his coach told him and what he thought everybody else did: bow to all four corners, and do it with your country's flag in your hand, and you'll get what you think you want.

Yet every time I hear him talk about 1968, he doesn't give any acknowledgment to the victory stand; he talks about how those young guys (again, he was younger than we were) were trying to do something and everybody understands that now, but back then he wasn't in a position like that, because all he wanted to do was box, and that's what he did, and he hit that Russian so hard he didn't know if it was the sixth round or the ninth round turned upside down. And he gets a big laugh. He's a big guy who intimidates people, and he disarms them with a funny phrase and gets them to tune in to him. What's not so funny is that he was in the same "position" I was. If that's his thought process, more power to him. Mine was the atrocities committed against us and the racist barrier that we had to break through, by militant reaction because civil action had not worked. I had a platform and I used it. He uses his platform to crack jokes and sell grills.

I've been asked many times how I feel about being a college coach while George Foreman is a millionaire on television. Who came out ahead? My answer is, I still have a mind, and I ask what sits on George's shoulders where his head is supposed to be. If he has anything in that head, I say, it's a lot of kitchen utensils.

Whether George had enough sense to mean it or not, what he did only hurt me when I returned from Mexico City. Every wall in black America didn't have that poster on it like he thinks; a lot of black people believed more in Big George and what he stood for than they did in what I took a stand for. What I did, did damage to them, the way Jimmie Hines tells everybody that I cost him a lot of money. The people that I had turned to for support left me with nothing.

That included other famous black athletes, including one for whom I had so much respect that I don't understand even now why he did what he did. I was drafted by the Los Angeles Rams in 1967, while I was still at San Jose State, and when I worked out for them, I thought that I impressed them enough that I might make the team, earn a few thousand dollars, and pay for my house. At that time, Jim Brown had an organization called the United Athletic Association —he was already retired then, and he was setting up his businesses, most of them aimed at helping young black brothers get some economic independence. This organization sought out young pro football players to represent as their agents. After I was drafted, he came to San Francisco and met me at a burger place, and we talked. I knew I wasn't going anywhere until after the Olympics, but I asked him about a loan, and he said, "No problem. If you're with us, we'll get 10 percent of your contract, and you're covered for the loan." His people drew up a $2,000 check for me, and I put it in the bank—I didn't spend it, because something told me to hold onto it and try to live off of what I was making, just in case.

I held onto it that entire time, until after I returned from the Games. I was supposed to have been contacted by UAA soon after, because camps were going to be taking place in February and March 1969, with training camp opening in June and July. I wanted to know how my contract with the Rams was coming, when was the next time we could meet, when and where I needed to report, everything. But I heard nothing. Finally, I called the UAA office in Los Angeles—I remember sitting in my kitchen on North 11th Street and making the call—and got Jim Brown on the phone. He was very vague. He did say that what I had done in Mexico City had made everything null and void. He also asked for his $2,000 back.

Here I was, 24 years old, without a job, without a degree yet, with a wife and an eight-month-old son, trying to finish school and get some sort of career started, and he asked for his money back. The great Jim Brown. I was very hurt, and I let him know how hurt I was and how disenchanted I was, and that what he had done and what he said was uncalled for, and I hung up on him. Denise called him back and kind of apologized to him, and told him his money would be in the mail the next day. It was, thankfully, because I hadn't spent it, and I paid it all back. But we needed that money.

I don't know if he got pressure from somebody, maybe the Rams, maybe the National Football League. He has never talked to me about it. I've met him a couple of times at different functions, particularly in southern California when I was at Santa Monica College. One time I remember very clearly was at a big fundraiser in Los Angeles. A number of big sports celebrities like Tom Lasorda had been invited. Jim Brown was at the head table, and he was introduced during the event, and he stood up and waved. I was sitting in the back, and when it was over, he walked through the ballroom, and there I was in front of him in broad daylight. I put out my hand to shake his, and he said to me, "Hey, man," and walked off.

I've tried to give him the benefit of the doubt and figure he just didn't recognize me, or that he just didn't connect me with the person that he did that to many years ago, or couldn't equate what happened then with what kind of person he represents himself to be now. Now, he's a very positive thinker who does a lot to help young black men out of trouble, off of drugs and out of gangs, straightening them out. He's all black now, wearing the African cap everywhere he goes. People now talk about Jim Brown this and Jim Brown that, on camera taking a stand and helping brothers out. That's not the Jim Brown I know, because that Jim Brown's mind wasn't on helping this young brother out. What he is to me is the guy who asked for his two grand back, money he had given me that I needed to stay solvent, because I had stood up on the victory stand.

That was the pattern that was developing, though. Two months after Mexico City, the San Jose chapter of the NAACP invited Julian

Bond to be the guest speaker at a big function they were putting on at the fairgrounds one night. They also asked me, John, Lee, and Ronnie Ray Smith to be on stage for the function, and we'd be given something for showing up. We thought they meant money, so we made sure we were on that stage, even though we didn't know exactly who Julian Bond was. Well, he stood up and made a speech about all the great things the NAACP was doing around the country, getting bills passed and getting things organized and showing the strength and togetherness of black people and the great accomplishments that can come of it. We listened, but we were thinking more about getting what we were promised and getting back to campus so we wouldn't miss class the next day.

He finished his speech by saying, "All you business entrepreneurs out there, we've got young men sitting up here who represented themselves as black men in the Olympic Games. I know they don't have jobs and they don't have money; three of them are married. You business people tonight, while I'm standing up here, come up here and give these young men your cards and give them a job, because they need them."

There had to have been 500 people in that audience at those fairgrounds. Did anybody come up there onto the stage? Not a single one. Julian Bond made a beautiful speech on our behalf, supporting and praising what we did, to a crowd that supposedly was interested in the betterment of black people. "Advancement" is in the organization's name. If we didn't have to be somewhere the next day, we'd still be sitting there waiting for someone to walk up to that stage. And the NAACP didn't give us anything for being there, as they had promised, so after the gas money we spent getting there, we left poorer than when we had shown up. We didn't get so much as a handshake when we left. I thought, "This is the NAACP?" I told Lee that this wasn't right, and he was kind of quiet, but I knew he was thinking the same thing.

Do you think I belong to the NAACP now? Think again.

I think I understand why black people treated me this way. I don't pat myself on the back for being on the victory stand, because I believe that anybody could have done it—but I also feel that everybody else would rather not do it, because they knew how it would affect them negatively, and they would hear and see how others might suffer because of them. But later, they reap the benefits of somebody else's sacrifice to break a racist law or to make a change in a racist system—when they get a job they wouldn't have gotten before, or live in a place they wouldn't have lived in before. I know it happens. I've seen it happen. Then they're thankful that someone else did it, someone they had no use for when he actually was making that sacrifice. That's a fact.

So nobody was helping; nobody was even calling. Jim Brown, the NAACP, even Harry Edwards had let me down on their promises to me; remember, Harry was going to set up my son and John's daughter for the sacrifices we made, and it never happened. Finally Denise, who hardly ever complained about what we were going through, said to me, "You're a proud man, but somebody's got to help us. I'm hungry, our son is hungry, he's nine months old and he's lost three pounds. We're behind on the house payments. We've got to do something to get some money." I didn't know what else to do; I could have gone out and started stealing, but I wasn't brought up that way. I want to cry sometimes thinking about what we went through—and that day in San Jose when they made plans to build the statue, I almost did break down when I was asked about it.

I decided that if one team, the Rams, wanted me to play football, then maybe another would, too. So while I was waiting around to hear from Jim Brown, I began checking into the possibilities. I contacted the Raiders up in Oakland, but I never go a response from Al Davis. I tried the San Francisco 49ers, but I never got anywhere with them either. It was Mexico City. Then a lawyer for the Olympic Project for Human Rights, who heard that I was trying to find a job, called a friend from his San Jose State days—Bill Walsh. This was long before he won three Super Bowls coaching the 49ers. Bill Walsh had coached at San Jose State when I was there, and he was now an assistant with the Cincinnati Bengals, working for Paul Brown. The OPHR lawyer told Bill Walsh about me, the guy from Mexico City, and Bill told him to get me to Cincinnati to meet Brown. I warmed up on San Jose State's field a little, caught a few passes to get used to it again. They filmed it to show that I had the ability to do it; I still have that film.

I got to Cincinnati and walked into Brown's office, wearing an Afro and a Fu Manchu mustache. Walsh was in the office as well. Paul Brown asked me if I wanted to be there. I said yes, and he asked me why. "I need a job," I said. "I've got a wife and son, and I need money." They scheduled me to go out to the field and catch some passes. I couldn't sleep that night; all I could think about was that I was going to make $20,000, I was going to be rich, I was going to put tires on the car and buy my wife a dress. The next day, I caught a few passes, ran some curls and out patterns, and a few times they threw it long, and I outran the ball. The quarterback took a seven-step drop, and by the time he took that seventh step, I was 80 yards downfield. The ball fell short by about 10 yards—thank the Lord. My leg was completely healed and it felt good. I had all my speed. I thought I looked pretty good.

I wasn't good enough to get that $20,000 contract, but they invited me to training camp and said that if I made the team, I would be paid $300 a week to be on the taxi squad, the scout team that did not dress for the game. If I was put on the active roster for a game, I would make $900 that week. I got no bonus. I found out after I got there that there were guys on the team, like the quarterbacks, Greg Cook and Ken Andersen, who made $150,000 a year. We all had to go down to a hotel downtown to pick up our checks every week because they weren't mailed home back then, and I knew there were guys picking up $1,500 a week or more. I was making $1,200 a month. It was outrageously unfair, I thought. But no one was rushing up to me offering to help me out.

I had not played football since high school; I never went out for the team at San Jose State. Harry Edwards had always said that we have to be captain of our own ship. So I packed our belongings into my '66 Chevy Nova and drove from California to Ohio. We didn't have enough money to fly, but I didn't want Denise and Kevin, who was 10 months old by then, to be in a car all that time, so I flew them out after I got there. The next year, though, we all drove out in that car. I had to do it. I had lived almost my whole life in California, but I had to leave the state to find a job. But even that would not have happened if not for Bill Walsh taking a chance on me, and Paul Brown continuing to give opportunities to black ballplayers based on their talent and character, which he had done long before other pro football teams had the idea.

I was reminded right away how brutal the game of football can be, and saw how much more it was when your job and your life were on the line. My first touchdown with Cincinnati came in a scrimmage during training camp. My roommate in camp was a defensive back named John Gillery, and we were both trying to make the team. He was defending me in the scrimmage, and there was a long pass to me down the sidelines. I was jetting, high-kneeing it, and I caught the ball. He hit me about 10 times trying to knock the ball loose. The ball was his ticket to stay on the team if he knocked it away, and his ticket home if he couldn't. Sure enough, a few days later, there was a knock on the door, and the man said, "Gillery, Coach wants to see you." And that was it.

So I found out fast that you had to fight to keep your job, and I had to keep this job, even as little as I was making. I got into maybe seven games in two and a half years with the Bengals, and I kept getting $900 when I played, and $300 to get knocked around in practice. So when I played for the scout team, which pretended to be the opponents against the regular players, I hurt some people. I had liked to hit people when I played in high school so that I wouldn't be the one getting hit. In fact, on the opening kickoff of my very first game with the Bengals—against the Buffalo Bills and a rookie named O. J. Simpson whom I had run track against out West—I got a 15-yard penalty. I was on the kickoff coverage team, on the outside to keep the guy returning the ball from going that way. Of course, they had a guy trying to block for him, and his job was to try to knock me out. So he hit me, and I wasn't used to being hit. I hit him back, and he hit me, and I said, "Damn, this is a fight." So I drew my arm back to hit him again, and out of the corner of my eye I saw that orange flag. When I went to the sidelines, I figured Paul Brown wasn't going to put me back in, but I guess he liked my tenacity. I didn't play much, and I didn't get many passes thrown to me, but I stayed for two full seasons and made it to training camp for a third.

If anybody on the Bengals or in Cincinnati was upset at me because of Mexico City, I never noticed. I suppose I was so immersed in trying to make the team that it didn't matter what they thought. I don't think the other players really knew. I hung out with white guys on the team also, like Chip Myers, Bob Trumpy, and Bill Bergey, and they never said anything about it. While I was there and for 30 years after I left, I never thought about whether they knew. I think more knew than didn't know, but I don't know if they were scared to talk to me about it or not. As for the fans, I vividly remember one hate letter I received in my first year. I took it out of my mailbox, I read it, and it scared the shit out of me. It was from Akron, and it read, "We know who you are, we know where you are, you will not play football for the Cincinnati Bengals." It mentioned death a couple of times and had "nigger" all over the place. I was shaking all over the place. I was in Ohio, out there in the open practicing on this huge field, surrounded by all this lush greenery. A guy could hide out there and get me with a single shot. I showed the letter to Bill Walsh, and he turned all kinds of colors. He gave it to Paul Brown, and he just told me, "Don't worry about it," took the letter, and kept it. I think of how scared I was then, and I get scared now.

I drove to Cincinnati by myself for the third season there in 1971; Denise decided to stay home and find a job. She had to; I wasn't making any money playing. Then I didn't make the team; I went through summer camp, and at the end, I got a call from Bill Walsh saying that I had been cut. I cried. He made a call to a team in Canada, the Hamilton Tiger-Cats, and suggested that I try there. I stayed for a few months but didn't play one lick, and they sent me home with $2,000, promising they would bring me back the following year. I haven't heard anything from them since. That was the end of my football career. I contacted the NCAA to ask if I could participate in track and field again, and they told me that I was now a professional athlete. I pointed out that I was not a professional in that sport, and they told me that it didn't matter. Several years later, the NCAA changed that rule, and track athletes like Willie Gault and Renaldo Nehemiah were able to play pro football and still compete in amateur competition on the track—but all the calling and petitioning I did couldn't change it fast enough for me.

Not long after my football career ended, so did my marriage to Denise. Being with me had brought all the pressures that I had to endure onto her. We both did things we shouldn't have done. It didn't have to end the way it did, but it was better for the both of us. It was a clean divorce. I moved out of our house—we had finally moved out of 55 North 11th Street and up to San Francisco—and moved in with Lee Evans. Lee welcomed me in, and then told me how much was my share of the rent.

It hurt to have to split with Denise and deal with what the victory stand had done to us, and it hurt to be finished with pro football and be without a way to support myself again. But nothing that happened during that time hurt more than what I lost in 1970, while I was still in Cincinnati. My mother died suddenly, my dear Mulla, at only 57 years of age. I will attest to this to the day I die—the way she and the rest of my family in Lemoore were treated after Mexico City contributed to my mother's death.

I got the call at about two in the morning from my older brother George. He told me she had been in the church in Riverdale, near Lemoore, listening to Liz, Mary, and Gladys, the three youngest girls, singing her favorite songs, and she just slumped over. People thought she was asleep. It probably was an embolism in the brain. She probably couldn't have been saved anyway, because once one of those happens, that's usually it. But when they called an ambulance, it came from Hanford, 12 miles away, and it took 45 minutes to get there. When it got there, it was just an empty van, with no resuscitation equipment. They put her in there, and of course by the time they got to Hanford she was dead.

Whether or not the hospitals cared whether black folks lived or died back then, Mulla should not have had to deal with the high blood pressure, worry, and stress those people in Lemoore put her through. A few years ago, one of my sisters visited me and told me that once, a friend of hers made jokes about having sent dirty, racist paraphernalia to the house on Jersey Avenue. My sister had gotten irate and asked the friend, why did you do this? And this fool said that since so much time had passed, she should have thought it was funny, too, and it was really nothing to get upset about. I wanted to go find that friend and shake the dookie out of her. I think it was just one of those things that sent my mother to the grave.

Mulla and Daddy and my brothers and sisters had begun to get hate mail, taunts, and threats around the same time that I had, before I went to Mexico City; there was a lot of talk about a boycott in the papers and magazines and all over the radio. Everybody in town read the *Lemoore Advance,* and I was in there all the time, but of course there weren't any black folks anywhere near that paper, nor any American Indians, even though there were more of them than of us in the town. It was nothing but white folks writing about me. So everybody knew, and they were letting my family know how they felt. The trouble only increased once I made the silent protest on the stand.

When I came back to visit Lemoore about a month after the Games, my father talked to me about what had been going on. He said that people around there had been saying that I'd done something bad down in Mexico City. "I don't know what that means," he said, "but you couldn't have done anything too bad, because you're my son. And whatever you did that was bad, you've got to understand something—everything that some people do, not everybody is going to agree with it." He wasn't an educated man, but I knew what he was saying: whatever I did, something positive was going to come out of it, because I was his son, but that people are going to think whatever they think no matter how true it is. My mother told me the same thing.

I knew that my family was too big for me to get everybody's okay on something like this. I also knew that whatever I did, I was going to try to make them proud of me. Besides, it was something I was called on to do, not something I had a choice in by that time. If any of them had said to me beforehand that they disagreed with my taking that stand, I would have listened, but I also would have tried to explain how this needed to be done because of who I was, what I had done, and the platform that was created because of it. But nothing I could do would have prepared them for what they went through. They had cow manure, dead bugs, nasty notes, all sorts of junk put in their mailboxes. My sisters living in Oakland were harassed at their jobs when coworkers found out I was their brother. The same went for my brothers who still lived in Lemoore or nearby. My younger brother Ernie was harassed on campus at Oregon State University in Corvallis; he kept being told that if he ever tried anything like that up there, he would get kicked off the football team. He actually did quit the team briefly.

I don't know if my youngest brother, Nudy—Eugene—has ever recovered. He was kicked off the Lemoore High team, and he felt then and now that living with the repercussions of what I did destroyed his life. He went to Berkeley for three years, because he's very sharp, but he detached himself from the family years ago, burned a lot of bridges, and had a lot of personal problems that kept him out in the street and away from everybody. Nobody in the family wanted to deal with him for a long time. It wasn't until a couple of years ago that I did much talking to him. I think Mexico City really kind of did him in.

Little by little, as time passed after the victory stand, I found out that most people in my family disagreed with what I had done and wished I had not done it—they thought it was a good idea, but they were ostracized in many places and endured a huge backlash. They felt that they were being made to suffer for something I had done wrong. That hurt me. All I had ever wanted to do was to go away to college, get an education, and come back as someone they would be proud of. I wasn't trying to stand out, but it just happened that I did while I was trying to be the best at what I did. I know it ended up hurting Ernie, because he spent the rest of his time growing up being known as Tommie Smith's brother. As great an athlete as he was— on any given day, he could have beaten me in the 100 and 200, and he also ran track at Oregon State—he was still in my shadow. Now, because of what I had done, he was dealing with notoriety that had nothing to do with him.

Even though he went away to college and then got his doctorate in education, Ernie's world was like the rest of my family's, largely limited to Lemoore and the surroundings. They could tell me how they felt about everything, but I was out there in the world; they weren't as social as I was. In a way, they didn't know me the way they knew all the brothers and sisters who stayed close to home, and they didn't understand how I had been called to do something like this. If I had come back to Lemoore and become a teacher or policeman or spent a 30-year stretch in the army, this might not have happened. I apologized to them, but that was all I could do. I had been sent to do what I had to do, regardless of whom it touched so deeply and negatively, and that was what happened.

I came back for Mulla's funeral, flying myself back because the Bengals didn't pay for it. All the white folks at the funeral had to say to me was, "How's the football going?" On the way back to Cincinnati, I didn't even know what to think, except for, "Why did I have to grow up in a place like that?" When I got back to practice, I just started hitting folks, legally. I did it so well that it's probably why I lasted the rest of that season and part of the next. That's what kept me sane, hitting people. My mother had died, a woman so strong you could almost feel her presence. I felt it in the field way back, making me pick that one more row or two more rows. I picked them for my momma, Dora Smith.

The pressure of Mexico City had taken my mother, had broken up my marriage, and had left me without a way to make a living. It was time for me to leave world records, victory stands, and silent gestures alone for a while.

10

Going Underground

I STAYED AT LEE EVANS' little house on Hawthorne Street in San Jose, in a bedroom in the back, for about a year and a half. I had to do it, to get on my feet after my divorce from Denise and after my football career ended. I needed to work. I wanted to teach, but even though I had graduated from San Jose State a while ago, I did not have my full teaching credential from the state of California. I received temporary credentials to work semester by semester, reapplying each semester. I taught the fifth grade at Ravenswood Elementary School in Milpitas, just north of San Jose, and also coached track at Milpitas High School. Early in 1972, I reapplied for my teaching credential for the following school year. I thought I was staying in California teaching elementary school for a while. But at about that time, through my old friend Art Simburg, I met Jack Scott.

I didn't know who Jack Scott was, but I soon found out. He was a radical-thinking man who had edited a magazine in Berkeley around the same time I was at San Jose State and had written books, such as *The Athletic Revolution,* that challenged the system that dictated coaching, authority, and athletes' rights and participation at every level of sports. That included the way that black collegiate athletes were exploited by the white administrators, officials, and coaches at white institutions. I could relate to that. When I met him, Jack was the athletic director at Oberlin College, near Cleveland, a school that was nationally recognized for its music conservatory, not for its athletic programs. But Oberlin, Ohio, was one of the first stops on the Underground Railroad, one of the first places in the North for slaves escaping the plantations. Oberlin was the first college in the United States to admit women and the first to admit blacks; among its alumni were Ralph Bunche, the Nobel Peace Prize winner, and legendary black journalist Carl Rowan. It has a great history.

Jack was trying to make history himself. He had been hired by Dr. Robert Fuller, who had become school president two years earlier when he was just 33 years old; he is still a great friend to me and is now retired out in Berkeley, writing books and lecturing about the reforms in education and society that still need to be made. Dr. Fuller was opening things up at Oberlin, including the athletic department. He had a new on-campus sports facility, Phillips Field House, and he wanted things to happen there, and taking a new approach was one way to do it. He brought in Jack Scott to bring that new approach, and did he ever straighten things out, by his mere presence. Jack was kind of white-boyish, but he was forceful, and he did things that weren't normal and figured he could get away with it.

Jack was looking for people to put his ideas in motion at Oberlin. He didn't know enough people who would follow him, who would believe in him and come with him to Ohio to get involved in a program and facilitate it to the point that made him happy. But he thought Tommie Smith might be that kind of person, so he asked me to come be an instructor and head basketball coach. Yes, basketball coach; he knew about my basketball background.

I didn't know Oberlin, but I knew Ohio, from my days with the Cincinnati Bengals. It isn't really South, and it isn't West, two areas I had done enough time in. The Midwest had worked out fine for me so far. I wasn't in California at that time by choice; I had left there happily once before, and now I didn't have a marriage to keep me there, although my son Kevin was still with Denise. The main thing was, there in San Jose I was running and ducking and hiding. No one noticed me, no one knew where I was, and a lot of people didn't know who I was. I could do that even more easily in Ohio. Oberlin was right. It was like Emancipation.

So I just left. I had a Porsche by then, and I loaded up that car with everything I owned. Porsches aren't very big, which shows you how much I owned. And a year after what I thought was my last trip to Ohio, after I was cut by the Bengals, I drove across the country again. I didn't have a place to stay, so I stayed with Jack Scott for a couple of weeks until I found faculty housing, in an old house, up a creaky flight of stairs—again, in hiding.

Once I arrived, I agreed to coach track as well as basketball, but my career as the basketball coach lasted one year; just as when I was at San Jose State, participating in basketball meant a shorter time to prepare for the track season. By the time basketball ends, you've done no recruiting, and two meets are already out the door without you being there. In my second year, I told Jack I needed to coach track full time so I wouldn't spend the whole season just conditioning them. And coaching track at Oberlin went beyond full-time, because for me, it meant making sure my team could practice in the middle of those Ohio winters. The snow would be six feet high, and I was the one shoveling snow off the lanes of the track, digging out the long-jump pit, and clearing the runway. That meant clearing snow for about 150 meters, all the way to the field house. That was the only way we could train. So I dug out the pit and brought sacks of sand to fill the pit and keep it covered so it wouldn't freeze over. That next year, I decided that it made more sense to practice indoors in the winter, and I found a space in the field house to put a long-jump runway—26 feet from the takeoff board to the wall, which meant that a really good long jumper would break his neck, but at least it was a place to jump. So in the middle of the night, I would dig up that sand from the pit, drag it inside, dig another hole, and dump the sand in it.

Nobody was helping me, because I was one of Jack Scott's hires, overturning the established order of the school and the athletic program. He was already becoming unpopular, so his hires were, too. They called us the Oberlin 11, coaches and assistants and administrators who didn't look and think the way coaches, assistants, and administrators in a college program were supposed to look. I was the first to arrive, and when I stepped away from basketball, he hired Pat Penn, another black coach, to replace me. Then, in the middle of my first year there, Jack hired my old friend from San Jose State, Cass Jackson, as the head football coach, the first black head coach ever at a predominantly white school. Not only did Jack hire Cass, but he hired him after consulting with the players on the team and making them part of the decision process.

That action was significant enough to bring Howard Cosell to Oberlin, to do a report on television for ABC News. Cosell interviewed the football players, Cass, Dr. Fuller, and Jack about the path they were taking and why they were taking it. Cass talked about how it was time that college and pro teams recognized that black coaches were qualified to be head coaches and got the opportunity. Dr. Fuller talked about how students deserved the chance to exert control over their own lives, and how this hiring process would teach them about shared responsibility and shared authority. I was interviewed out at the football field; I have a picture of him and me sitting in the stands. I told him that I thought that the college was there to serve the students, not the other way around. Cosell asked me if I was a militant, and I asked him back, "What does militant mean?" He explained what he defined it to be, and I nodded and said, "I am a militant."

Cosell later asked Jack Scott the same question, and Jack answered, "In the sense Tommie Smith says he's a militant, I'm a militant, too." He also pointed out that hiring Cass wasn't all that radical, because under the white coaches, the football team had gone nine years without a winning record. So he thought it was funny that people were questioning that he had an agenda, that winning no longer mattered. Cass had a winning record that first year, 1973, and they haven't had a winning season since they got rid of him. He brought in coaches, black and white, who were known for going against the establishment culture, including George Sauer, who had the personality during his pro career as a wide receiver. He also brought in a different type of player—two of his former players from San Jose State were Willie Martinez and Jay Greeley, both Hispanics with long ponytails. That was heavy duty in Oberlin.

Jack didn't just hire black people, either; he hired a lot of white coaches and administrators, some of them from California, who thought the way he did. He also directed more money and resources to the women's programs and hired a women's athletic director— Lynda Huey, whom I also knew from San Jose State. She was one of only two women competing for San Jose State when I was there; Denise was the other. Schools didn't have full women's track and field teams then, not before Title IX went into effect; the only school that regularly produced great women track athletes was Tennessee State. But Jack had big plans for women's sports, and he brought in Lynda to run the program. She was bright enough to do it, and we are still close friends today, but she came there with the wrong idea in mind —to hang out with me and have fun. That was a no-no. I wasn't catering to that, and she got offended and eventually left and went back to California. She could have gotten the job done with the right mindset and could have been a real asset—but as it turned out, she might never have had that chance, once the administration started rebelling against Jack and his programs and started running all of us off.

The track team was good, too. We competed against much larger schools with more money and facilities, schools in or near Ohio like Wooster, Carnegie-Mellon, and Baldwin-Wallace. It was tough for a little school like Oberlin to compete with them, yet some people saw the great Tommie Smith, with a team of nine guys who look like little ducklings, and expected him to turn them into world champions. But we won. And we looked good when we won, because I designed their uniforms, the baddest-looking uniforms in our conference.

I was just relieved to have a job. I was making $14,000 a year, after making $3,000 teaching in San Jose. I had so much money I was giving it away—I called my sister Sally, in Las Vegas with her husband, who was a preacher and not making any money, and offered to send her money. I told her I had so much I didn't know what to do with it. I ended up sending her $150 a month for years after that, and I know it helped her.

I also had the time and money to get my master's degree in sociology. I found a program at Cambridge College in Massachusetts; it cost $2,000 just to get into the program, so I saved to get in and to keep paying the tuition. I did a lot of the work over the phone and through mail correspondence, but plenty of times I had to fly back and forth to Massachusetts, and later to Goddard College in Vermont when the program relocated there. With everything else I was doing at Oberlin, I was working so hard on that master's, researching, writing, and typing papers, that I felt like quitting sometimes. One reason I didn't quit was Micki Scott, Jack's wife, who was in the same program. We did a lot of work together in person and on the phone. One time we flew to Massachusetts together, and on the way back, we got harassed in the airport. We were standing on line at the gate, and we were ordered to get off the line and into another room. I just stood there, and they kept telling us to come with them. I got mad, and Micki told me not to show any anger or fright and to just go ahead and see what it was about. So they took us and separated us and questioned each of us. It was all because they saw a black man traveling with a white woman; they wanted to know why. By the time they let us go, we barely made it back in time to get on the plane. We didn't fly there very much after that, and when we did, we went separately.

After three years, I had done enough work to get that degree, but during the time they were reviewing my coursework I was sure I was going to get a letter saying I had been denied. When I got the confirmation that I had indeed completed all the requirements for the master's, I wrote back and said that with the hundreds of hours I had spent earning this, I want more than a letter of confirmation; I wanted at least a certificate to hang on the wall. They sent it, and it hung on the wall of whatever office I worked in from then on—lifetime teaching credential in sociology and physical education.

I did all of this while teaching and coaching and, soon after I got there, being assistant athletic director at Oberlin. How did I find the time? I had no social life. Not long after I moved to Ohio, Denise and I agreed to have Kevin live with me, while she pursued the life she did not have while she was supporting me. So I raised him, and I got students to babysit him while I was teaching, coaching, and studying. I needed as much help as I could get; I had about enough time left over to fix Kevin Hamburger Helper for breakfast, lunch, and dinner. He won't eat Hamburger Helper to this day. The babysitting worked out for the students because Kevin, who had not turned six yet, would sleep most of the time they were there, and they would have a place to study until I came home and took them home. I was just Tommie Smith the teacher and coach, not Tommie Smith the guy who raised his fist in Mexico City.

I was also Tommie Smith the teacher and coach who couldn't date a student, even if I had wanted to, which I didn't. The only lady I had spent any time with there was a woman named Myrna, of American Indian descent. We got together a couple of years after I came to Oberlin, and we became an item; we were seen around the town, which basically meant we were seen at a restaurant called Prestie's. On weekends, we'd usually be gone to Cleveland. It was perfect for me—I felt protected from anyone who could get to me, play games with me, or talk about seeing me up in this house or that house. But one summer, I drove back to California to see my old house in San Jose, and I was thinking so much about Myrna, I stayed in San Jose one night and turned around and drove all the way back. When I got back, I found out she was seeing somebody else, and that was the end of that.

But then Denise Kyle came onto the scene. When we first met, she was a 20-year-old student at Oberlin, I was 27 and a single black male college instructor, and she was in my bowling class. She was from Cleveland, born to a white mother and a black father but raised by a black couple and raised as black, although she was so light-skinned a lot of people took her for white. She was a good student and very sociable and popular around campus, including around black students. She was easy to notice in class, as well, because she was pretty talkative. She introduced herself to me one day in class and wanted to know if I needed a babysitter. I wasn't hiring women because I didn't even want to raise a little bit of suspicion about me, but I needed someone to come watch Kevin on weekends when I had to attend a meet or go on some other athletic department business. I had just lost Kevin's favorite sitter, a kid named Gerald, because he just couldn't do it as often as I was gone.

So I agreed to let her babysit, and we became friends—but I still couldn't fraternize too closely with her. When I returned, any time of day or night, she would go back to her dorm rather than stay overnight. She wouldn't take money for sitting with Kevin, either. We were friends long before we became husband and wife. We didn't become anything more than friends until after she had graduated in 1974, and I could then openly walk down the street with her. She moved home to Cleveland after graduation, but she visited quite a bit, and I visited there and met her mother; that meeting really sold Denise on me. We got married in 1976, and we stayed married for 24 years and had four children together.

Denise—or Akiba, the name she took on during her final year at Oberlin—got a good job in administration at the telephone company and within a couple of months had a telephone card and a gas card, which was a big deal back then. Eventually she was making

$22,000. We still lived in faculty housing. It had an open space in front of the house, and you could sit on your lawn all day long. There were no fences, no parking meters, and no stoplights, and in the summer, when the students were gone, it was quiet, nothing around but trees and green grass. On one of those warm summer nights when it rained, I would wait for a break in the rain, grab a pole, head for the reservoir, and catch some crappies; I'd come back just when the rain started up again, and we'd fry them up, eat them, and sit up all hours until we'd go in for the night. It was almost heaven.

Best of all, I was underground, as I call it. No one knew where I was. Nobody bothered me about Mexico City, at least not the students, although a few faculty members did once in a while. But nobody else knew. I didn't want to hide, I had to, and God had given me a blessing by getting me out of California and into the perfect state for me to hide. I had to be that way to maintain sanity within the system. Now, I had found who I thought was the person I should be with, and if I had ever thought before then that I would ever have to leave and go back to San Jose, I might not have even been with her.

This was it. I had found what I needed. I thought I would be in Oberlin the rest of my life.

I already believed that I was still alive by the grace of God. I've been in too many places where I've felt death and it's turned out not to be me that got shot. Even then, I had been in places at night and seen guys I didn't know but later met or spoke to 20 years later—and they tell me they had been in that place to keep an eye on me. I know of a few that came up to me in Santa Monica later, laughing and telling me they remembered me from some party or function; I wouldn't know what party, but they'd tell me they had been hired by some group to keep their distance and report to them on what I did, and they'd laugh again and tell me what a bad motherfucker I am. I know they came from some white group, probably the government, and I'd think, "Oh my God."

During what turned out to be my last year at Oberlin, the FBI found me. That wasn't a surprise; the FBI finds everybody, and I found out later that I spent a long time on their top-10 list of subversive characters in the athletic world. I actually got the government's file on me years later, through the Freedom of Information Act, but so many things on it were blacked out that there was nothing I could use from it. At that time, they were keeping an eye on me and Jack Scott, but Jack was gone from Oberlin already, so they caught up to me. I was at a barbershop on the other side of the tracks, in the black part of town. I was sitting in the shop, tired, watching cars pass by in the street, and I noticed that this old, raggedy, nasty, gray and brown Ford with two white dudes in it kept passing by real slow. I figured somebody was just passing through town. Then they stopped next to my car, the Porsche, and started looking in it and looking at the license plate, and I thought I was going to have to go out there and cuss them out. Then I noticed that their car had a small antenna on the trunk. Back then, everybody had antennas on their cars, the big ones for their CB radios—but not those little ones. I immediately thought, Fed, and I sat back down. The two white guys came into the shop and asked who owned the Porsche, as if they didn't already know. I saw their coats bulging on the sides, and I knew what was making them bulge. So I told them the car was mine, they asked me if I was Tommie Smith, I said I was, and they told me they had just driven by and noticed my car (bullshit, I thought) and would like to talk to me about a couple of issues. I said I had no problem with that, but I'd like to finish what I was doing and invited them to meet me in my office in half an hour. Now, I didn't tell them where my office was, but sure enough, when I got back, they were standing by the door.

They were very polite, and so was I. They told me why they were there, and when they told me, I said, "You've got to be kidding me." It was the Patty Hearst case, the kidnapping, and they were investigating Jack about harboring a fugitive and illegal transportation across state lines. I thought, "This case is so hot they had to look me up?" I didn't know her at all, I told them. But, they told me, Jack knew her, Jack hired me, he was gone, and I was next, as the athletic director who replaced him, so they had to talk to me. We talked for an hour, and when they left, they told me that they had learned a lot about me, and that they could use a guy like me on their team. I answered, "Well, better some team than no team." They laughed, and then they left.

I had tried to be Mister Bad while all this was going on, but in truth, it scared me. Here I was in Oberlin, Ohio, at this little school in a town of 5,000 when school wasn't in session, where nobody knew who I was, and a big case like Patty Hearst comes up—a case where they were still putting people in jail 30 years later—and the FBI tracks me down. There was nothing to get out of me, but it reminded me that in their eyes, I was still as hot as anybody, that they could catch up to me anywhere for anything, for a speeding ticket or for some woman telling them she had my baby, and they could have put me in jail and there wouldn't be anything I could do about it.

Even with all of that, I didn't think I would ever leave Oberlin. I was as safe there as I would be anywhere in the world. I should still be there right now, retiring from there instead of from Santa Monica College. Almost 30 years later, it's as big a shock as it was when it happened; it hasn't hit me yet and it probably never will. It shouldn't be such a shock, since I wasn't there long before Dr. Fuller was forced out as president by the school administrators. Next, they forced Jack out, and one by one they got us all.

Before Dr. Fuller and Jack Scott, there was no reason for anybody to come to Phillips Field House, not with all the deadheads in the physical education department there. When Jack came, he brought new classes, a new vibrancy, and new black folks in new positions. There had been only 36 black students enrolled there when Dr. Fuller arrived, and now the black population was up to 10 or 12 percent out of almost 3,000. They came not just to play, but to be students. They even had black people taking swimming classes.

We were teaching students things that had not been taught before, there or many other places. My belief always has been that the impact of Mexico City was greater than the impact in my classroom, but it is only part of the experience I bring to the classroom, and it complements what the students have in their textbooks and what I teach outside of the book. I want to bring about in the thought process of the student an understanding of the book and of the instructor, how I bring the textbook to life and get them to express in their own terminology what they get from it.

My classes were good, they were standing room only, I was on time, and I was good at what I was doing in the class and on the track. The track team had never had a winning season before I got there and had one the very first year. Jack backed me on everything.

Things just kept rising and rising all the time—until it plateaued. I should have known something was happening when an instructor told me to slow down, that I was moving too fast, that I was too good, that if I didn't slow down, I would become too visible, and that wouldn't be good for me. He was right. I was too good. Everything was too good.

Jack knew. Dr. Fuller had warned him before being forced to resign. "Calm it down a bit, or else they'll get rid of you too," he said, "and if they do get rid of you, the guys you hired will catch hell because you're gone. If I'm gone and you're gone, they're gone too." That's exactly what happened. They got Jack out—basically, they paid him to leave—and they began to tear down everything he and Dr. Fuller had done. The black folks there were left wide open, and they laughed and cut us one at a time—*whack,* Cass; *whack,* someone else; until finally there was me, the last one. In 1977 they told me they would not grant me tenure, and that when the academic year was over in the spring of 1978, I would be gone.

I had been promoted from assistant athletic director to replace Jack, but I caught hell the entire year. It was the most devastating year of my life administratively, because no one believed in me, since I was Jack Scott's protégé. They had so much power over me, Cass, and the basketball coach, Pat Penn, who really didn't say a whole lot the way Cass and I did. I had no support whatsoever. The administrators who worked under me were only attending the meetings I called because I would write them up for nonattendance—I was adamant about attending and being on time. Their hearts weren't there. They decided I was incapable of being the AD—I was Tommie Smith, the militant, Jack Scott's guy, and I couldn't tell them what to do. Once the board denied me tenure, there wasn't anything I could do anyway.

Their reason for denying me tenure was that my teaching and coaching were below departmental standards, and that I was not able to do what I taught. They had to be laughing when they said it, because they knew it was bogus. Not be able to do what I taught? I was head track and field coach and taught physical education classes. There's no way I should have been fired for that. I had done things for that school that you couldn't pay people to do, digging out long-jump pits and shoveling snow off the track in zero-degree temperatures in the middle of the night, and then they give an excuse like that. But what could I do? And once I was gone, every trace of what Dr. Fuller and Jack Scott had done was erased. Before I left, I had constructed a board to list the school's track and field records, and had it displayed in the foyer of Phillips Field House, along with one of the uniforms I designed. Years later, when I went back, it was gone, taken down; I don't know when or by whom.

Not long ago, Cass called and told me he wanted to set up a reunion of the old Oberlin group, at the school. But I wouldn't go back there for something like that if you paid me. I have no warm feelings about that place whatsoever. When we did have a reunion, it was for a sad reason: it was a memorial service for Jack Scott in Berkeley in the spring of 2000. He had died of cancer a month earlier. The reunion was held on what would have been his 58th birthday.

I had gotten a year's notice that I was not getting tenure, so Denise and I moved into her mother's house in Cleveland. That made her mother happy. We stayed for almost two years, and I drove back and forth to Oberlin. The drive was so beautiful, scenic, and peaceful that it reminded me of back home, except I didn't have to pick any grapes. I also spent that year trying to get a job at another college; I had hoped I could stay in Ohio because it was Denise's home, her mother was there, and I had done so well hiding out there, but I looked for a job everywhere. I turned a corner of the basement in the house in Cleveland, near the washer and dryer, into a little office. I sent out hundreds of résumés, spent hours and hours duplicating them and mailing them. Some never got an answer. Some of them came back with an "I'm sorry." A lot of them came back with, "You're who? And you want what? Are you kidding?" The college presidents knew who I was, and they were the ones telling me no way. A lot of the ones I called directly laughed into the phone and then hung up. Others never called me back.

A few of them did say that they would keep my information on file, which was at least polite. One of those responses came from Santa Monica College, a two-year college: it said that they thought my résumé was very interesting and that they would love to have me, but Proposition 13 has prevented them from hiring anybody at all. In case there was an alleviation of their financial problems, it added, they would contact me. At least that made sense. I knew about Prop 13; everybody in America knew by then about the revolt by California property taxpayers that led to budgets being slashed for everything, including education, to make up for the lost revenue. Still, it meant there was no job. Meanwhile, Denise was pregnant with our first child, Danielle. I was back to having a wife and child I couldn't feed, back to wondering if I would have to try sweeping streets again. As a last resort, I tried selling insurance, but I couldn't sell ice in the Sahara in July.

Suddenly, in the late spring of 1978, a possibility surfaced, back in California, of all places. The Muhammad Ali Track Club, based in Santa Monica, called me. The guy who ran the club was named Harold Smith. You might remember him: he was Ali's promoter for a while, and later he was busted in the big Wells Fargo embezzlement case, when it was learned that his real name was Ross Fields. Someone had recommended me to Harold Smith, and he called me and said, "Look here, we've got a kid here, Houston McTear, and we need you to coach him. You've got to come out here right now." Houston McTear was one of the best young sprinters in the world back then. I could see myself out there working with him, money flying into our pockets, my wife driving a new car. The man told me to come out in June and he'd put me up in his luxury hotel, and we'd talk. I drove out there in my green and white Thunderbird —the Porsche was long gone—so I could have a car already there when I moved. I got to Los Angeles and phoned Harold Smith, and ended up on the street on the phone waiting on him because he was so hard to get in contact with. When I reached him, he put me up in something other than a luxury hotel—it was an apartment that Ali owned in a building near Wilshire Boulevard. I shared the apartment with a man that worked with Ali named Tom Peters—whom I began calling Funky Peters, because of the odor he carried wherever he went.

I kept trying to get back in touch with Harold Smith and stayed in that apartment for three days. Finally, one morning, I got ahold of him, and he said, "Yeah, Tommie, come on over and we'll talk, I'm waiting for you." I put on the black suit I had cleaned and pressed for the occasion, grabbed the briefcase I had used at Oberlin to bring my lunch to work (and which didn't have anything in it now except the smell of sandwiches), hopped into the T-bird with hardly any gas in it, drove to where he was, and knocked on the door. I was thinking he would be dressed and ready to negotiate, but he answered the door with no shoes on, hair all over the place, and his kitchen looking like there had just been a war in it. Then, out walked this white woman. I thought, "Oh shit." I didn't know who she was, or who he thought I should think she was, but I wanted to walk out right then and there. I didn't, out of respect for him and for the fact that I'd driven 3,000 miles to talk to him. The meeting didn't last long anyway. He said, "You're a good man, and Houston doesn't need somebody like you; he needs his ass kicked, and he's not going to get you." I said to him that I needed a job, and he said back, no, I didn't need this job.

I think I know why he did that. I think he saw his wife look at me and see something there, and he didn't want me around for that. She had just looked at us and gone back to what she had been doing, but I think he saw something and felt like I didn't need to be around. So I didn't get the job.

There still was nothing for me back in Ohio. Denise and I realized that my chances were better back in California after all. So she flew out to join me at my family reunion in Fresno, and we started looking in the newspapers for an apartment and a job. We saw some possibilities in the Los Angeles area, but nothing was working out, not for a family with one son and a baby on the way. Finally, we called about a place, and the folks renting it said they could meet up there the next day. We were on pins and needles all night. We got over there and nobody was there; we knocked and knocked, and finally gave up, thinking it was another bogus lead. We got back in the car, went up the street, and were about to make a left turn when I saw in the mirror, the last thing I looked at on that street before turning, that a car was pulling into the driveway. We did a U-turn and went back, and it was the guy coming to meet us, running late. If I hadn't looked when I did, my life would have gone in another direction. The man, Mr. Yang, then asked me if I had a job, and I said of course I did, I was a college professor, which pleased him, and which of course wasn't true. Denise got out of the car and liked what she saw, and Mr. Yang said yes, we could have it: two bedrooms, a huge office with one of those Murphy beds in the wall, full kitchen and dining room, wash room, front porch, and back yard, for $400 a month.

We flew back and packed everything we owned into a trailer. We brought Denise's mother with us to California, so we sold her house (and only got $12,000 for it). I drove the truck, and Denise drove her car behind it, driving while pregnant with Danielle in a car without air conditioning behind a truck that couldn't go faster than 50 miles an hour, all the way from Cleveland to Los Angeles. It took forever, crossing those big empty Midwest states, coming across the Rockies, stopping at night so Denise could rest.

We got there, with only enough money in my pocket to pay that first month's rent. I went to the police department, I went to the sanitation department, I went to the public schools, and I went to the stores in the neighborhood asking to sweep floors. But I had a master's degree, and I was overqualified to do any of those things. One day, I was sitting in the house by myself; Denise was out shopping with her best friend in California, Michelle, and I was glad I had enough money for her to do that. I was just sitting and stressing, thinking, what am I going to do? The phone rang, which was significant because we had just had it put in the day before. It was the president's office at Santa Monica College, telling me I was one of three finalists for the job as head track and field coach. When could I come in? I said I could come in any time—and when they got off the phone, man, I hung up and flew to Santa Monica. The other two candidates were there, and one of them was Joe Douglas, who was the head coach of the Santa Monica Track Club, the amateur club that was producing Olympic athletes and would keep producing them. I was sure I wasn't going to get the job, so I went defiant. I went in telling the people exactly how I felt about education and the needs of athletes and students, all the things I had stood for at Oberlin and my entire life before that.

I went home and picked up the paper, wondering if the police department was hiring this time. The next day, the phone rang again, and on the other end I heard the words, "Congratulations, you're hired." Denise and Michelle were out again, so I left a note on the front door that read, "You are entering the home of the head track and field coach at Santa Monica College." It sort of solidified things to me. I thought all my troubles were over, although I eventually found out during my years in southern California that they were just starting again.

When I started at my new job, I was the new kid on the block. I went in working; I wanted to win, and I wanted to prove myself. My office was a cubicle about the size of a living room rug, but it was an office, with a desk and a phone, which sat on a wall between the offices. But I had a job, man. Then after a few years, I began to get accreditation; I was recruiting, I was handling my team every year, and people began to get to know me. One of my runners, Johnny Gray, set the American record in the 800 meters, and he went on to college and made the Olympic team five times. I coached about 50 athletes who won conference or state championships, and several went to the Olympics, from the United States and from other countries. One of my favorite athletes was Chris Faulkner, a sprinter who was born in Jamaica and made his country's Olympic team. All of my athletes can tell stories about running at Santa Monica College, because I got in all their butts something fierce. I got a lot of these kids out of the ghetto, in southern California or elsewhere, and I was able to coach them to championships. Besides excelling as athletes while I was their coach and afterward, many of them became coaches as well, and they come back later and thank me and tell me that what they learned about becoming a coach and a teacher can be attributed to me. Of course, whatever I learned about coaching track and field I learned from Bud Winter.

No one knew about any of this because they didn't make it great the way someone like Marion Jones did. The closest was Johnny Gray, and he did not become known until he joined the Santa Monica Track Club after he wasn't able to become academically eligible at the University of Arizona. The Santa Monica Track Club isn't as prominent as it used to be, because other clubs have sprung up around the country and in southern California, clubs that have money and endorsements and corporate tie-ins. But if athletes wanted to be educated, there was a place for them at Santa Monica College while I was there, because I made sure they paid attention to the classroom.

I was not worried about being out of the loop in terms of recognition. I was still happy to be in hiding. Santa Monica was an extension of my blessing from Oberlin. Oberlin was my saving grace, taking me away from the riffraff in California. I went underground for six years, and when I resurfaced, it was back where I had started, at the end of what had started there. It was a triangle, San Jose to Ohio to Santa Monica. I had to go away first to be saved.

Families Lost, and Found

A LOT OF PEOPLE still don't understand why it would be important for me to go underground, to keep my distance, to lose myself and get myself lost in where I live and where I work. That group includes my family, my parents and brothers and sisters and the nieces and nephews and cousins. It also includes my wives, plural—Delois is my third. When we met, she didn't know what it meant to be around Tommie Smith, the good and the bad. I think that anyone who has ever gotten involved with someone like me, with a background like mine, is going to both suffer and reap benefits, because of who I am and what I represent.

Delois sees this, but she doesn't. I do things now to make money, with her help, and much of it comes from what happened to me in Mexico City. So I get a lot of "Oh, you're Tommie Smith! Can I shake your hand?" She's standing there, and of course she's proud, but I'm saying, "Hey, come on, let's not." All it takes is one—one shot, one stab, one anything. She doesn't see that; all she sees is that I'm Tommie Smith and I'm important.

It has been hard on all of them: Delois, whom I married in 2000; Denise, who also was known as Akiba, whom I was married to for 24 years; and my first wife, also Denise, whom I married while we were both in college and while she was carrying my eldest son, Kevin. They all suffered. The first Denise suffered the most. She's the one that people tormented on the street in San Jose; she's the one who got the phone calls while I was out of town because I had to travel to make some money; she's the one who didn't go to school because she had a child and chose to stay home and take care of him. She's the one who saw me early in life struggling, trying to get going, who saw me not making it in Cincinnati with the Bengals. And she struggled right along with me; she was the one making 25 dollars a week cover everything—food, clothing, everything.

Denise was the only family I had in Mexico City. No money; Mulla and Daddy had to find out what I did from back in Lemoore. I'm still wondering how Denise got to Mexico City; that really escapes me, I don't know where she got the money. I just knew she was coming, and she was bringing me some gloves. That would never happen today; the shoe company would pay, or some other sponsor, or the USOC would make arrangements. These things were not possible in 1968, I don't believe, but Denise was there.

Before I met Denise, I had not been out looking for a wife. I was interested in the opposite sex, of course, and I did have a girlfriend at San Jose State, Valerie Yates, the girl I looked for in the gym when we marched to San Francisco during my sophomore year. I had female acquaintances, probably more female ones than male. Some of them I still have to this day, such as Lynda Huey, who came to Oberlin to join Jack Scott in the athletic department during the years I was there. We knew each other when we both ran at San Jose State. It did not work out for her at Oberlin, but she went on to start her own business that dealt primarily with using water workouts in athletic training.

But I generally didn't have time for friends, period. I was quiet, and I spent my time studying and training. Socializing was not part of my plan. Valerie was very social, and while we shared the same belief in academics and in being engaged in activism, I could not take time away from what I was doing to be a social person the way she could. In fact, because Valerie and I had different ideas about parties, we ended up parting ways during my junior year. We actually had gotten engaged; I had put a ring on her finger, and one weekend there was a big party being put on in Palo Alto by one of the fraternities. I didn't much want to go, partly because I was very tied up in the middle of training, and partly because to get to the party, it would have taken gas money that I didn't have. But she wanted to go and asked if she could go without me, accompanied by a male friend of hers from Los Angeles. I didn't say no, but I got suspicious, and I decided that I would go anyway and keep an eye on her—accompanied by someone I knew, a young lady named Gwen Ribbs, I still remember, someone I had known from around campus but had never asked out. My brother George in Oakland loaned me his car and put gas in it, and off we went to this party. Everybody noticed when we walked in, because I was 6 foot 3 and Gwen about 5 foot 2, and because everybody knew who I was.

After we danced a few times, I walked over to where Valerie and her friends were sitting, and I noticed there was an empty chair at their table. We talked, and I said that on the next song, I should come out and dance with my date and she should come out and dance with hers. No, she said, she couldn't do that, because her date hadn't shown up. I felt like she had gotten what she deserved, but I also felt like a dog—and since we now knew what both of us were capable of doing to each other, that was the last night of our engagement. I've never been mad about that, though, because a few months after that, early in my senior year of 1966–67, I met Denise Paschal.

It was more or less Denise finding me rather than me finding her, although it was several years before I found out from someone how much had gone into her finding me. What was certain then was that at the time, for me, there was studying and training and sleeping, and I had little time for anything else. But I did come to know Denise, because she was one of the nation's best track athletes. She was a pentathlete, which today would translate into a heptathlete—she long-jumped 19 feet and shot-put almost 40 feet, and was a sprinter and hurdler. She was 5 foot 9 and 145 pounds, all muscle, not an ounce of fat, not an imperfection on her body—just a beautiful dark-skinned woman, beautiful enough to become a model later, after we had split up.

She was from Detroit, but her family had moved to San Francisco when she was young, and she had turned down a scholarship to the University of Hawaii to go to San Jose State—she and Lynda Huey at one time were the only women running for San Jose State. She was a freshman practicing with the team one day when I drove over to the track in my old blue Volkswagen to find Coach Winter. I saw Denise there, tall, athletic, everything in the right place—but I had other things on my mind. As I passed, though, I noticed she was looking at me, and I overheard someone say something to her about me. She laughed and told her friend, "I didn't think he would ever straighten up from getting out of that VW." I thought that was pretty funny, too, and we started talking. That turned into visiting and spending time with each other. Besides being a world-class athlete, she was very smart and academically inclined. But jeez, what a great athlete. She was in the films that Coach Winter took of the team; you can see her in a clip that was used in the *Fists of Freedom* special on HBO, with me and Lee and Ronnie Ray Smith and Kirk Clayton and Sam Davis, coming around the turn on the track at San Jose State. God, she was beautiful to watch, and I used to watch her a lot, watching her run, especially watching her long jump, how hard she'd hit the board and how hard she'd land in the pit, sand flying everywhere, and me wondering whether that sand all over her would scar me up when we got together later. But she was good. If we had had the money and the surroundings then that are available now, I would put us in the same category as Tim Montgomery and Marion Jones. She was that good.

Still, I know most of my reason for marrying the first Denise was that she was pregnant with Kevin. I was not through with my degree, and she was 18 years old. I felt it was necessary. I think I would have done it anyway, but that pushed it a little early. It was my responsibility. In those days you didn't say to a woman, "You're having a baby? Oh, it ain't mine." I wasn't going to do that. I know what kind of person she was.

I didn't know exactly what type until a long time later, some 35 years later, although I had suspected something before. I knew that she had known me and had been looking to meet me before I knew her—that she really had the inclination to hunt this guy out, find this guy out, and find out what he was all about, which is probably why she chose San Jose State over Hawaii. Some of her friends told me that not long after we divorced, and decades later I met another of her friends at a function for the 100 Black Men. The friend walked up to me and asked me if I was Tommie Smith, the one who was "married to the gold digger." Of course, I didn't know what she was talking about, and she asked me if I had been married to Denise Paschal, from San Francisco, tall and dark-skinned. It turns out that she had known her in high school and had been told that Denise had turned down that scholarship to go to San Jose and "hook" this runner named Tommie Smith because he was going to make a lot of money. The friend even asked Delois if she was the one, because Delois also is tall and dark-skinned.

That's actually not the only trait my first wife and my current wife share; they are both intelligent, strong, educated, successful, ambitious women—in fact, my second wife Denise also fits that description. Delois was not an athlete, though. She also did not know me when she met me, and that apparently was not the case with the first Denise. It was interesting to hear that about Denise, even though it was too late to do anything about it. Of course, if Denise had hunted me down thinking I was going to be rich, she would have hunted down the wrong man.

Even if that all were true about her, though, she did not deserve what she went through while we were married. She was still young when she had Kevin, and she quit school to take care of him while I went out trying to support us any way that I could. It was a good relationship for a while, but then the pressures of 1968 mounted. I wasn't exactly the model husband, because I never was around very much. When I went to Cincinnati, she and Kevin went with me, just a young black girl, only 19 or 20, following her husband with their baby. But she noticed right away that most pro football players drove nice cars, and I was still driving an old Nova, fixing it up so I could make the drive back and forth to San Francisco. That told you I wasn't making any money, and I know she never got used to that. Finally, in that third year in Cincinnati, before I got cut, she decided not to come out with me, choosing to stay in California and find a job. My football career and our marriage ended at about the same time; we thought it was best for both of us and for Kevin. It's not that we didn't want it to work out; it just didn't, and we had to get out of it before it got too sour. It got to the point where she thought she had to watch me to make sure some woman, especially some white woman, didn't try to take me away, and I had figured she was seeing another dude, a white dude, because I was never around and never had any money.

Denise got the house I had bought in San Francisco, on Peralta, up on a hill. After the divorce, she told me to get to stepping, just said she was tired of having nothing and being with someone who was never going to have nothing. She was right; we didn't have anything, and she had endured every bit of the hard times, from Mexico City to the final months of college, the Jim Brown situation, and the years going back and forth to Ohio. It still hurt, though, and when she said for me to pack up my one bag because that's all I had, that hurt, too. I was mad, but I didn't want to hit her, and since Denise was a big, strong woman, I definitely didn't want to go that way. Our separation was loud, and it could have gotten violent, but it didn't.

That was when I moved in with Lee Evans back in San Jose. Denise's mother lived in the house on Peralta for several years, and Kevin later took it over and turned part of it into a studio for his business arranging and producing music and singing a little bit. That shows you the Detroit in his blood; he knows the Jacksons very well, as well as the Winans family, from his mother's side of the family. He also coaches track, after competing at Cal-Berkeley, and he later joined San Francisco State's staff as a volunteer assistant. Kevin grew up to be very talented and successful, even though he had to go through the Hamburger Helper years in Oberlin.

When you lose a marriage and you lose a parent, the way that I lost my mother a year before Denise and I divorced, you begin to wonder if what you went through with Mexico City had been worth it. Everything I had done as we planned for Mexico City, I had done for my wife and child; I had sacrificed for them, but I had lost them anyway, at least until I was able to bring Kevin to Ohio with me. I had wanted to have a family to raise and support the way my daddy had done, and I had thought that even by stepping out of that life in Lemoore and into a broader segment of society, the system would at least allow me to keep a family together even if we presented a challenge to that system. I still had a family when it was over, but it was not a family of my own to support.

The family I had was still strong, though, and it gathered every summer in Lemoore for a reunion because most of them had settled into their own lives there. Now they have it closer to Fresno, but they still have reunions, and I always go. They usually have about 500 people show up; even the smaller ones have about 200. My oldest brother James had 11 kids, and those kids have kids. Only one of the 12 of us didn't have kids, and none of us that had kids had just one—

we all had two or more. We don't even know who's who every year; we have to introduce people to each other. My younger sister Mary is now the program coordinator, because the reunion is so big we can have organized programs every year. We've got a heart surgeon in the family, as well as a lot of PhDs. A lot of us drive up in Benzes and Cadillacs. Many of them are people I used to pick on when I was in my 20s and they were three or four years old.

I see all that, and I know that what I did in Mexico was worth it, man. Some of those kids still don't know who I am or what I did until someone tells them; they think they know, and they look at me kind of funny. When they find out that I'm that Tommie Smith, that I did that thing they've talked about and heard about their entire lives, they can't believe it. They seldom understand it, either, the pride that went behind that stand and the motivation, which wasn't money. They'll say to me, "Man, you must have lost a lot of money." And, "I don't know if I could've done it." My answer is that they probably couldn't, because times are different, but that they don't have to worry about it because it's been done. And by the way, what kind of car are they driving there? They'd usually be driving something nice. I remember back when I was borrowing the cars I was supposed to wash at North American Pontiac, and the cars I would borrow from my brother, and the intense wish I had for a little $6,000 Chevrolet. Back then I would have given everything for a GTO to drive home and surprise my mamma. But those world records I held couldn't buy me a GTO, so what kind of sacrifice was I really making?

But my parents and brothers and sisters sacrificed a lot because of what I did. I'm not the prized kid in the Smith family because I caused so many problems. Ernie was harassed and threatened at Oregon State because of me. Nudy was kicked out of Cal-Berkeley because of me, and I know that with the problems he has had since, he blames a lot of them on me. My sisters were tormented because of me. My parents endured a lot of stress, and it killed my mother. My first wife endured it, and my second wife did, too.

Denise Kyle had been a 20-year-old student at Oberlin when I was teaching there. She had helped me survive my time underground, we had gotten married, and she had been brave enough to leave where she had lived her entire life, to leave her family, to move to

California with me. But she was a strong person, and that came from the way she was raised. Denise was half-white, and to look at her, you would think she was white. She had a white mamma and a black daddy; that's whom she got her last name from. Her mother was a very pale Lithuanian woman, and because she had her with a black man, she did not want Denise. When she came out of the womb, her mother didn't even look at her. She immediately gave Denise away to an old black woman nearby, not caring whether she could be taken care of or not. Had Denise stayed in that house another night, she would have died, but the father's brother came by and saw her and told her mother, "We'll take this baby." He took Denise home to his wife, and they raised her, and that woman, the wife of her uncle, became Denise's mamma. When I first met Mrs. Kyle when Denise took me back to Cleveland, she told me that Denise was tiny and red as a beet, and looked like a piece of cooking meat. They raised a beautiful, intelligent daughter. They raised her black, and she had a phobia about white people, because of what her natural mother had done. She didn't like white folks.

That was intriguing to me, because when I first met her, I didn't want to deal with her because she looked white, and I wasn't looking for a white woman. It wasn't until she had told me the story, after she had introduced me to her mamma, that I felt I had the freedom to be with her—that is, to be seen with her. It was pretty heavy for people to see a black man walking around with a white woman, no matter where you were, in California or Ohio or anywhere else, and it was extra heavy to be Tommie Smith and walking around with a white woman. I ran into a lot of hell for a long time, and I had a problem with it in the beginning until I realized something: that the problem was not with her being white, it was with me being black. Denise and I were married for 24 years and I became accustomed to it, but I noticed how different it was to be married to someone who could be confused for white when I later married Delois. All of a sudden, when I walked down the street with my wife, white people looked and kept going, and so did black people. No more of them saying to themselves, "Oh man, he's married to a white woman." No more black folks saying, "Oh, this nigger's with a white woman." Delois still takes offense to that, but it's true.

It was troubling enough to me that I couldn't make up my mind about marrying Denise. In the end, I didn't make up my mind; my sister Sally made it up for me. I had brought Denise to the family reunion, and the first thing I heard Daddy say when she and I got out of the car—I didn't see him right away, but I heard him—was, "Another one?" What he meant was another white woman. There were white women all through the family, and there still are; my brother Nudy drew attention around Lemoore for years for being around white women, and every year another cousin or nephew would come to the reunion with one. One reason there are so many now, though, I think, is because the family thought it was okay from seeing me with one— they only thought Denise was. Years later, when we had separated and I came to the reunion without her, a lot of my relatives who had white wives or very light-skinned ones thought, "Oh, if Tommie abandoned his, what am I supposed to do?" I didn't know I had set the standard or become a trendsetter. I do know that they thought it was okay to do it because I had stood up for blackness and fought the white man and now I was marrying one of his women, so I was opening the door for them. It was Delois, actually, who pointed out to me that they were following my lead depending on whom they saw me with.

But after the family had first met Denise, I was still struggling to decide whether to ask her to marry me. So one day, as Denise and I were sitting at home, she decided to call Sally and ask her what she thought. Sally immediately told Denise to put me on the phone, and she said, "Tommie, you'd better marry her." What helped seal the deal—and it put my mind at ease, too—was that Sally called her Akiba, the name she had taken on her trip to Ghana during her junior year at Oberlin. Her friends were all calling her Akiba, and when Sally called her by that name, she felt accepted. In the future, everybody at the reunions knew her as Akiba.

We actually got married when we went to the family reunion in 1976, at my brother-in-law's church in Fresno, my sister Willie Jewel's husband (whose name, if you can believe it, is Willie Pearl). The reception was the reunion—it wasn't at the reunion, it was the reunion.

We were together through the final years in Oberlin when they refused me tenure, through the time living in her mother's house where I was copying résumés in the basement, through the trip to Los Angeles for that job with Harold Smith that didn't really exist, and then through the years at Santa Monica College. All together it was 24 years, but I count the years up until the divorce was final in 2000. In actuality, we separated on January 10, 1997, when she ordered me out of our house, and I filed for divorce in 1998. Basically, she told me—and I believed her, even if I didn't like it or agree with it—that I had raised her, marrying her when she was just 20, and it was time for her to move on and do different things.

By then, in 1984, we had settled into a house on 78th Street in Los Angeles, a nice stucco house that was built during the 1932 Olympic Games in LA. It had three bedrooms, because we had two children, and we had a fishpond with 200 pounds of koi fish in it. I had a red light shine on it at night, and it shone on the fish in water so clear you could see all the way to the bottom. It reminded me of home. I thought, "This is me; I'll never have to leave." Everything was going well at Santa Monica. Life was great, I thought.

Denise and I had four children. Danielle, whom Denise was carrying in her when we drove from Ohio to California for good in 1978, turned 27 in 2005; then come Anthony Kyle, Timothy, and Joseph. Four of my children are grown, including Kevin, and Joey is a teenager. Dani finished college a few years after her mother and I split up; Denise had the other three with her during that time. She got the house, and they were all jammed in there for a while, along with three dogs. It's a beautiful house, and it should be with all the work I put into it over the years. I look back, though, and I realize I didn't put enough time into loving Denise the way a man should love a woman, giving her time. I should have known that, since I had seven sisters. But I didn't know, and that's why I've had three wives. It's a job all the time, but I enjoy the challenge.

I don't know exactly when things went bad for us, but I do believe that Denise was seeing somebody else by the time she told me to leave in 1997. Maybe I'm wrong, but she changed so drastically so quickly —all of a sudden she was wearing short skirts and a new hairdo and was coming in all hours of the night. I used to wait up for her, and I would hear her car roll in, and it would be another 20 minutes before she would get out of the car and come inside. When she'd see me still up on the patio, she would tell me that I don't need to do that, I'm not her daddy. We were having arguments night after night for a year before I left.

Then, one night late in 1996, while we were talking and then yelling, I said, "Wait a minute, do you want me to leave? Because I will leave and give you your space." She had never heard that from me before, and she was silent for a long time. That was my answer. I told her I would do it as soon as I could put things together, organize my brain, and find a place to live. That's all right, she said, she'd already found a place for me. She was planning to move out herself, with the boys; she had been looking for an apartment and had found a three-bedroom, but it wouldn't be ready for two more months. She was ready to move everything and everybody out and put them all in an apartment deep in the ghetto. I wasn't going to have that. So I moved out instead.

There wasn't much I could do about it. As I said, I believed she had someone already, and I knew she had a lot of friends on the police force, because that was where she worked. She was attached to those uniforms, to that power. I knew I couldn't go up against her and do anything against her will with all those police friends of hers.

The apartment I moved into—that she was going to move into—was near Crenshaw High School, where the kids went to school. At least if they had an emergency or just wanted to walk home, they could stop at their dad's place. For me, it was just a place to lay my head, get out of that ruckus, and have a place for the kids to come if they had to. I was too busy working at Santa Monica to worry about how it looked. But I did have to go into the apartment through the back, past the old raggedy garages and garbage dumpsters, because I didn't want people to see me coming through the courtyard in the front. The time I spent there, I spent killing roaches. I made sure that place was roach-free. It was hard when I had to go out of town for a while, because they would invade from the other apartments. I was embarrassed to invite anybody over, but Denise and the kids would come by, and when they were gone, I had to clean everything up as soon as they left, because the roaches would feast on what was left.

I had to do that because I wanted the place to be clean just in case Denise wanted to come by and spend some time. I wanted her to come over so much, so she and I could just sit, talk, and watch a movie together for a couple of hours. It never happened. I wanted her to ask me back, to tell me yes, I could come back to our house. I stayed in that apartment, near a dump, killing roaches, hoping she'd invite me back. But the only things that ever happened were my getting robbed and the police showing up because she had told them I had threatened her with a gun.

She had filed a harassment complaint against me, claiming her life was in danger and that I had threatened to shoot her. There also was a restraining order that prevented me from coming within 100 feet of the house. So one day, I heard *bam bam bam* on my door, and, "Open up. It's the police." I was the quiet guy in that complex, so I quietly opened the door. They asked if I was Tommie Smith, and they asked me to have a seat. I wanted to say, "This is my house, you have a seat," but they had their hands on their guns. They told me there was a complaint against me and so on, and asked me if that was my gun on the table. It was on the table because I had been broken into two times in three days. But they told me not to go near it, because of the complaint against me. In all the time I was involved in the Olympic Project for Human Rights and all the meetings I had been in and all the harassment I'd received from white folks, I had never had the police called on me. And then my wife called them on me. I cried for days. I could not believe that my wife of 24 years and mother of my four kids called the cops on me. I had never touched her in anger. But some of her friends had gotten to her, telling her, "You better watch that nigger." I know they did, I can hear them.

When my place was broken into, they got all my rings, all the gold I had received over 30 years of competing. They didn't get the gold medal, but they took almost everything else—South Pole coats, my shoes, more than $30,000 worth of watches that I had won in meets all over the world, and about $700 in quarters. The things I have now are new; if you see them, you see they're too good and shiny to be 30-something years old. They're five or so years old, not 35. They stole my college rings, too, and my pro football players' association ring. And they stole the ring I received for participating in the Olympics, and my track and field Hall of Fame ring.

When Delois came on the scene, she told the Hall of Fame people that my ring had been stolen and got me another ring. She also got the Olympic ring replaced, and nearly all the rest except the pro football ring. The fact that she got all these rings back after some nigger had come in and stolen them—that's when I married her. If you can do that, you're the one for me.

I had met Delois in the administrative office at Santa Monica College not long after I filed for divorce from Denise; she was a sales representative who had never heard of me, and she began representing me in business deals soon after we met. Denise was kind of hurt, telling me that at least I could have waited until the ink was dry on the divorce papers. I thought that more than two years out of the house was long enough for me, a man from a big family who wanted kids and a wife and a home and a job, who wanted to come home and watch television sitting in his chair.

I did get all of those things, because I inherited a family when I married Delois. I paid child support for the kids that were still living with Denise, and I am still paying for Joey until he's 18. Does that sounds like a deranged husband or one that loves his family? It was hard for Delois to see me doing that at first, but I was doing it before we met and now it's part of me. She has two daughters of her own, and I paid for the wedding for the elder one, Tracy. In the first year we were married, I spent $30,000 on Delois's daughters, Tracy and Jennifer, who is in college, and I am taking care of Delois's mother, too, just as I did with Denise when we moved from Ohio. Plus I started paying off $65,000 in loans when Dani graduated from Pitzer College in southern California. So we both brought something into this marriage. Delois grew up in the South, in Alabama, was raised by her mother and grandmother, and also has been married two times before, to the father of her two daughters and to a man who was killed not long after they were married. Plus, she had a son while she was in high school—Montell Jordan, the singer. So with all these families, I taught year-round, including summer school, and did coaching and speaking just to make ends meet. Everything has met pretty well so far, well enough that I could afford to retire in 2005.

The second Denise was a good businesswoman, but Delois truly understands business. That fact was important to me, because I had always had the business done on me. Now, I am the business; that is, I am her business, Delo2K Enterprises, which markets Tommie Smith. I am what she works on, and she knows that. We have argued before about who Delo2K really is, but there really is nothing to argue about. I am the business, the one signing the shirts and giving the speeches, but it's her coming in and orchestrating things that were there but were not orchestrated. One of those projects is this book. When it comes to business, she goes out and gets what she wants, and she doesn't stop, she doesn't let up. That's how she runs the company; she runs me, because I'm the company. That's what she does. That's why this book is going to go and why this movie that we're pitching about my life is going to go. When Delois and I travel, she makes all the travel arrangements and contacts with where we're going. She gives me a list of what I need to know, topics that might be asked about, length of topic, and what time we leave and I come back. There's a lot of arranging that takes place, and I don't really deal with that. I deal with the subject matter.

In marrying me when she didn't know anything about me and in doing what she has done with me, Delois has done a commendable job of absorbing things about me, reading everything about me and talking to me. But she is still learning what it is like to be married to me, as well as to represent me. She's a very strong personality and has a very strong presence, so it's hard for her to hear me tell her something she's unsure about or doesn't know. It's very hard for her to realize that even when they see and hear her, they still want to turn and shoot me. I tell her she has to be careful about what she says, because she really doesn't know who she's married to. She'll say, "Well, I love you and I married you," and I have to stop her and say, "No, no, no, no—people want to gun me down because of their racist background, and they don't care who they have to take out to get to me. They're still out there." She'll say, "Do you really believe that?" Well, of course I do. I'm still getting threats more than 35 years later; I got threats in my neighborhood in California and I got them when it was announced they wanted to put up the statue. Delois has never been in a scary situation; being from the South, she has seen white folks torment black people, but she has not been close to death the way I have.

If I am not facing death in my surroundings, I am facing it inside myself. Curt Flood wrote his book, and so did Vince Matthews, Harry Edwards, Howard Cosell. I have all of those books, but I don't have one by Tommie Smith. Now, Curt Flood is gone, Cosell is gone. Jackie Robinson died young. The stress will take you out. I have to sit and calm down at times. My heart beats about twice as fast as it should when I'm resting, when I'm just sitting in my office or something. It's hard to believe that one of my keys to running fast is relaxing. I'm blessed that I've lived as long as I have, and please, God, don't take me away just for talking about it. I've now gone back to practicing relaxing, and that comes in handy, because at this point, being married to Delois is not relaxing, I guarantee you. It's because she doesn't realize how things affect me. She'll come up in the bedroom when I'm sleeping, and she'll be thinking of something and all of a sudden say, "Tom," and I'll jump up screaming, "What, what?" A couple of times when we lived in our house in Baldwin Park, she did that, and I jumped out of my skin and reached for my gun, or at least the drawer. It would terrify her, but it would scare me. I had to explain to her that it's a reaction from where I'm from, that I'm very protective, and that when I get scared I don't jump up and try to hug her, I try to protect her. It's my background. I could be wrong in doing it, but it's how I react.

This is why this has to all go onto the record now, once and for all. This is the end, the omega, for me. I gave away so much stuff, even to other book writers and filmmakers with proposals. Tapes, letters, artifacts all got lost. I'm down to nothing but words now. I understand that my legacy is being preserved, or at least remembered, which is one of the reasons Delo2K exists. I have been places, and I have seen the picture from the victory stand on shirts. I've also seen a picture of Martin Luther King and Malcolm X and an eagle, and Tommie Smith and John Carlos with the raised fist. My sister sent that one to me and asked me if I had ever gotten money for it. I said no and began looking for it where I lived, and I found it. I asked the man who was selling it, "Hey, this is a nice picture, but what does it represent?" He said something about the two guys at the Olympics that were shot for protesting, back in 1972. I said, "Shot? What were their names?" He didn't know, but he knew it would take $19.99 to get the shirt.

When Delois told him I was the one on the T-shirt, the man said, "Yeah, right, and I'm Little Caesar."

So the education continues. All the years that I had the photo hanging on the wall of my office at Santa Monica College, students paraded in and out and never knew who was in the picture. Every once in a while, one of them would say, "Coach, you ran track before?" I point to the picture and to a picture of me crossing the finish line. One of the students not long ago was the daughter of Otis Burrell, a high jumper who was one of my teammates in college. I told her that I had gone to school with her father, and she saw the picture behind me and said, "That's you? You're Tommie Smith? What are you doing in Santa Monica?" My thought was, Where was I supposed to be?

In 1999, I decided to make one last big leap at trying to do something for the young folks—a foundation that bore my name. I wanted it to be in my hometown of Lemoore, and I expected that others would like to see the same thing. After all, two other Olympians from the same area, Rafer Johnson in Kingsbury and Bob Mathias in Tulare, had all sorts of things, schools, streets, and others, named after them. But Tommie Smith had held more world records than both of them put together. So I started driving to Lemoore once a week from Santa Monica, sometimes twice a week, 203 miles each way. I talked to people there about starting the Tommie Smith Youth Foundation and organizing activities, beginning with a march in the spring and a walkathon in the summer. I did this for six weeks, four hours each way, making it back in time to teach a 10:15 A.M. class.

My plan was to oversee the whole thing and have a committee of civic and athletic leaders in the area handle the fundraising and sponsorship and operation of it. But the people I was looking at to organize it wanted it the other way around: I would provide the money, and they would basically spend it. Out of a committee of 12 people, including judges, teachers, and business owners in Lemoore, they couldn't raise $2,000 to provide the basic expenses for the first walkathon. Then someone had the idea of going to the nearby Indian reservation; it had money, and it gave money to civic causes like this one. I had gone to school with some of the chiefs of the reservation, and some of my sisters worked there. I thought it would be no problem—and it wouldn't have been if I had not suggested that my old teacher, coach, and principal, Mr. Focht, go with me. I thought it would work because everybody respected him. The committee grew silent at that suggestion. It turned out that Mr. Focht was instrumental in the reservation's not having a school of its own, having said that a school there would not be up to standard. Once we got there and sat across from the chief, I found that out—it was like walking into a refrigerator, because they saw Mr. Focht. The chief spoke very cordially to me and said that he liked the idea and the fact that I was connected to it, but that there was a lot going on there and that he would have to think about it. I didn't catch what he meant, but when Mr. Focht spoke, and asked the chief if he was still thinking about not having a school there, it was all over. I was shot. The chief said a couple of more words and left. I was shocked at how much money was available on that reservation—I found out from my sisters that each child in each household gets a certain amount from the government—and shocked to find out that we could not get them to part with $2,000 to start a foundation they agreed with, because of the presence of that white man who had done that to them.

When it came down to it, my name meant nothing in my hometown, not the way Rafer Johnson's or Bob Mathias's did in theirs. All these years later, the social climate, the attitudes, the implication of truth, still leave their mark. No athlete in Lemoore ever truly gets recognized by the white people of the city. They will invite them back to help them celebrate one thing or another, or to help them bring attention to a cause, as they do when they hold functions for pro football players from the area like Joey Galloway and Lorenzo Neal. The white people in Lemoore will honor a city council member or someone in the police department or an administrator at the high school, but not an athlete. Even the athletic fields and facilities have nothing that honors anybody, certainly nothing for me. There is a plaque commemorating the fact that I ran there, but you'd have to look hard to find it. Besides, I have pretty good degrees from pretty reputable sources, but if anybody recognizes me at all, it's because I was an athlete. I tell them I'm a college instructor, and they say, "No kidding, really?" Nothing has changed since I came back there 30 years earlier for my mother's funeral, and they asked me how my football career was going. I'm nothing more than Richard Smith's son, the kid who used to clean classroom floors and dig for tadpoles. I had come there to gladly give my time to build a foundation to get kids off the street, and it never came together.

IT WASN'T UNTIL THAT SITUATION came up that Delois and I started talking about auctioning off my track and field artifacts. I still had a few things that could raise enough money for what I needed. I had the warm-up suit I had worn in Mexico City, the singlet and shorts, and the olive branch I was awarded on the victory stand. Delois is a good salesperson, and she had started a Web site for me, tommiesmith.com. It was easy to set up an online auction. But the items we put on there weren't enough; I needed 10 times what they would draw just to handle the basic needs, to provide a staff and an office for the foundation. People were not going to work for nothing; one time not long ago, Jean-Claude Van Damme actually came to me about working as a trainer for the foundation, but I had nothing to offer him besides Tommie Smith's name, and you can't eat that. When I asked people to donate money and invited them to be on the board of directors of the foundation, they would say that they would love to do it if I could do something for them in return, like give 10 speeches for them. I didn't have time to give 10 speeches for anybody, not for several people; I had to work. I couldn't understand why a youth foundation wasn't a good enough reason for people to just give the money. I could have started the foundation with the money I had made from speeches, which is the way that I make money for Delo2K. But I didn't want the foundation to cost me money and send me into debt. I couldn't believe that no one was dedicated enough to the cause of the foundation to just write a check.

It was at that time that we decided to put the gold medal up for auction. It was the most valuable piece of memorabilia that I could offer, and we decided to ask $500,000 for it. In the corporate world, that is not a lot of money. People spend twice that for a small car or a small ring or a piece of property that they don't stay on, or on memorabilia they put in their house under glass and no one ever sees. The baseball Mark McGwire hit to set the home run record got

$3 million, and Barry Bonds' baseball, which he hit to set his own record, got about half a million. They're sitting someplace now where no one can enjoy them. But the bottom line on this was that no one offered the $500,000 price. I was insulted. We took the gold medal out of the auction, and now we won't put it back. It's better off this way, anyway, because I believe some people would have bought it and thrown it away, jut for the heck of it, so I wouldn't have it. There are people that are still mad, without a doubt, and there are enough people with money who would spend it to satiate their own hatred. But still, I sure wish I could have found them, if they were willing to spend the money. For some people, 500 grand is not that much money, like $500 to someone else.

I have other items from Mexico City and elsewhere that I'd like to see someone have if they want it. It really doesn't mean a whole lot to me. I still have my ceremonial uniform from the opening and closing ceremonies, the red coat and white pants and the Puma hat. Miriam Makeba and Stokely Carmichael gave John Carlos and me each a cane made of an ivory tusk; I got the female one, John the male. It's irreplaceable. But if someone wants those items for a contribution to the Tommie Smith Foundation, I can part with them. I have my gate entry pass to the stadium in Mexico City. I have a pin given to those of us who competed at South Lake Tahoe for the altitude training, a pin we all wore very proudly. You'll see more Olympic pins than you'll see of those "altitude" pins. I didn't even know I still had that; there were a lot of things I didn't realize I had until I put it all together several years ago.

I've also got the torch I carried in the relay for the 1996 Olympics in Atlanta. I worked for that, too, and became good enough to be called back to do it, and to call attention to it and make it bigger. It was a big deal to see Tommie Smith in the Olympic torch run. It was the first thing I had been involved in with the Olympics since Mexico City, with the exception of a program in Laguna Hills, California, back in the late 1970s and early '80s called the Olympic campaign, which was a series of camps for kids that the city ran. I don't know if it was affiliated with the IOC or the USOC, because they have appendages everywhere, and they made such a profit from the 1984 Games in Los Angeles that this might have come under the control of one of the programs started with the surplus money. Still, nothing official with the Olympics came my way until I was invited to run in the torch relay through Santa Monica. They charged me more than $400 for the torch, but so what—I have it now, and it will be here after I'm gone, with me or with whoever wants it.

I don't have the gloves; I had never felt it was important at the time to keep them, never thought to give them to someone for safekeeping or to put them in a vault, just in case. The other items I've acquired over the years would solidify the things I want to do for young people. So many things have gotten lost or broken through all the times I've moved, or they were stolen and either got replaced or were unable to be replaced. I've got four or five full trophies that I don't even have on display; they're stored away someplace in a case I built back in high school.

But now, my gold medal is not going anywhere. The price is too high for me to get rid of it now. I'm not like Muhammad Ali, who threw his gold medal into the Mississippi River when he realized it didn't get him treated any different in his hometown of Louisville. When the Olympics came to Atlanta in 1996, they gave him another gold medal to replace the other one, but once mine is gone, I won't ever have one again. I also am not like John Carlos, saying the gold medal didn't mean much to him, so he let me win it. That's very negative, and that's John Carlos. The gold medal does mean something to me.

I won't make money off that gold medal. My money comes largely from the appearances Delois and her company set up for me. Sometimes I think about how speaking was not my strong point, and in the beginning I had to come up with ways to do it right. In the beginning I would stand before an audience and I would need to calm down, and I didn't know how to do it. The very first trip I ever took with Delois to speak, at an Ivy League school, I made a big mistake that I learned from right away. I was really looking forward to this; some nice articles had been written about my visit, they were expecting 500 students, Delois had brought a bunch of T-shirts for me to sign and sell, they had a limousine for us on a misty, rainy night, and there was a dressing room. I had spent about 28 hours on the speech I was going to give. Delois went out and began the program with a song, as she always used to do before my speeches. Then I came out and saw maybe 50 people out there, mostly students, just looking at me. Every once in a while I'd scan the audience and see someone writing, then I'd see someone looking away or looking down.

I was hurt, just cranially interrupted by madness. I started picking on them, asking who they thought they were, just sitting there like that while I was trying to give them some history. Some people got up and left; others sat up quick, then slumped down again. There was a young woman sitting right up front, and I started on her, talking about how her hair was too long. As soon as I said it, I said, "Tom, you're dead in the water." But I was so angry, from spending so much time on the speech and flying all night and dealing with the rain and the airport and the hotel for 50 people when there were supposed to be 500. It was the last time getting mad. From then on, if only one person showed up at my speech, I was going to speak to him as if it was a million. I also came up with a way to calm down when I lost track of my subject or got distracted. I spoke at an awards dinner for a youth track team in the Los Angeles area a few years ago, a club coached by one of my former Santa Monica runners; I was to speak to the kids and their parents. I looked around the room and I started prancing around like a preacher, focusing in on the parents, who were really into what I was saying. Then I looked at the kids, and they were looking at me like they were thinking, Whatever. I went up to one kid directly and was about to say something to him, but the other Tommie in me—the one who had learned his lesson at that Ivy League speech—said, "Back off, don't do it." So I turned around, made a crack about the women in the audience, and did a little dance, and it calmed me down. It works: do something else to get your mind back on track.

The Ivy League trip was also the last time I accepted an invitation for free. I figured that if I was paid up front and received a first-class ticket, then at least I would enjoy the trip no matter who came to the speech. Still, I don't ever ask for a lot, just enough for me to live and to be happy. I don't need a lot. I've retired now; I've moved to Georgia and bought a house there. I'm going to have that recreational vehicle and I'll just hook the car up behind it, be on the road, travel the country, and let that be my home.

I got full tenure at Santa Monica, got what I did not get at Oberlin. People had asked me over the years why I never went to a place like UCLA; I answered, I would make $58,000 at UCLA and made $95,000 at Santa Monica, so why would I leave? They would say, money isn't everything, and I would say, no, money is not—and I would leave it right there.

Now all I want to do is settle down with my wife in our home, have some peace, and make a book and a movie out of all of this. I want to say what I want to say and then go away. It's my last chance to pull myself out of the muck and mire that I've been stuck in since the Mexico City Olympics, that I tried to hide from in different places for all those years.

12

It Will Outlive Me

I HAD WANTED FOR A LONG TIME for Santa Monica College to be my last professional stop. This is where I wanted to retire, and in the summer of 2005, I did, and Delois and I moved back to the South, to Georgia, near her home and her people. I've gone into partial retirement, actually; I would never just retire and go fishing, it's not in my blood to do that. When I do stop speaking and writing for a living, I probably will keep on moving. But I was blessed to have found my place for a period of 27 years, and nothing happened to uproot me.

Some have said that I settled for it, a small community college with a small athletic department, a small athletic budget, and a small enrollment, which produced a small group of athletes whose lives I could affect. I would not say that I settled for anything. For one thing, I fulfilled one of the dreams I had growing up. Remember, as a kid, I had yearned to be a soldier, a policeman, or a teacher—a man who had authority, a man who could provide a service to his community. I have done nothing but teach for more than 30 years. Teaching is all I wanted to do once I completed college, regardless of where my athletic exploits would take me. And regardless of the location or the size or the prestige of the place where I teach, I will always be glad that I was able to do this.

Why would I say I am settling for anything? Some have asked if the victory stand has prevented me from coaching or teaching at bigger schools—if any of us involved in the protest found their paths blocked to better jobs that would have paid more money. I understand the question, although it presumes that I am controlled by the almighty dollar, that I make decisions based on giving into the system and getting paid to compensate me for the compromise.

True enough, I will never forget how many rejections I had gotten and how many times I never even got a response when I sent out all of those applications in 1978, when my tenure at Oberlin was denied. I will never forget, either, the way no one in San Jose would hire me or John when we began to get involved in the Olympic Project for Human Rights back in 1967, or when we came back from Mexico City—how I struggled to feed my family, the lengths I went to, after taking my stand.

But being at Santa Monica College was not settling for anything. My fellow runners from 1968, and my teammates at San Jose State, did not settle, either—on the contrary. What we have done since 1968 indicates not only that we were the best Olympic track team in history, but also that academically we were rated among the top. We are all still working in the professional education field, in coaching or teaching or both. My old partner Lee Evans joined Bud Winter's staff at San Jose State after he was finished running, staying from 1970 to 1972. Later, he coached the national track teams of four different nations over a span of 22 years, from 1975 to 1997. He developed athletes for Nigeria, Qatar, Saudi Arabia, and Ghana. Six of his athletes became Olympic medalists. In 2001 he joined the coaching staff at the University of South Alabama in Mobile, a Division I program; the head coach there now is one of my Speed City predecessors, Ron Davis, a distance runner back in the early 1960s when blacks were not supposed to excel at distances.

Larry James, who finished second to Lee in the 400 at Mexico City and joined him on the victory stand in the 4-by-100 relay, became a coach and then the dean of athletics at Richard Stockton College in New Jersey. He also is on the board of directors for USA Track and Field, and he was on the staff for the U.S. team at the world championships in Paris in 2003 and in Helsinki in 2005.

Larry also was inducted into the National Track and Field Hall of Fame in 2003. That was a long wait for a member of one of the greatest teams in Olympic history, but he made it, and he was at the ceremony at the new home of the Hall of Fame in New York City. I was inducted several years ago, and a part of that victory stand is also there; some of what I wore on the stand was donated to the Hall when it was based in Indianapolis. Not the gloves, of course. Also inducted with Larry were two men whose careers crossed mine. Mike Larrabee was one of the great 400-meter runners against whom I would have competed in those Olympic Trials in 1964, had I not been so young and isolated and confused that I missed my heat. Mike Larrabee went on to win two golds in Tokyo. He passed away not long before his Hall of Fame selection.

And John Carlos was inducted. I couldn't help but think: now, what did he do to get into the Hall of Fame? He didn't win a gold medal. He had the 100-meter world record for about a minute. He had that bogus world record in the 200 in South Lake Tahoe with the illegal shoe, which was never counted. He didn't finish college. I know that his name is there because of the victory stand. It's another thing he has because of being on that victory stand with me.

Still, John is one of the members of that 1968 team who is teaching and coaching. He is still in Palm Springs, coaching and counseling at a private high school. We're all spread out, and we're doing things. We stayed in teaching. We all did what we had set out to do, even if it was not at the biggest venues and at the largest institutions, where someone with our accomplishments would normally go.

True, nonblack athletes who were not involved in the Olympic Project for Human Rights have attained higher-level, higher-visibility positions. Bruce Jenner and Bill Toomey have never had to think about regrets as far as where their careers have taken them. I understand that these people also worked to get where they are, just as we did, but they got where they are a long time ago, and they are making a lot of money, and they were making it long before Lee or I. Even though we were qualified, we had to wait in line, and we had to wait there to get what no one else wanted, or to get what we wanted a lot later than we should have.

I am proof of that. I spent those 27 years at Santa Monica, but I had to wait until 10 years after Mexico City to get that position. It was the only place I could go. In my four years at Oberlin, I was a track coach, a basketball coach, and at the end an assistant AD, although Jack Scott was the type that did everything himself. I was full AD for a year after Jack left, and I traveled all over Ohio that year, going to different meetings and gatherings and that sort of thing. After that, I told myself, "No, this isn't for me." But once they refused to give me tenure—after they ran me out and everyone else from Jack Scott's regime—I couldn't get a job doing anything, coaching or teaching, until Santa Monica called, and even then I had to wait until they had enough money for my position.

In those 27 years at Santa Monica, opportunities were never available to me at the bigger schools. The job as head track coach at Cal-Berkeley opened up in 2003. My son Kevin had been on the team at Cal, as a jumper, so I knew the program. I sent my résumé in, I did all the right things, and eventually the school said there was no use in my going any further, because they were going to hire the assistant coach, Chris Huffins. Chris Huffins was the in-house choice —he had performed there, had competed in the 2000 Olympics in the decathlon, and had coached elsewhere before returning to Cal. They were all set to hire him; all that stood in the way was his completing his degree. I understood quickly enough that they had an in-house preference that would get the first crack. Otherwise, I don't see why I couldn't have gotten the job if I had the chance in an open competition.

My responsibility at Santa Monica grew soon enough, anyway— in late 2003, I was asked to take over as athletic director, along with my other athletic duties. It was strictly a financial move for the school. The entire state community college system was essentially out of money. If you remember the recall of the governor that year, when "The Terminator" was elected—and I still can't get my mind around that, another actor running my home state, Arnold Schwarzenegger, following my old "friend" Ronald Reagan—you know about the California budget crisis, and you know that higher education took one of the biggest hits. At Santa Monica, a lot of the managers didn't have enough people under them to be called managers anymore. So the school just started cutting positions. The physical education department wasn't spared—we were cut 30 percent, and we lost people in several positions through attrition, reassignments, layoffs, and forced retirement. We also had employed six athletic directors in five years because of the demands of the job.

Now, the vice president asked if I was willing to take the job. It's a position I could have had 10 years earlier, when the school president had asked me. I turned it down because I didn't want the hassle, and

I didn't want to give up instructing. This time, I told the vice president, whom I knew well, that if necessary I would take the job, for a while. I knew the department was in shambles. I also soon found out that, because of the way the rules work with the teachers' union, I would have to give up instructing classes in order to take over as AD, because I would then be considered management. Making that sacrifice was not something I necessarily enjoyed, since teaching has meant, and does mean, so much to me.

But I took the AD job—which meant I was not teaching a class, yet I was adding to my athletic department workload, operating under the financial strain of the budget cuts, while still running the track program. I also was managing a staff, getting used to a new secretary for my new position. I was back to attending endless meetings and dealing with the different personalities with the different agendas. And for all of that, I was rewarded with a $6,000 pay cut—because of having to give up instructing and because it was the reality of the financial bind. With what I've gone through the last 50 years of my life, the athletic directorship would not be a problem. In fact, it would be a worthwhile challenge to me. I could get the department running the way it should be within a couple of years, and I'd find avenues to raise money. But not for a $6,000 pay cut. Not after more than 25 years there. I knew right away that I was not going to be doing this for long. It gave me even more reason to think about my retirement.

Giving up classes was almost as painful to me as the pay cut. I've done it before, giving up a class so that a younger coach can have a class in the summer. I've given up a lot of money at that school in order to help younger coaches out. Of course I want the money—who doesn't?—but my profession is teaching. I have proven many times the benefits I bring to the various positions.

Yet I was passed over a number of times right there at Santa Monica, despite my accomplishments, my history, and my sacrifices. It has been clear over the years that I have a rapport with students, especially with athletes, a mentor-type relationship. The students know me. There's no more effective vehicle for learning than for an ethnic person, in this case a black person or a black student athlete, to talk to someone who has been where they are. They can relate their own experiences to the teacher and ask questions relating to their future and to how I dealt with a particular issue, questions I can address because of my background in athletics and politics.

Not long after I was asked to take the AD job, I learned about a position in the sociology department. I contacted the people hiring for it and told them I had a master's in sociology and have taught sociology at Santa Monica and at Oberlin, and the woman said, "I'll bring it up at the table." Maybe she did or maybe she didn't, but they hired a white blond-haired blue-eyed woman for the job—to teach sociology at Santa Monica, where the student population is significantly black and Latino and, increasingly over the years, Asian. They never contacted me at all. All the places I've been and the people I've known, it wasn't even worth a call back to me. It had happened to me there before, and it had happened at Oberlin, where I was pushed out because, they said, my teaching and coaching were below departmental standards. I know that if I had been chosen for the position at Santa Monica, I would have gotten a lot of athletes into the particular class and could have spoken directly to them, as well as to the other students. They could have looked at me as a role model. I could have affected students that otherwise might not have been affected.

Well, people make bad decisions, and that time, Santa Monica College made one. Yet there I was, giving up a class, taking a pay cut, and lengthening my hours, in service to a school because of my belief that I can impart my knowledge to young people who need it. I love teaching, I love coaching, I love the school, but I couldn't keep doing that.

The welfare of students, their future, and their educational opportunities will always be important to me. I have no choice but to stay engaged in what they are thinking and how they are acting—and how they are thinking. It drove me as a teacher at Santa Monica, it drives me at the places where I appear and lecture, and it dominated my thoughts that day in October 2003 on the San Jose State campus.

I wish I could say that the spirit and passion shown by the three students on the panel that morning—Justin, Ambra, and Mary—permeated that campus, as well as other campuses. I can't say that their courage was that evident on this campus even in my day, at least not throughout the population. Those of us in the middle of the struggle were passionate enough, but the rest of the campus was more content to stay out of the line of fire.

They are the same age that I was when I began to realize the power I had and the problems in society that could benefit from it. Now is the hard part. They have stood up and acknowledged us and the victory stand, and now they have to use that to catapult their ideas into the world. I hope that they do their homework, get in the trenches, and make sure their own platform is solid so that they don't run into a stone wall and be stopped. Tommie Smith and John Carlos couldn't have been stopped; the whole world saw us from our platform. We had something the whole world could identify with.

These students are taking off from what we did. Just as the past had laid out for us what we had to do, their past has to do that for them. We, and our action, are their past, and they have a chance to build on it and go on, to realize fully what that stand represented and carry it the next step. It is easier for them to lay it aside—to discuss it a little and engage in the celebration and then go home and forget about it—than it was for us to go home and set anything aside. They could just let the victory stand go back to being a famous picture— but they can't allow themselves to do that. That picture is what they build on, and they have the task of continuing the task of the men in that picture.

I thought of that as well when, later in the day, at the end of the banquet to honor John and me at the Fairmont Hotel, I walked close to the stage and looked at the model of the statue they planned to erect. All day long, I had heard about Tommie Smith and John Carlos, the sculpture, as I walked around campus. Everybody was talking about it, but a lot of those students were also looking at me as we passed each other, and they didn't know who I was. Yet they knew the victory stand; they knew what the statue meant and what the men on that statue meant. That's amazing, to know that I don't have to be there for them to recognize the importance of that stand. It's not the two of us in person that's going to make this happen; the idea of it is what will be represented. But at the same time, it had become obvious by the end of that day, as the students reacted to us as they realized who stood before them and spoke, that our being there in front of them made it more eventful. We were there, and they could see us. We're not 90 years old, we're not on crutches, we're not in wheelchairs—we're still vibrant, moving and working in the system. So as they walked past that stage that night, they saw the model of the statue, but they also saw us.

I made a point of this to the audience for that morning panel discussion, at the very beginning, before answering the questions and describing what it was like for us on campus, on the victory stand, and in the midst of the struggle.

"We knew not very much, but we did know something: we were human, and we wanted to be treated as human," I said. "But we did not know how to go about fighting for this. We were students like most of you are, so we had no tools to fight. I was put in a position I didn't want to be in. I was sacrificed because I believed later in life that it would become a complete circle, and it has made a complete circle, several circles.

"I am here now because of that," I continued, "and because of you wanting to see living history. And I'm here to let you know we're both still alive and well. We're not perfect, but we were there. We were the ones who lived through it."

I believe those young students grasped the full meaning of completing the circle. It's not just my coming back to San Jose State; it is the entire situation in society. We're even fighting a war that's similar to Vietnam, almost the same. Ironic, isn't it? It's more proof that humanity and history can only go so far before it starts to repeat itself. What was happening in 1968 is happening again—a little differently, in ways that we might not even know about yet, but the similarities are obvious. And the people are going to have to make a move to do something about it all, just as the people did in 1968 when all that upheaval was taking place. In some way, that all had to take place—the assassinations and murders and breakdown of the old social order—to ensure that things would change. But will people actually join together to make those changes this time, in a time when personal connections are lost because of the age of computer technology? No one knows.

Our act, Tommie Smith's and John Carlos's, was one of those upheavals. Plenty of people agreed that something had to be done, and they agreed with what we were saying, but they disagreed with how it was done and where it was done. "Why couldn't it have been done around a conference table?" they would ask. Well, because too many things don't happen around a conference table. This had to be a world event to provide a spark that caused the fire to burn away the injustices that were occurring at the time. It will have to be a fire again, and possibly a bigger fire this time, because the same injustices are still alive today, but they are very hard to find.

It would take an extra effort and an extra commitment, even stronger than the one we made. We laid the groundwork for the later generations. Even the students at San Jose State are building their foundation not from the base of the events of their day, but on the stand we took, and they will take off from there to build further and effect change. We were like the old cars, and the old technology that made those cars run. The later generations can build cars, and build better cars, but they have to build them from the parts we had. And to understand how to build the new cars, you have to go find the parts of the old car to find out. Even if you look at the new car, you can't understand it without knowing about the old car. But the old parts don't fit that well with the new cars, especially with the computerized parts of the new. Again, computers alter the way something runs, whether it's mechanical or flesh and blood. Rely on the technology too much, and the humanity dies. See how many people want to blame failures and faults on the computer—but where does the knowledge that is programmed into the computer come from? It's just another way to push off responsibility and another way to separate ourselves from our humanity and from other humans.

I truly believe that the students heard and understood John and me, but we were that old Chevy with old Chevy parts, and they're in the Lexus dealing with the computer parts, and they tried to put it together and couldn't. How we looked, how we walked, and how we talked were more interesting to them than what we had to say.

Even to the students who care, who understand, who want to engage themselves, the challenge is greater now. Man is growing weaker and wiser. The brain process is infinite now, and it now is capable of taking on more issues, so a person must decide how his or her brain can be used best—devoting a lot of time to a few issues or becoming devoted to many issues but with less time for all of them.

You don't have to be a rocket scientist to know there are needs in this system. You don't have to be a rocket scientist to know that if you stand up for one cause, there will be others waiting for you to address. Because of the one stand we made, John Carlos and I are now addressing a lot of causes. That stand was like a mustard seed; it was planted and it grew. Yet a lot of people are not taking part in the festive eating of that mustard plant. They don't understand all the things around them.

For certain, the magnitude of what John Carlos and I did is too large for them to comprehend. At a basic level, these students—even the ones who cared enough to see us—do not understand how they are connected to us. They don't see John Carlos and Tommie Smith playing a part in their being there on a college campus in the 21st century, but we are that link of social war that caused them to be free enough to get that seat. Yet I could see, on the San Jose State campus that day, at the campuses at which I have lectured over the years, and on the one where I taught for 27 years, that they take their seat in class for granted. It's another example of how we, as black people, are still sometimes our own worst enemy.

They are not the only ones who fail in this, but black students especially have a problem giving tribute to those who have gone on before. I believe they think they're there because they signed a piece of paper and were accepted. There are too many people who have gone on before them who have given up life, family, and status for them to be there. We don't realize that sometimes to attack something—and I mean attack, because that often is the only way—we have to use a dull knife and sharpen it as we work through the mess. When you are on the outside, you have to beat the hard surface to make it soft, but once you get on the inside, you cut your way out. That is what I did. I stood on the victory stand, but I stood there as a man without my degree, and I knew that fact meant that I was still not what I was supposed to be. The victory stand did not give me that BA either. I understood that others had sacrificed so this could happen, and what I did not want to do was make this stand and then turn my back on it when I stepped down and came home. I got my BA, I got my master's, and I maintained my family as best I could, and I stayed in the system that allowed me to continue my pursuit. That didn't mean I was willing to be dehumanized, of course, but I had to stay within that system. That meant education.

That is why it hurts me to see these students not taking that baton, not making education a priority, going through college the way they do. I know because I see them, not listening to the instructor because they don't believe in what he is teaching them, or sleeping through a class, or not showing up at all. They go through their time in school knowing nothing more than the bus schedule, their computers, what corner to hang out on and get into hoo-rahing, and what they're wearing, with the baggy pants and the skirts and hip-huggers and very little else, showing as much of their bellies as they can. Not that I don't understand it. I know that very well. I tell students this all the time—I know you're bored in class, because so was I. Fake it! Sit there, look at the teachers, come up with a way to stay awake in class. You don't have to believe what that teacher says, just understand it. Don't hide behind a hat or sunglasses. Hats and sunglasses are not allowed in my classes, for a reason. That might be the only thing your instructor remembers from your entire semester with them, that they caught you sleeping, and that will make the difference in your final grade. Yes, I wanted to go to sleep, and no, I didn't want to go to every single class, but I did.

And if you don't like what they say or how they say it, you're not the only one, either—it was worse when I was going to school, because everybody talked different from the way I did, and it made me not want to be there. Instead of tuning out, try to understand why people talk the way they do. Listen to the person, dissect every word that person says, and if you don't understand it, ask him to please repeat it. You could be wide awake and if you're ignorant of a fact, that's the same as being asleep, so do not let anything just slide past you. I can see this going on when I talk to my students— oh, my goodness. Have you ever been in a conversation with some-one and realize that you're not talking to them, but they're talking to you? No matter what you say, their next sentence will be a continu-ation of the last sentence they had spoken. You're the dash in their conversation. They don't understand the most important thing about a conversation—the conversing, rather than making the other person the dash.

I open my students' eyes to this when they come into my office at Santa Monica and see the wall, covered with history, from Jesse Owens to Malcolm X to Martin Luther King to Howard Cosell to myself and all my world records, and finally, to the photo of the victory stand. They see it and say, "You did all of this? Can you coach me, can you help me do all of this?" They want to be great, and they see a path to it through me; they weren't dealing with me, but with their own thoughts. But then, I tell them that the victory stand was my lowest point. I tell them that I did not set those records or take that stand or come in contact with those people without sacrifice, by a lot of people and by me. And it did not happen by me not taking class seriously, but it happened because I listened to everything and everybody and reached my own conclusions and convictions. Suddenly, I was more than the dash in their conversation.

Suddenly, listening and remembering becomes important—I have kids come back to me and tell me about something I told them at 3:22 in the afternoon back on June 15 eight years ago. They take that into their classes and in front of their instructors. All they retain might be a mustard seed's worth. They might hate every word out of that teacher's mouth; they might believe he is the racist to end all racists, and they might fight only to make that teacher believe that he understands the information being given. If it gets you the grade you need, you do it. One day, long after you grunted and griped your way through that class and finished it, you will see how that mustard seed that was planted has grown.

The sad truth is that, like everything else, our lack of understanding of what we are being taught is a continuing cycle. It has been our problem since Day 1. I had that problem throughout my educational years in the 1960s, and black students have the same problem today. I sat in the back of class; I was always behind, continually catching up, because by the time I figured out what was going on up front, with my short attention span, the class has moved on to something else. The children that have followed since then have done the same thing, gotten bored and disinterested and turned our focus onto things that won't help us as much as what's happening right in front of us in class. It was a fight that all of us from 1968 never stopped fighting. This is why so many of us stayed in education, even John Carlos, who still takes it as some sort of source of pride that he never got his degree, emphasizing how we're different. Yet I know he still cares about education, for himself in a sense, and definitely for others, because as a young black student in that day, he had that same problem.

Now, part of the education of those youngsters, those students at San Jose State, that next generation of Americans that will try to make America listen just as we had tried—part of that education will be a statue of me and John Carlos. That model that I gazed at in that ballroom would one day, very soon, stand on the grounds of my campus. It was difficult for me to comprehend, and the statue is of me, and I was the one who did something that warranted a statue in my honor. So imagine how incomprehensible it all was to the students, even as they had gone a long way to recognize and grasp the fact that what the statue symbolizes was worthwhile.

Here we are now, alive, dealing with something that's going to last forever. We were so young when we began our quest, and so young when we climbed atop that victory stand. And 35 years later, we were still here, and we were going to witness a symbol to us and our action that will last another 35 years, 40, 50, 70—it will be infinite. Those students, and all the ones that follow them, will have plenty of time to absorb and understand what that means—that it was more than two athletes standing with our fists in the air. In fact, our standing with our fists in the air isn't the most important thing about it, although it's what everyone knows. We could have been standing on our heads, we could have been raising white fists instead of black ones, but the message we were sending comes from the context, not the act. It happened at a certain time and place in history, and because of that, it was done a certain way. It could not be ignored, and it was done silently, so that anyone could take from it his or her own message.

People all over the planet can look at that image and can identify with its message: not just in America, but in Africa, Europe, Asia, every part of the seven continents. I am reminded of this every day and in every trip I take in this country and around the world. In other countries, I have seen replicas of the victory stand, on T-shirts, on posters, in works of art, on murals, on magazines and in books, and on album covers. In 2003, I spoke at a Black History Month dinner at DeAnza

College in California, not far from San Jose State, where several of my old San Jose State friends and teammates, such as Robert Griffith and Eb Hunter, have converged as teachers and administrators. They invited me there as the keynote speaker, and after I spoke, a group of dancers from South Africa, I-Themba, performed several routines that were drawn from their experiences both living with apartheid and living in the aftermath of its demolition and the expansion of democracy to the native Africans. It was an interracial group of young dancers, and they were spectacular and colorful and full of the passion youth should have everywhere, in this country and everywhere else.

After they had performed, several of them spoke to the audience about their lives, and one young white woman spoke about how apartheid had done terrible damage to her life and the lives of her family, even though they were part of the ruling class. Her family, she said, had turned their backs on her sister because she had married a black man and had given birth to an interracial child. She herself had been ostracized because she had made friends with blacks. She had seen terrible oppression and dehumanization firsthand. And one of the factors in her brief life that had inspired her to continue to fight, against the wishes of her family and the constrictions of her own society, was the image of John Carlos and me on the victory stand—an act of democratic protest that took place 10 years before she was born, an entire hemisphere away from her, during a sporting event. The young lady was in tears by the time she finished her testimony, and so was the rest of the audience, including Delois and me, smiling through our tears as we listened. When the dinner had ended, that young lady and the other members lined up to speak to me and embrace me.

That was not an uncommon experience for me. So many people around the world are moved by the sight of those fists raised and that head lowered. Yet again, it is not something everyone fully understands. Right here at home, I will see a kid wearing, say, a T-shirt, and as I did on San Jose State's campus that day, they walk past and have no idea that the man they passed was the one on the shirt. I have been approached by young men in Los Angeles, at the open markets and vendor stands on the street or at cultural events, holding up a T-shirt or cap or jacket with the image, telling me I really should get one of them. They'll point to it on their own chest and say, "You want one of these? This is a righteous picture." And I tell then, "That's me on you. Why would I need the shirt? I'm the one on the shirt." That blows them away.

It is just a case of their not having the knowledge of what had happened, or how it happened, or how the man on that shirt connects to them. That's me being the old Chevy whose part doesn't fit into the new Lexus, but who made the new Lexus possible. They do not understand: there might not be a you now, if not for me then.

Will they understand it all when they see that statue? I admit, I can't understand that—it's hard to envision the new thing they are going to create out of the old parts, by way of building that statue. I mean, a *statue*. They don't have statues of black men, unless it's at a historically black college—and most of those colleges, and the statues, have ended up being taken over by the state because of budget cuts. But I have to admit that I'm a victim of low expectations for myself, something a lot of black people are. One of the perks of being athletic director at Santa Monica was my own secretary—a white woman. My phone would ring, both in my office and out in the main office, and she would pick it up and say, "Tommie Smith's office," and I would whirl around to look at her, amazed at the sounds of those words and who was speaking them. My first instinct was to say to her, "Why are you answering my phone?" I also had white coaches who worked under me, who came into the office to ask me for things. This is how it is done.

It was a whole different life for me, and for all I have said about how we want and wish and strive for better things for ourselves, we really don't expect it. That was beyond what I could have envisioned; I've seen it all my life but I couldn't have imagined myself in it. That's how we think. Considering the time I was there, I shouldn't have expected any less of myself. But as black folks, we think too little of ourselves, and we have to learn to respect ourselves in relation to the position that we are in and the position that we can someday be in. It took me until I was almost 60 years old to reach that realization, until I was in that position, when my phone rang, and when coaches came to talk to me, and when I went into meetings and realized I was the head of that meeting.

This is what centuries of exploitation by a system can produce, though. This is black people making it clear to white people that no, you are not always in charge. I had to realize that as unusual as it felt for me to be sitting behind that desk, it was just as uneasy for them to be the ones standing in front of the desk, talking to a black man behind that desk. One reason the victory stand was an athletic shock as well as a social and cultural shock was that this was an image of a black man few had ever thought they would see. When I played for the freshman basketball team at San Jose State, I did not start the very first game. I was there on a scholarship, I was 6-foot-4 and could out-leap our 6-10 white center on the opening tap, I was definitely good enough to start for that team, and I had started every single game I had played at Lemoore High. But that coach, Danny Gline, would not start me in the first game—no way was a black kid going to start for his team in the very first game. I started every game after that in that season, but not that first one. I didn't even know how to sit on the bench, because I had never done it before; I didn't know whether to sit straight or cross my legs.

I learned an important lesson that day: white folks have a hard time dealing with folks other than themselves because they have always ruled, and they have always done what they want. Having a black kid start in front of a white kid was too difficult, for the coach and for the white kid whose starting job was gone. When you have everything your way, you do not want to give it up, and you will resist giving it up. They have to be trained, and white folks don't understand being trained because they had never been trained by anybody but themselves. It's that simple. In 1968 we were telling the white man a new way to operate his country, reminding him that it wasn't only his country but others' as well. It was like telling him how to run his family, and you can't tell a white man how to run his family—but the white man has told other people, black folks in this case, how to do it, what they can and can't do, and how to do it. He could not, and cannot, take his own medicine. When we stood on the victory stand and said, "Look at things from my standpoint for once, because I've already seen it from yours," his response was "Don't stand there and tell me about my system; you ought to be glad that we let you into it." To a people who are used to telling everyone else what to do and how to do it, nothing is harder for them than to hear someone else tell them. In fact, they cannot deal with the fact that they are not the ones doing the talking.

Conversely, we are not accustomed to being in the throne of power, and we wonder how long we will be there and what we are doing there. I'm not on the victory stand anymore, a young kid standing there, waiting for someone to throw shit at me or shoot me or say something bad about me. They can't touch me now. Of course, now that I have it, I'm getting out of it. But that's just that one instance of power. Then there is this statue and what will come with it, and after it, after I am long gone. Just like the thought of a white woman answering my phone for me, the thought of this statue scares the heck out of me. The only statue I revere is a statue of Jesus. Yet there's going to be a statue of me on campus. Me on the victory stand.

I can't help but think that what happened to me on the stand will, in its own way, happen to that statue. Birds are going to shit on it—in fact, I don't want to think about what people are going to do to it. I feel that it's going to be defiled quickly. Burned up, shot up, peed up. I don't want to think about what might happen to that statue. It's going to be standing up there, and no one is going to protect it. Do you think I can forget what was done to me and my family, and think that this statue is going to somehow be universally and unquestionably revered? Oh my God. They took the Ten Commandments out of the state courthouse in Alabama, right around the same time San Jose State was proposing this statue. If that couldn't stay where it was, how is this going to make it? Those people that did not want me on campus or on the victory stand will not stand for that statue, either.

But truthfully, I know that is out of my control. I cannot get upset, and no one else should get upset because people will look at it and say, "What's that?" and not get its meaning. Or get upset about it being defiled. Or even that it might not be talked about at all, that it might only be treated as a social or festive occasion, that the day honoring us or the day it will be erected and dedicated will be considered just another day, a chance to skip a class. It won't just pop up in conversation among white folks sitting around at the dinner table; it probably won't even pop up with a lot of black folks around the dinner table, because a lot of us are very lackadaisical in our social awareness. People might walk past it and just think of it as something else standing up on campus that no one thinks about or understands, representing something that happened too long ago to mean anything or to have any connection to their lives today. Even if, as I believe, 1968 does come back, as it is slowly doing already with the situation in this country and in the world and within our own families, a lot of people won't recognize that statue as the bond that connects our 1968 to the one that is coming.

I hope that they, or future generations, grasp it soon, because the statue has to be protected. I don't mean physically, someone there to scrape off the bird shit or keep people from peeing on it. The historical strength, the historical value, of the victory stand needs to be guarded. I'm not saying this because the statue is a depiction of me. Any stand in history needs to be guarded; it needs to be guarded by law, it needs to be guarded by social entities, by everything it will ever affect. It cannot be played with or played down. It would mean a lot to the system if the statue becomes something that falls, is taken down, is made to disappear—if the memory of the statue and of the victory stand is that of its being torn down. If something bad happens to the statue and the historical recollection of it, while these students are trying to build it up and preserve it, what will be remembered from it? Doesn't everybody remember that statue of Saddam Hussein falling down in Baghdad during the war? Of course everyone remembers that, and it is valuable to the system that the sight of the statue falling is what is remembered forever, rather than the bombing of innocent people and the body bags of our own soldiers coming back, after we were told everything was cool, all the trouble was over with. If this statue falls, if what it represents is allowed to fall, then was the sacrifice we made even worth it?

I sacrificed a lot back then for the victory stand, and I sure would not want to see it fail because someone had other reasons to build it up, reasons other than pride and justice. It might be rather harsh for me to say it, but it is me that's up there. I know what I sacrificed to get up there. My life was sacrificed; I suffered physically and emotionally and financially. It's an important entity in history, even if it's a history a lot of people won't want to teach or put in the history books. But still, it was me up there, and I want what I suffered for to be protected. Honoring it one time is one thing; preserving it in a real way, not just as a stone or marble object, is more important.

I know people are still afraid of what we did, and they are still afraid of the fact that this has come back to life. I don't believe the people who organized this whole thing knew it would be this big. I believe they are finding out. I met the young man who was awarded the contract to design and build the statue, an artist named Rigo, and one thought that came to mind as I saw him was, There probably were not a whole lot of people bidding for this. I also knew that it would be no easy task for them to raise the money. They were talking about $250,000, and they did not want major corporations trying to attach their names to it with big contributions. They wanted to keep the process clean and raise the money individual by individual. I knew they would find out how difficult that really would be.

I knew the answer, but I asked myself anyway: Why was this causing so much trouble? What's so bad about this project? Is it not strong enough? Is it too strong? Is it because it's about athletics and it's dealing with black athletes? There is no other image like it—can anyone remember a stand like that one? Muhammad Ali had many different poses that reflect and represent him, in the ring, outside the ring, making speeches, knocking people out. He was a tremendous figure, but not even his most famous poses are as well known as the victory stand. But for 35 years, people have run away from it. What is it about the victory stand that makes people still run away from it?

Actually, that very question ran through my head all day long— as I had walked all over campus, and as I sat at that dinner, the culmination of everything, listening to this man I had never heard of talking off the cuff. Why? Very simply, why all this? I enjoyed it, but I said then, and I say now, Why? More specifically, Why now? Why all of this now? Why not a little bit of this all the way through down the ages?

After all that the victory stand had created for me in my life, all of a sudden this young white kid voiced an opinion and it caught on, big time, all over campus and even with Associated Students, who never got behind anything unless it was going to make money—and here is this big thing for us, on our campus, 35 years after the Olympic Games. But why? Am I the first to ask why? Do I even have the freedom to ask why? I want to be gracious. It's all good for me. I'll take it and smile and go on. But why?

I know I will never lose that feeling I have that someone will decide to end it all where it started. It is San Jose; it is where I experienced all the joy and pain, and now the embrace after the rejection. That feeling is with me now. There is something more to it, that's all I can feel. Watch out, my mind tells me, the hammer hasn't fallen yet. Maybe the statue is being put up just to be blown up.

I can't *not* accept the graciousness of those who now are thanking us for what we did 35 years ago. The people who are doing it now weren't even there; for them, it's a historical search and recovery. But if it's a person my age doing it, I'd have to ask the question "Where were you when I needed you?" Maybe if that person is my age and he is in the administration, he knew that if he squeaked back then, he would be fired—even for doing so much as speaking of the positiveness of 1968. But 35 years is a long time to stay silent. Thirty-five years later is a hell of a time to stand up and recognize me. More likely, people my age and older are still angry; they still see John Carlos and me as two niggers that got up there and embarrassed us. Not two people who stood there to educate and improve America. That thought process had to come from these kids long after the fact, or from those who finally have the courage and pride to speak up. Still, it was a long time to wait.

It was all great, the tables, all that money, people coming in—I felt like I was coming to see someone else, yet I walked in and everyone was smiling at me, applauding me. It was special. I knew it might not have happened at all, and that at almost 60, I'd better appreciate it. But 35 years—not three plus five, *thir-ty-five*—for something like this to happen about an event that so many people felt was so great. To be very elementary about it, I was saying, "What's going on?"

Long after the fact, I'm kind of dumbfounded. I shook a lot of hands that night, but no money passed hands, not any. Why not write a check to us for $200,000 and say, "This is for reparations, we know you've suffered"? I'm sure people will see that and think, "Oh, it's just about the money; all he wants is money." I will not apologize for that. I have a need for money, just like other people have needs for money. I can tell you for certain that I needed money back in 1968 when I couldn't feed my baby son and support my wife. I have a need for money now, even if my need is not as great at other people's needs. I can use it more than I can use a handshake, though.

I sacrificed my life to do what I am shown to be doing on that statue. When I look back at how I suffered physically, mentally, and financially, I think, "If I had to choose between a statue and a foundation to spend that money on, I would take the foundation." Think about it: The San Jose chapter of the Tommie Smith/John Carlos Foundation. Every year, the foundation would give five scholarships, for $1,500 each, for student athletes, all athletes, not just blacks. Make the criteria talent and academics—don't give it to a guy who ran a 10-flat 100 and has a 1.8 grade-point average. Hold a banquet then and hire a speaker to honor the winners each year.

Would that last as long as a statue? Maybe longer, knowing what might happen to a statue of us. Once again, I am gracious about all that has been done for me. I am grateful for what they are trying to do. But I also knew as I watched and listened to it all: the statue is not up yet. I am not ready to stop being nervous about it.

I say these things and I continue to speak out about 1968 and all the years that have followed, and I hear people wonder why, even in the middle of all the accolades, can I not let the bitterness go? Just forget about the mistreatment of you because of your race, they say; don't think about that anymore, you're beyond that now, you're in the mainstream now, you were at Santa Monica all these years—you're almost us now. I've heard it so much.

Oh, do I come back on that, very hard, sometimes with words I really regret having used. Not the intent, just the words. Years ago, an older white woman that I knew and worked with—someone who apparently was very fond of me, who used to come up and hug and kiss me when she saw me—talked with me about a number of social issues, including 1968. She said to me, in all sincerity, "Tommie, you did what you did, and I'm sure you regret it because it didn't do anyone any good." She softened up her stance later on, saying that what happened in Mexico City benefited some people, but that I, Tommie Smith, didn't get anything out of it. "Put it behind you," she said. "You have to live for yourself, you're a beautiful young man."

They just don't get it, people who think like that. And I get that from black folks as much as I do from white folks. They all need education. I talk all the time about how my own people need education, but clearly white folks need it also. But just as they believe they can tell us how to live while not accepting that anyone else can ever tell them about themselves, they don't want you to tell them what they need. We can't even suggest, "Maybe you should see it from a black perspective." Their response will be, simplistic as anything, "But I'm not black." Or, better yet, "It's not a black thing."

All I can do is separate a man's faults from the color of his skin. Otherwise, white will become a negative in itself, in the way we view it and in the way the white man knows he is viewed by us. He knows that he has not done right by us, and he knows that we look at him in a negative way. He fights that; he knows what the term "white" means to us. I look at what such a large number of individuals with white skin have done for me, especially as they fight the uphill battle to honor me and my legacy—starting with that white college student at my alma mater who did nothing wrong, who in fact did something very right and very courageous, without knowing what the consequences might be. That kid and so many others have done nothing wrong. They are left with the legacy of what that color has represented. But I do hate what that color has represented.

So to those who say, "Let it go," I ask again, "How? And why? This has been my life." I tell everyone who has ever asked me and will ever ask me: I do not regret taking the victory stand. I have lived long enough to see people who were born long afterward take up the challenge and build upon that victory stand. I don't know if I will see that statue, but I did not think I would ever see what I saw that day on San Jose State's campus exactly 35 years after Mexico City.

They say they will build it. But even without a statue to it, even before I knew anyone wanted to build it, I knew that the victory stand would outlive me.

Epilogue
Silent and Eternal

THIS TIME, when Tommie Smith and John Carlos returned to San Jose State University, 500 people greeted them with warmth, love, and admiration.

And with a 25-foot-high likeness of them, made of fiberglass, ceramic, and bronze.

On October 17, 2005—37 years and one day after Mexico City, two years and one day after Smith and Carlos gazed upon the model of the statue in a downtown hotel ballroom—the two men sat on a stage set up on a normally serene lawn in the middle of campus and gazed up at the memorial to their sacrifice, at that moment covered by a black tarp. The lawn, bearing the unassuming name of Sculpture Garden—coincidentally, located near the campus building named for Dr. Robert Clark—was not serene on this day. At dusk, it was packed with students, reporters, and onlookers from all across America, and the stage was crammed with speakers, dignitaries, and celebrities.

If the crowd didn't all share the sense of shock Smith and Carlos felt at the unlikely scene unfolding before them—and some of the spectators indeed were old enough to grasp how improbable it all would have seemed in 1968—it did tingle with anticipation. Living history was present on that stage, and soon a monument to their deeds would be unveiled, in the place where the seeds of it had been planted.

Among that crowd were Smith's wife, Delois; four of Smith's five children; his first wife, Denise Paschal; and six of his 10 living brothers and sisters. More of his legacy also sat in the crowd—members of the Tommie Smith Youth Track and Field Club of the Bay Area. That club, and several meets throughout California each year, had come into existence since the statue fundraising ceremony two years earlier.

Smith's father was back in Lemoore, unable to attend. Seven weeks later, on December 5, James Richard Smith, who had told young Tommie years ago that if he ever finished second in a race he would have to return to the fields, died at age 94.

On stage were, among others, Lee Evans, teammate at San Jose State and at the Olympics and lifelong friend; Dr. Harry Edwards, the professor who helped light the spark of the protest; Erik Grotz and Alfonso de Alba, the students who turned a classroom idea into the reality before them; and the athlete who at the time was an unexpected accomplice on the victory stand. Peter Norman, the silver medalist in the 200-meter final who wore the "Olympic Project for Human Rights" button on his uniform as the anthem was played, had made the trip from his Australian home. Norman is not depicted on the statue, but well into the night, he posed for pictures atop the silver-medal stand, intentionally left empty by sculptor Rigo23 to inspire future visitors to likewise fill the space themselves.

The seating section filled up quickly, and students who made late arrivals or who stopped as they wandered by climbed atop fountains and railings, scaled trees, and crowded onto walkways and the sloping hill on the right side of the lawn. As everybody in the crowd and on stage got situated, a band led by local trumpet legend Eddie Gale played music from the 1960s. Eventually, mistress of ceremonies and local television news anchor Janice Edwards officially opened the ceremony by proclaiming that all were assembled here "to celebrate a moment of destiny."

The procession of dignitaries began soon after. The current president of the Associated Students of San Jose State, Alberto Gutierrez, who acknowledged that on this day, Tommie Smith and John Carlos "will become a permanent presence on campus." The president of the university, Don Kassing, who remembered being a high school freshman at the time of the victory-stand protest and thought it was "simply cool"—and who described the meaning of the statue to the campus in particular, saying, "You've created a whole new generation of student activists."

Proclamations and commendations were read from several area politicians. Dr. Edwards presented commemorative plates to Smith, Carlos, Evans, and Norman.

The most riveting guest speech was delivered by Dr. Ethel Pitts Walker, campus theater professor, playwright, and activist; her most impassioned statement was a plea to the students: "Don't entomb Tommie Smith and John Carlos, keep them alive."

Actor Delroy Lindo, an Oakland resident, brought personal recollections of the meaning of the protest, how it raised the fundamental question of whether one was "a house Negro or a field Negro." In taking their stand, he said, "Tommie Smith and John Carlos told me, I am somebody."

The honorees were introduced to the crowd by Norman, who said he had always stayed in touch with his fellow medalists over the years and never let up in his support of the cause. His final words, in his sharp Aussie accent, before bringing Carlos, then Smith, to the podium: "These two men gave away that Olympic glory in 1968. San Jose State University, you're giving them back that glory today, and I'd like to thank you for that."

Just shy of a year afterward, Norman passed away at age 64. Smith and Carlos traveled to Australia to serve as his pallbearers.

When their turn came to speak at the unveiling, the two men slipped easily into character as they reflected on what was taking place in front of them. Carlos was expressive and verbose. He called for Evans to have a statue in his honor as well. He talked of the honor of competing against, and teaming up with, another world-class sprinter like himself. In making the gesture, he said, "I stood up and said, 'America, I'm your son, and I'm wounded.'"

Smith was more in awe of the entire scene. He acknowledged the large gathering of his family. He spoke of how happy he was that the members of his youth track club were there. And he echoed his thoughts from the moment he heard the university was considering him for this honor. "The history of what happened will live on long after we're gone," he said. "I'm just glad a part of it will live here."

Finally, it was time for the statue to become public. A soloist sang, of course, the national anthem. The crowd sang along quietly, respectfully. It was a mild surprise that no one seized the moment to raise a fist in the air. It didn't matter, though, because the fists that would be raised forever were coming into view. Slowly. Unnervingly so. The huge tarp, lifted off by a cherry picker, got caught twice—once on each fist. Then, set against the darkening sky and lit by hundreds of camera flashes, the entire statue came into view in its full majesty.

After 37 years, one day, and a couple of anxious minutes, Tommie Smith and John Carlos were back home on campus, for good.

David Steele

Acknowledgments

FIRST AND FOREMOST: to my Heavenly Father who chose me to be a vessel in this season, thank you for giving me the opportunity, the strength, and the knowledge to Stand Up for Peace, Love, and Equality for ALL.

David Steele, thank you for your great writing and listening skills and your patience with me. If I remember correctly, we cooked you a steak dinner, and we sat on my patio and talked for hours and hours. Now you can buy me a steak dinner. Thanks again.

To my wife, Delois Jordan Smith, you were relentless in finding the avenue to see this book completed and published. The race is not given to the swift, but to the one who endures to the end. My lady, job well done.

To my sister Sally Mae Gamble, who worked alongside me in the cotton fields in the San Joaquin Valley and pushed me to continue my education. Rest in Peace.

To the rest of my brothers and sisters: Willie Jewell, James Richard, George, Lucille, Hattie Mae, Ernie, Mary, Gladys, Elizabeth, and Eugene. Let us not forget from whence we come. "Faith is the substance of things hoped for and the evidence of things not seen."

Dr. Tommie C. Smith

MY ROLE IN TELLING THIS STORY would not be possible without the trust and faith placed in me by Tommie Smith and his wife, Delois, who selected me to be the chronicler of a long-awaited, important chapter in history and showed the patience and perseverance to see the work through. I can only hope I have rewarded that faith.

This work would not have been completed without the help and support of the following:

Urla Hill, who first pointed out that Tommie Smith was planning to write his autobiography, and whose knowledge of and passion for the history and legacy of "Speed City" were invaluable. Also, Derek Toliver, Otis Bess, and George Wright, who shared that passion and passed along their resources and support.

Several generations of the San Jose State University family, including St. Saffold, Lee Evans, Frank Slaton, Ray Norton, Eb Hunter, Robert Griffin, Bill Walsh, Lawrence Fan, Alfonso de Alba, and Erik Grotz; as well as Robert Poynter, Payton Jordan, and Arif Khatib, longtime integral members of the San Jose and Bay Area sports community.

The resources of the Dr. Martin Luther King Jr. Library at San Jose State (especially Steven Groth, head of special collections), the Moorland-Spingarn Research Center at Howard University, the Amateur Athletic Foundation Library in Los Angeles, and McKeldin Graduate Library at the University of Maryland, College Park.

Dr. Robert Fuller, who was generous with his time and recollections of Smith's tenure at Oberlin College.

The newspaper writers, authors, and editors who encouraged me directly and by example, including Bill Rhoden, Ron Thomas, Michael Wilbon, Randy Harvey, Ron Bergman, Michelle Singletary, Huel Washington, and the late Ralph Wiley.

Joshunda Sanders, Pamela and Rod Alston, Sharon Smith-Mauney, Felicia and Morris McDaniel, Karen Moody, Mark Stewart, Teri Washington, and all my friends who kept up the encouragement when it was needed most.

Micah Kleit and Dr. Amy Bass, whose enthusiastic embrace of this book made the years of toil worthwhile.

And, most important, my sister Alexa, brother Renard, and my entire family, to whom this all is dedicated.

David Steele

Index

About the Authors

Tommie Smith, one of the most celebrated track and field athletes of all time, is a member of several athletic halls of fame, including those of the Olympics and USA Track and Field. Born in Clarksville, Texas, in 1944 and raised in Lemoore, California, Smith won the gold medal in the 200-meter dash at the 1968 Olympic Games at Mexico City in a world-record time of 19.83 seconds. He is best remembered, however, for the gloved fist he raised from the victory stand during the playing of the national anthem after that race. After earning his bachelor's degree in social sciences from San Jose State College in 1969, Smith played professional football with the Cincinnati Bengals for three years. He later earned his master's degree in education from Cambridge College, and from 1972 to 1978 served on the faculty of Oberlin College in Ohio, as a physical education professor, track coach, and athletic director. In 1978 he became track coach and professor of physical education at Santa Monica College in California, where he served as athletic director from 2003 to 2004 before retiring in 2005. He is still in great demand on the lecture circuit and by the national and international media for his recollections of his historic stand. In 2005 he was awarded an honorary doctorate in humane letters by San Jose State University for his "courageous efforts on behalf of human dignity, equality, and civil rights." Smith and his wife, Delois Jordan-Smith, divide their time between the Los Angeles area and their home in Stone Mountain, Georgia.

David Steele has been a sports columnist at the Baltimore *Sun* since 2004. Previously he had spent nine years at the *San Francisco Chronicle,* the last five as a columnist—the first African American to hold such a position at a San Francisco daily newspaper. Before becoming a columnist, he covered professional basketball for eleven years at four newspapers. A 1985 graduate of the University of Maryland at College Park, he has written for the *St. Petersburg Times* in Florida, the *New York Post,* the *National Sports Daily,* the Stamford *Advocate* in Connecticut, and *Newsday* in New York. Among the notable sports events he has covered are the Summer Olympic Games in Australia, the Summer Olympic track and field trials, the Super Bowl, the NCAA men's basketball Final Four, the Atlantic Coast Conference and Southeastern Conference men's basketball tournaments, the major league baseball playoffs, the Rose, Sugar, and Gator bowls, a heavyweight championship fight, and thirteen NBA Finals. In 1988 he was honored by the Associated Press Sports Editors, the Florida Sportswriters Association, and the Southeast Chapter of the Society of Professional Journalists for his part in a three-piece *Times* investigative series on blacks in coaching and sports management. In 1992 he was honored by the Associated Press Sports Editors for his writing about middle-school athletic recruiting, and in 1999 he took part in the *Chronicle*'s coverage of the school massacre in Littleton, Colorado— an effort that received recognition from the California News Publishers Association. His work has been published by *ESPN The Magazine, ESPN.com, The Sporting News,* and *USA Today Baseball Weekly.* In 2003 he co-authored a book, *Four Generations of Color,* with sports agent and former major-league scout and coach Dr. Miles McAfee. A native of Washington, D.C., Steele lives in suburban Baltimore, Maryland.